OCEAN RACING AROUND THE WORLD

Ocean racing around the world

ADMIRAL'S CUP
by Paul Antrobus

SOUTHERN CROSS CUP
by Bob Ross

SOUTHERN OCEAN RACING
CONFERENCE and *ONION PATCH*
by Geoffrey Hammond

PRENTICE-HALL INC.
Englewood Cliffs, N.J.

Black and white photographs (pages): Anderson, 103 (top); Antrobus, 139 (bottom), 223 (inset); Australian News and Information Bureau, 95 (top); Bahama News Bureau, 173, 177 (bottom), 183, 201; Beken, 2, 9, 13, 15, 21 (below), 31, 35 (top), 49, 157; Bermuda News Bureau, 217, 221, 223, 225; Central Press Agency, 55 (top), 59; Cork Examiner, 28; Cruising Club of Australia, 84; Daily Express, 57; Eastland, 45, 65, 135; Fisher, 113; Gurney, 203 (inset); Hammond, 159, 185 (bottom), 189 (top, bottom left), 195 (bottom), 201 (inset); Hobart Mercury, 55 (bottom), 89, 115, 125 (bottom), 143; Hoyt, 67; Kuenzec, 177 (top); Miami News Bureau, 163, 166, 167, 169; McQuillan, 119; Modern Boating, 81, 91, 95 (bottom); Nautical Publishing Co., 84 (inset); Nakajima, Japanese Yachting Association, 214–215; Qantas, 97, 109, 110; Ramsay, 35 (below), 103 (bottom); Rosenfeld, 185 (top), 189 (bottom right), 195 (top), 205, 211; Ross, 127 (top), 137, 139 (top); Ocean Publications, 209; Sefton, 109 (inset), 125 (top), 127 (bottom); Simpson, 21 (top); United Press, 27; Veit, 171; Watney, 71; Western Morning News, 12; Yeldham 7, 77.

Maps, diagrams, and drawings (pages): Camper and Nicholson, 20; Alan Gurney, 181 (right); Hicks, 155; Miller and Whitworth, 131; Gary Mull, 193; Myers, 39, 87, 99, 219; Ocean Publications, 209; Sparkman and Stephens, 37, 107, 181 (left); German Frers, 227.

Colour photographs (captions): Amey, 7; Clarke, 18; Fisher, 4, 16, 17; Hammond, 22, 24, 25; Hashimoto, 23; Motson, 6, 9; Rosenfeld, 26; Ross, 10, 11, 12, 13, 14, 15; Simpson, 5; Van Mesdag, 3; Watney, 1, 2, 19, 20, 21; Woolley, 8.

First American edition published by
Prentice-Hall, Inc., 1975

First published by Angus and Robertson (U.K.) Ltd. 1975

Copyright © Admiral's Cup by Paul Antrobus 1975
Copyright © Southern Cross Cup by Bob Ross 1975
Copyright © Southern Ocean Racing Conference and Onion Patch by Geoffrey Hammond 1975

ISBN 0-13-630400-1

Library of Congress Catalog Card Number: 75-9193

Printed in Great Britain

Contents

PART ONE

The Admiral's Cup

The Pioneers

In August 1925, seven yachts raced from the Isle of Wight to the Fastnet Rock, off the south-eastern tip of Ireland, and back to Plymouth in Devon. With the blessing of the Royal Western Yacht Club in Plymouth they were racing for a challenge cup presented by Lieutenant Commander E. G. Martin, who won the race and his trophy in his 12-year-old converted Havre pilot cutter *Jolie Brise*. That same year George Martin became the first Commodore of the new Ocean Racing Club, formed by a breakaway group of the Royal Cruising Club. British ocean racing had taken its first faltering steps.

In 1973 no fewer than 258 yachts raced those 605 miles around the Fastnet Rock, the climax of the biggest ocean-racing challenge in the world, the Admiral's Cup. 'Ocean' racing is perhaps a misleading term as there's not much ocean in the majority of courses in the British programme sailed by those yachts today. 'Off-shore racing' is a more accurate description, and the important thing is that they do go offshore, rather than hugging the coasts.

Surprisingly, it was considered quite a feat for those seven yachts to go out of sight of land in 1925. It is also surprising that ocean racing has such a short history in Britain when you consider its seafaring heritage. The first 'offshore races' could well have been the chases between the revenue cutters and fast smuggling vessels in the 18th and 19th centuries. Later these same boats were used for actual sporting races.

Coincidentally, the earliest yacht club formed in the British Isles is almost stone-throwing distance from the Fastnet lighthouse—the Royal Cork, in Ireland, founded in 1720. It took another 100 years for clubs to establish themselves in England, Scotland and Wales but gradually the Solent, the stretch of water off England's south coast protected from the English Channel by the Isle of Wight, became the centre of British sailing. Sailing, not racing, because although there were some pretty large cabin yachts on the scene, they were used for cruising. Racing was confined to the keel dayboat classes built specially for it.

Possibly because Cowes on the Isle of Wight was patronised by royalty, certainly because it was a fashionable spot, regattas there were always popular. When the Royal Yacht Squadron—the elite club which still fires the starting guns for many important races from its grey, turreted walls—was formed there in 1820, even the cruiser owners enjoyed the odd race or two, but the craze died out until the schooner *America* sailed across the Atlantic and won that fateful race around the

'Jolie Brise', the 48 ft. cutter which won the first Fastnet Race in 1925. She was owned by the first Commodore of the R.O.R.C., George Martin.

Island and the rather cumbersome jug which has stood ever since in the New York Yacht Club.

The Americans became our traditional yachting adversaries from then on and, because they have always enjoyed bringing their yachts across to race at Cowes, they have sparked off some of the best racing in the world.

It was in the 1920s, when the 'Big Class', and the Twelve, Eight and Six Metre yachts were racing in the grand Cowes Week regattas, that a few people became aware of a sport catching on in America in a big way. It was ocean racing, 'also known as the king of sports by those who understood how high are the qualities demanded from it . . .' This was a quote from Weston Martyr writing in 'Yachting Monthly' in December, 1924.

He went on to say: 'We have plenty of boats fit to go to sea . . . but in spite of this, we simply do not do it. We seem content to race around the buoys in our enclosed waters or to cruise quietly round our coasts, putting into port every night or whenever the weather looks threatening.' He described a New London to Bermuda Race that he had taken part in Stateside, with entries ranging from 35 ft. to 70 ft., and commented that professionals in the crew were the exception.

The new sport sounded too good to miss and Martyr, Martin and their friends decided to hold their own ocean race, the Fastnet. Other races were then organised under the auspices of the Ocean Racing Club (given royal status in 1931). It is interesting that the first Channel race was held in 1928 for yachts considered too small to enter the Fastnet.

Now the Channel and Fastnet Races form the major part of the Admiral's Cup, the world championship of ocean racing. In 1973 teams from 16 nations competed for this coveted trophy. Germany is defending champion in the 1975 series, the jubilee year of the Royal Ocean Racing Club.

But in those pre-war years, racing was fairly haphazard. Owen Aisher, present Admiral of the R.O.R.C., who regularly lends his boat to Prince Philip to race during Cowes Week, began racing in about 1936. He had a 30-ton ketch and says the attraction as far as he and most others were concerned was that it gave them an excuse to get to foreign ports from where they could go cruising after the race. Boats were bigger and more solid in those days and many carried paid hands to do the hard graft. The owners and their friends had only to sit back and enjoy the pleasant sensations of sailing, attractive scenery and pink gins. That amateurs should race the boats in the new sport became established more quickly in the United States than in Britain. The situation has since been reversed and modern American yachts seem to carry more paid hands, professionals, than the British yachts, perhaps because they have longer delivery trips to get to races.

Today Owen Aisher, who at the age of 75 is still dedicated to the cause of racing and has campaigned in many top competitions including the 1973 Admiral's Cup trials (he was unsuccessful but his son Robin won a place in the team), believes the sport became more competitive just before the second world war mainly because of new foreign interest in racing, from Germany and France as well as America. Clearly international competition has always been a stimulating factor in the development of British offshore racing, even before the Admiral's Cup was dreamed up.

The 1939 Fastnet Race was won by Isaac Bell's 63 ft. yawl *Bloodhound*, built in 1936. Like her sistership *Foxhound*, she was a Charles E. Nicholson design, Camper and Nicholson built, and destined for a long, distinguished ocean racing career. All racing was stopped during the war, but certain names had already made their mark and were to influence the sport for many years after it was revived.

The 'Yachtsman's Annual' for 1938/9 carries reports of a young, energetic Naval officer who was a champion in the offshore fleet with a Laurent Giles design called *Maid of Malham*. Captain John Illingworth was his name and he possessed a *racing* spirit rather than a cruising sailor's mentality. This 'spirit' was to help shape the future and style of British and foreign ocean racing.

There was a lot more to Illingworth's contribution. The *Maid* carried her jib to the masthead, considered then so outrageous that Chris Ratsey, the leading sailmaker of the time, refused to make any headsails for her. He said it would be 'ruining a lovely boat'. Luckily for ocean racers of many nationalities, Illingworth has been 'ruining boats' ever since, his own and others he designed when he took it up as a fulltime job with Angus Primrose, until his retirement in 1972. He sailed his last full season in 1969 on the French masthead-cutter-rigged Admiral's Cupper *Oryx* before settling himself in the Mediterranean.

Also mentioned in the 'Yachtsman's Annual' for 1938/9 were the successes in America of boats designed by Olin Stephens. In 1928, at the age of 19, he had formed a partnership with a yacht broker called Drake H. Sparkman to design yachts. Olin had no experience, but it wasn't long before he was designing Six Metres and other smaller craft. His first ocean racer of note was *Dorade* in which he, with his brother Rod and their father, won the 1931 Transatlantic Race to Bergen in Norway and the Fastnet. The 1938 Bermuda Race was won by a 78 ft. yawl *Baruna* with its designer, Olin, on board, quoted in the Annual as an 'experienced and astute offshore crew'. The 700-mile race was hard on the wind all the way and five out of the first six boats overall were Stephens designs. (Rod had joined the business in 1933 and Drake Sparkman continued running the brokerage end of the business and was President of the company until his death in 1964, when Olin succeeded him.)

Years later, the ability of Sparkman and Stephens designs to go fast to windward was another important factor in the evolution of a competitive racing fleet in Britain.

The first ocean race after the war was in 1945 when a race to Dinard, near St. Malo in Brittany, was held. It's still a popular event on the R.O.R.C. calendar and these days attracts a fleet of 200 or so, divided into five classes. In 1945, as before the war, there were just two classes, known as the 'Big Class' and the 'Small Class'. In 1946 more races were put on, adopting the more businesslike names Class I and Class II.

However, those early post-war fleets were very much a continuation of the sport as it had been in the '20s and '30s—racing came secondary to cruising—

and perhaps more than anyone it was John Illingworth who stirred things up.

Illingworth was the first person to build a boat specifically for racing. More than that, he built a boat to win races, with no regard for looks or traditional style of construction, layout or sailplan. The boat was *Myth of Malham* and in 1947, her first season, and again in 1949 she won the Fastnet Race and Class II. She was a success 'because we were more thorough in our approach than anyone else had been,' Illingworth has said. He owned her until 1959.

The construction of *Myth*—her lines were drawn by Jack Giles and the rest designed jointly by Illingworth and Primrose—was a departure from the conventional with a heavy accent on functional simplicity and light displacement, achieved through double-skinned planking, a method pioneered by Laurent Giles. He stuck to his masthead cutter rig, still unusual for those days. The masthead foretriangle was to remain Illingworth's special trademark for a number of years.

But although *Myth of Malham* was extremely successful, there was not a great rush by other owners to build boats like her, or to try to copy her revolutionary design features, as happens today. Illingworth experimented alone while his rivals would not abandon traditional styling, Lloyds A100 construction and seven-eighths foretriangles.

Peter Nicholson, Hampshire designer, builder and yachtsman, from the same family as Charles E. Nicholson (Peter's father, Charles A., also a designer, was a nephew of Charles E.), describes the *Myth* with a note of admiration in his voice: 'She was ugly, a machine, but she won everything offshore, just as she was built to.' Illingworth far preferred racing offshore to inshore, because of the greater variety it provided in weather, courses and crews.

Nevertheless, it is curious that the *Myth* was never very successful in the round-the-buoys racing in the Solent. 'Everyone thought that was the thing in those days,' says Peter Nicholson, a Solent expert himself. 'If you didn't win in the Solent then you were nothing. Now, of course, much greater importance is attached to offshore performance, although Solent performance has not diminished in importance to the same proportion.'

Perhaps that was why others were slow to copy Illingworth's approach. To be seen racing at Cowes gave you social prestige. There was nothing to be gained from winning offshore. Such niceties didn't bother Illingworth. He was proud of the *Myth*, fast and seaworthy, suiting the R.O.R.C. measurement rule and, he reckoned, a bit of a pacemaker.

Owen Aisher eventually did rise to Illingworth's challenge. He responded in 1950 by building *Yeoman III*, the first of a long line of ocean racers. *Yeoman* is the traditional name for all the boats in the Aisher family, the first being the cruising ketch mentioned earlier and the second, a Six Metre Yacht, both designed by Charles A. Nicholson. In 1951 Owen won the Fastnet Race in *Yeoman III*, also a Nicholson design, 35 ft. on the waterline, but she had a seven-eighths rig which meant there was still no encouragement for others to follow Illingworth and go masthead. A comparatively heavy displacement boat, she was built to Lloyds 15R

Prince Philip sailing 'Bloodhound', the 63-footer built in 1936.
Seated astern of him is the bearded designer, Angus Primrose

and was traditional enough to keep the conservatives happy and of no incentive at all to the revolutionaries.

One difference, however, was that Aisher had teamed up with a crack crew experienced at racing, not cruising, large boats. He was Stan Bishop, a leading hand on Twelve and Eight Metre yachts which he skippered for Sir William Burton. Crews still tended to be friends of the owners and it was some time before they recruited people known for special skills to sail for them.

The sport of offshore racing was seeing changes but not very rapid ones. The influence of Illingworth reached a suitable peak in 1957 when *Myth of Malham*, by then 10 years old, was one of the British team in the first Admiral's Cup contest.

Another member of that team was Geoffrey Pattinson with *Jocasta*. Like Illingworth, Pattinson had the racing bug and went offshore to win. *Jocasta* was designed by Robert Clark and built in 1950. She was 51·5 ft. overall on a 40 ft. waterline, beam 11·85 ft. and draft 8·2 ft., and for lightness the frames and beams were aluminium. Following Illingworth's lead, she was cutter rigged but was not masthead. She set 1,335 sq. ft. of Ratsey sails, still the most favoured sailmaker.

Jocasta won the R.O.R.C. Class I trophy for the 1954 season. Class II was won by *Uomie*, an Arthur Robb design owned by Selwyn Slater, the third member of that first Admiral's Cup team and another man anxious for offshore racing to develop.

Thus there was emerging a new attitude to offshore racing by a few of the participants. Ashore, too, there had been a similar recognition of the growing importance of the new trend, and of the need to encourage it in British waters.

Cowes Week had always drawn the cruiser classes, but with the increasing emphasis being put on offshore racing rather than around-the-Solent cans, the attractions of The Week might have faded for the new breed of offshore boys had not this tendency been checked. The new incentive was the presentation of the Britannia Cup by King George VI in 1950, and the New York Yacht Club Cup a year later, specifically for ocean racers as opposed to the 'cruiser classes'.

The Britannia Cup was for a race around the Isle of Wight to retrace the course sailed by the *America* and the *Aurora* in 1851. The New York Yacht Club presented their challenge cup for ocean racers to mark 100 years of Anglo-American competition in yacht racing. The Royal Yacht Squadron set the size limit for both these races at between 30 ft. and 60 ft. rating. Now the two trophies are raced for over Solent courses on the Tuesday and Thursday of every Cowes Week, and they have been Admiral's Cup events. They are still the most prized trophies for the big classes.

An atmosphere of change was taking a hold, but it was only a change in the reasons why owners went offshore racing—because they wanted to race. They were beginning in a few cases to build boats especially to race, but so far the importance of refining their craft in terms of design, equipment and crew was not acknowledged. They had not yet realised—or if they had they didn't want to take advantage of it—the extent to which an offshore race is won on the shore, in the designer's office and in the sail loft, before the race even begins.

To gain an edge over another boat through technical advances in such areas as sails, ropes and other equipment seemed slightly unfair, too big a break away from the traditional sport. So it is doubtful that anyone took these things seriously, except to buy the gear which did a job safely and satisfactorily. The go-fast drive had not yet arrived.

The Admiral's Cup changed the whole attitude dramatically. In a short time this gave a status to the sport which attracted some first-class yachtsmen, which is itself a self-compounding thing. By raising the standard of the challenge, more serious-minded people wanted to have a go and this, in turn, attracted more and more. Now one sees Olympic dinghy champions sailing in Admiral's Cup fleets, drawn to it by the quality of the competition rather than the opportunity of going

'Myth of Malham', the first British yacht specially built by Captain John Illingworth for offshore racing

foreign. These men are actively recruited by owners in search of talents which will help them win.

The founders of the Admiral's Cup may have had the development of the sport in these terms unconsciously in their minds. However, their declared objective was to build up international participation in British races, especially the Fastnet and Cowes Week. Both of these were already international occasions. The Americans loved to pit themselves against our tricky tidal conditions. Now there was the opportunity to enlarge these events, give them more weight, and to give the British fleet a chance to compete more formally against boats and skippers with different experiences from those they normally faced.

The Admiral's Cup became the catalyst in making ocean racing in the United Kingdom the highly competitive sport it is now. The goal of all dedicated off-shore yachtsmen was—and still is—to win a place in the team. The successes or failures of boats to achieve this aim affected future trends in all aspects of the sport.

The challenge of the sport draws men like moths to a light. It's a love-hate relationship, according to Ron Amey, owner of 10 ocean racers since he started sailing in the '50s with an Arthur Robb design, the 34·9 ft. *Cloetta*. Between 1958 and 1974 he had nine boats called *Noryema* (Ron Amey backwards), several of which have represented Britain at home and in America, and he spent much of the '74 season planning number 10.

He says: 'Some people have more love than hate when they're racing. Not me, though. I certainly don't enjoy it for a lot of the time and I hate the cost. I much prefer going motorbike scrambling (*which he does mainly winter weekends*) and I can buy *two* bikes for the price of a new jib. But it's one big horrible challenge. Once you start you don't want to be beaten and so many people are involved—crews, boatbuilders, designers and so on—that you carry on. That's why I do it, I suppose, because it's something I can share with a lot of people. It's not anti-social like dinghy racing.'

For a man who doesn't even enjoy it, he's spent a great many thousands of pounds to give others the pleasure of sharing the challenge with him. But Ron, who is also an expert snow and water skier, also feels that, as with any growing sport, racing has become much keener as more competitors have entered it and one of the biggest changes he has seen is that now the vast majority of crews are 'professional in attitude'. Quite different from the 1950s.

'Is every man a tiger?'

The Admiral's Cup was originally a private challenge to American yachts coming over in 1957 to race in Britain. The £300 cup was presented by Sir Myles Wyatt, Admiral of the R.O.R.C. at the time which gave the Cup its name; John Illingworth; Peter Green who shared *Myth of Malham* with Illingworth; Geoffrey Pattinson and Selwyn Slater. After the first series, the donors decided to open it to three-boat teams from all over the world, and the Americans agreed to this.

Sir Myles was keen, according to one of his crew on *Bloodhound* which he owned by then, to encourage our own ocean racing skippers to harden up their approach to the sport. His four partners in the Cup were already in the van in this area and it is easy to see why they gave him their support. In fact, these may well not have been his real sentiments. In later years he frequently said he regretted the effect the Admiral's Cup was having on the sport as it became increasingly serious.

Whether he meant what he said or not, he was genuinely pleased with the performance of the 13-year-old *Caprice of Huon*, an Australian team member in the 1965 series, and again in 1967. She proved 'the old-fashioned way', to quote Sir Myles, could still win. True, she was built to a design Robert Clark had first devised before the second world war. It is not recorded, however, whether Sir Myles knew how much of the internal comfort had been stripped out of *Caprice*'s hull, nor how carefully food and water rations were measured to keep down weight. The only thing 'old' about *Caprice* was her age—she was fitted out entirely in the modern idiom.

The three American boats which accepted that first Admiral's Cup challenge in '57 were all well known international campaigners: Dick Nye with *Carina*, Bill Snaith with *Figaro* and C. W. Blunt-White with *White Mist*. The British had Illingworth and Green in *Myth of Malham*, Pattinson in *Jocasta* and Selwyn Slater in *Uomie*. Obviously, none of these contestants had been built especially for the series and there were no formal selection trials. Until 1963, the R.O.R.C. committee simply nominated the three boats they considered the best available.

The Channel Race was the opener to the series and has been to every Admiral's Cup since, counting double points. It's a 225-mile race starting at Southsea, near Portsmouth, with a leg east to the Royal Sovereign light tower near Beachy Head, across the English Channel to the Le Havre light vessel, then back to the finish at Southsea. Two inshore races during Cowes Week would count single points: in 1957 the Britannia Cup and a special race laid on by the R.O.R.C. (subsequently the New York Yacht Club race) until the Admiral's Cup fleets were finally given their own separate Cowes Week races in 1971. The last race, for treble points, was of course the Fastnet.

Myth of Malham just won the Channel Race with *Uomie* second after some close racing with *Carina*. *Carina*, winner of the 1955 Fastnet Race and two Transatlantic Races, saw the two British boats as her special rivals. She led them on an exhilarating sail across the Channel and back but, being biggest of the three, could not quite save her time on overall positions. *Figaro* did not start, giving the Americans a handicap from the outset. On points, Britain led by 22 points to 14.

The Britannia Cup went to *Uomie* with *Myth* third, increasing Britain's lead to 11 points. On Wednesday, light airs caused a postponement for all the other classes but the R.O.R.C. sent off the intrepid six on time and *Figaro* gained maximum points with *Uomie* second, *White Mist* third, *Myth* fourth, *Carina* fifth and *Jocasta* the tail-ender on handicap. This gave the United States 12 points to Britain's nine, but on aggregate they hadn't caught up enough.

That year's Fastnet was a tough one, the wildest on record, and only 12 yachts finished out of 42 starters. *Carina* knew the way all right and finished first to repeat her overall victory of 1955. By all accounts her crew were pretty wild, too, but they were trained and worked on board for one thing only—first place—and her team spirit and crewmanship were almost faultless. They even had a war cry to help them along when things got really bad.

(Left) The Admiral's Cup. The hands are Mr. Heath's

(Right) Ren Clarke's 'Quiver III' was the first yacht designer Charles A. Nicholson built purely for offshore racing. 'Sylphide' is astern

'Is every man a tiger?' skipper Nye would shout, spitting out his cigar.

'Gr . . . gr . . . gr . . . gr . . .' would come back the roar, and they'd throw even more energy into winning that race.

The other two American yachts backed up *Carina* well with a fifth for *White Mist* and sixth for *Figaro* on Admiral's Cup placings, but the *Myth* and *Jocasta* kept up the British side with a third and fourth. Unfortunately, *Uomie* had retired during the Fastnet Race because she was leaking badly, so points were very close. America won the race 33 points to 27, but Britain took the Cup by the slimmest margin, 70 points to 68.

This narrow margin wasn't a big enough incentive to bring the Americans back to take up the challenge in 1959. It seemed they thought it a great idea if any boats happened to be over the other side of the pond, but not something to be entered at all costs, perhaps not an unnatural reaction at this stage. *Carina* came again but no American team proper. Nevertheless, enough interest had been created to bring teams from Holland and France, and the Dutch very nearly carried off the trophy at their first attempt.

The idea of an official international contest seemed to have stirred the con-

sciences of the R.O.R.C. committee. At the annual dinner in 1958, they announced they would exercise their right to inspect yachts to ensure they complied with their Special Regulations regarding safety, soundness of hull, gear and sails. These included lists of the equipment that should be carried, including storm sails, lifelines, life-buoys, first-aid equipment and fire extinguishers, and regulations which dealt with anchors, navigation lights, fog signals and so on. Until then the R.O.R.C. had simply stated it was 'contrary to the spirit of ocean racing to save weight by sailing without equipment normally carried while cruising'. Now they realised it was even more important that racing yachts should be fitted out for safety as they were less likely to shelter in bad weather, and any that did not come up to standard could be disqualified.

In those Special Regulations there was a new item permitting the use of echo-sounders on racing yachts, the first of the new-fangled electric aids. Up until then depth had been measured by swinging the lead, a primitive practice for that size of yacht when you consider the rows of instrument dials which face today's helmsmen.

The forerunners in the British fleet hadn't been idle in the meantime and during the 1958 season caught the travel bug. John Illingworth skippered one of his designs, *Belmore*, in the Bermuda Race and other British entries included Max Aitken's lovely new *Drumbeat*, and *Uomie*, not in the hands of Selwyn Slater but those of Geoff Pattinson. Fruit-farmer Pattinson had real itchy feet. He took *Jocasta* on the Brest–Canaries Sail Training Ship Race, while *Uomie*, which he had bought from Slater, was being shipped to America. Then, after a spell in the States, she was shipped by steamer to Australia where he sailed her in the Sydney–Hobart Race, the first British entrant since John Illingworth started the whole thing and won the first race 13 years before.

The British didn't shine in their ventures abroad but something significant emerged from that Bermuda Race. 'Yachting World' magazine commented that out of over a hundred starters, six had glass fibre hulls and it was reckoned that about 75,000 would be built during that year. 'Glass fibre construction seems to have caught on in the United States,' they said, a sure sign that it wouldn't be long before it reached British shores and opened up yacht racing to hundreds more people.

The defending British team for the 1959 Admiral's Cup were Illingworth and Green again with *Myth*, Selwyn Slater with his new yacht *Ramrod*, and the R.O.R.C. club boat *Griffin II* (formerly Owen Aisher's *Yeoman III* which won the '51 Fastnet), skippered by Major Gerald Potter with a 'picked crew'.

Ramrod's overall win of the Channel Race plus a Class II victory for *Griffin II* put the British team in a strong initial position ahead of Holland.

The Britannia Cup course that year was right around the Isle of Wight. It was a slow race and many didn't finish until the following morning. The leaders which cleared St. Catherine's Point before the tide turned against them were okay. One of these was the Dutch team boat *Zwerver* and she beat *Carina* for overall honours. It was a disaster for *Griffin II*, and the *Myth* was spotted struggling close in by the

'Griffin II', a member of the 1959 and 1961 British Admiral's Cup teams, was originally Owen Aisher's 1951 Fastnet winner *'Yeoman'*. Aisher, and subsequent owners Charles Gardener and Sir Giles Guthrie, presented her to the R.O.R.C. as the club boat in 1957

rocks, trying to cheat that relentless adverse tide. The New York Yacht Club Cup race was the second inshore event counting for Admiral's Cup points and put Britain only three points ahead of Holland. All depended on the Fastnet Race.

Unlike the rough one of two years before, weather conditions were mixed for the record 59 starters. Calms early on meant many yachts had to kedge; then fog brought bad visibility and later on there were gales. All three French yachts had to give up, suffering from broken gear.

The Dutch did well. *Zwerver* and her team mate *Olivier van Noort* were second and third at the Fastnet Rock and on final corrected times *Olivier van Noort* was second in Class I, *Zwerver* was fourth and *Zeevalk*, their third boat, ninth. But *Griffin II* was second overall and second in Class II and *Myth* was fourth in that class, with *Ramrod* third in Class I. Thanks to this performance, Britain held on to the Cup with 135 points to 123.

Five countries were represented in the 1961 series. Sweden made an appearance and America returned to the fray. Competition was keen to get into the British team and some new boats had been built specifically for racing, including Ren Clarke's *Quiver III* and Geoff Pattinson's Stephens-designed *Zarabanda*, with an

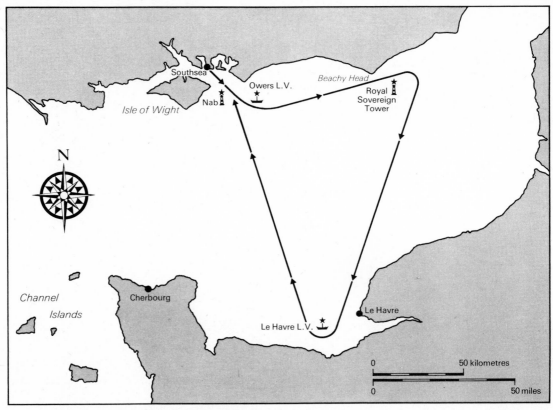

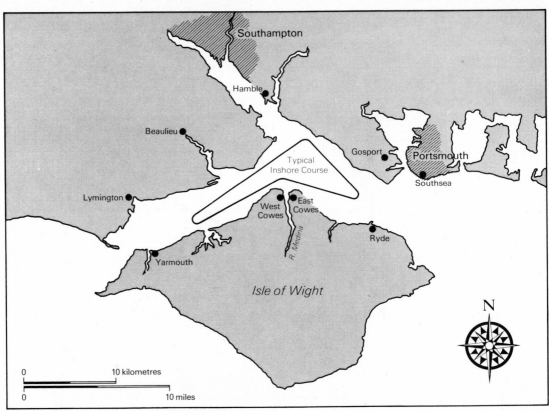

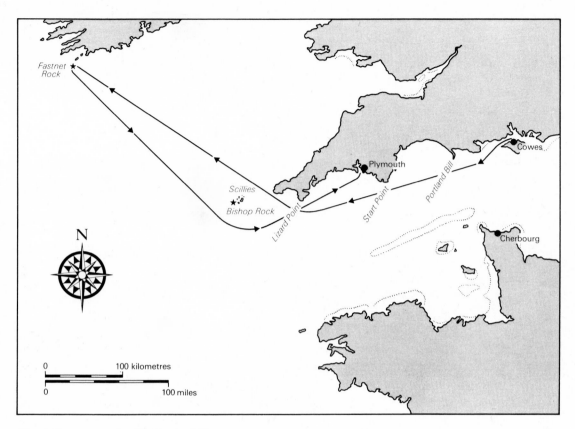

(Top) The course for the Fastnet Race,
approximately 605 miles

(Opposite, top) The Channel race course, approximately
225 miles

(Opposite, below) Courses for the Admiral's Cup
30-milers are determined on the actual day. There is
insufficient room in the Solent for the Olympic
courses as used in the Southern Cross and Onion
Patch series, and courses are laid round navigation
buoys

American-type stainless steel pulpit/bowsprit. He had taken her to the 1960 Sydney–Hobart Race.

Only one of the new yachts won a place in the team although all had featured in the prize lists at some time or another during the season. The Camper and Nicholson *Quiver III* was chosen, and her team mates were, incredibly, the *Myth* again, then 14 years old, and *Griffin II* again.

The Establishment was hard to break but this year was to show the old attitude just wasn't good enough.

The Americans went into a big lead in the Channel Race with an overall win for Jakob Isbrandtsen's *Windrose*. She was followed in Class II by the French *Eloise II* and Sweden's *Staika III*, which had decisively beaten *Quiver III*. Second and third in Class I for the other U.S.A. yachts *Figaro* and *Cyane*, when *Griffin II* and *Myth* could manage only fifth and tenth in that class, gave the Americans 76 points to Britain's 46. Only four points behind was Sweden even though one of her team, the '59 Fastnet winner *Anitra*, hadn't started. France was lying fourth and Holland fifth.

Britain scraped up three more points than the United States in the Britannia Cup with a second place overall for *Quiver III*, but America was strongly placed. At the start of this race yachts had to kedge against the tide and *Anitra*, bringing the Swedish team more bad luck, was dragged over the line. She took 40 minutes to recross and did not complete the race.

Quiver III again took maximum Admiral's Cup points for the New York Yacht Club Race, *Windrose*, *Staika* and *Eloise II* retired, the French *Striana* was disqualified and on aggregate the race went to Holland. Nevertheless, the United States went into the Fastnet Race with a 13 point lead over Britain.

Zwerver won the Fastnet Race and the British team scored most points for it, but again only three more than the United States. So at their second attempt the Americans won the trophy by 220 points to Britain's 210. Holland was third, Sweden fourth and France fifth.

This break of the dominance of a single country was one of the best things that could happen as far as the series and its status were concerned. It had been showing signs of becoming a British benefit. The American win put an end to that and gave Britain a much needed impetus to fight back. The British had to allay any fears that America, having once won, would be too strong in terms of monetary resources and technical advantages to be beaten again and the Admiral's Cup would go the way of the America's Cup.

1

1 Some close Admiral's Cup sailing during the 1973 series between Australia's 'Ginkgo' (KA 252), Argentina's 'Matrero' (A 709), and the German wonder boat 'Saudade' (G 33)

2 (Overleaf) 'Foxhound', a sistership to 'Bloodhound', is still going strong and represented Portugal in the 1973 Admiral's Cup

3 A puff of smoke from the Royal Yacht Squadron starting cannon and another race begins at Cowes

3

2

The last of the cruisers

Developments now came piling one upon the other. The next seven or eight years were to see spectacular and significant steps of progress. In the face of the American win of 1961, the leaders of British ocean racing decided that dynamic action was needed. A proper selection system was introduced for the 1963 Admiral's Cup series. Five of the regular R.O.R.C. offshore races and two inshore around-the-buoys races were nominated as trials. Contenders for a team place had to compete in three of the offshore races and both inshore events. The team would be decided not on a points basis, but still on 'selection' in the opinion of the committee.

There were a number of new boats on the scene, too, as owners cottoned on that there was something worth building for.

At Cowes a Sparkman and Stephens design, *Clarion of Wight*, went into the water for Derek Boyer, Commodore of the R.A.F. Yacht Club, and his partner Dennis Miller, and *Outlaw* was launched for Sir Max Aitken. An Illingworth and Primrose designed cutter, she had a typical Illingworth rig and at 48 ft. 6 in. overall a displacement of only 14 tons, achieved by her one inch thick, cold-moulded hull. Maurice Laing, who had done well previously with *Vashti*, had another Buchanan design, *Hephzibah*, built at Burnham-on-Crouch, Essex, and also on the east coast Kim Holman designed and sailed *Whirlaway* for R. 'Wilkie' Wilkins.

There were two new ones from Camper and Nicholson's, *Musketeer* for R.O.R.C. Commodore Peter Green, with a clipper bow like the American *Windrose*, and *Noryema III* for Ron Amey, a copy of *Quiver III* but carrying more sail. Her mast was about a foot taller. Charles A. Nicholson, designer of *Quiver III*, had intended her for ocean racing whereas before he had always concentrated on yachts that do well inshore. Peter Nicholson, his son, who was closely involved with both boats, design-wise and sailing on them as inshore helmsman, feels they were the last of the genuine cruiser/racer designs to be built in the context of world-class racing.

Even though the sport was now reckoned by owners to be more than just a game, they had still been building boats resembling the older designs built for cruising. After all, they used them for family cruising as well as racing. They also built with one eye on the secondhand value. It's a strange fact that second owners are rarely successful on the racing circuit, however successful the boat they buy has been, so they are more likely to want a comfortable boat for cruising. Interiors, therefore, were important.

Nicholson's had always given a good deal of consideration to the design of yacht interiors. Their idea was to provide dry and comfortable accommodation below

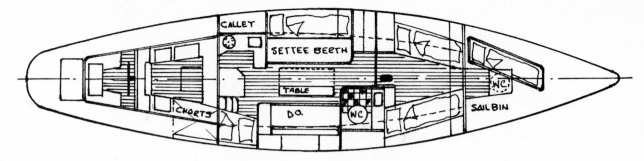

The interior layout of 'Quiver III'

for the off-watch crew and to provide excellent galley facilities so that, conditions allowing, food could be served in as civilised a style as possible. Many yachts carried a permanent cook, and crews sat round a saloon table to eat. When you consider this was probably built of solid mahogany, it comes hardly as a surprise to know racing men have now discarded this extra, needless weight and are content to eat off their laps!

On deck, too, the idea then was to keep the crew as dry, warm and comfortable as possible, rather than putting them where they could work most efficiently on a deck designed for speed rather than comfort. Sheet winches were placed by deep cockpits with generous coachroofs which had an overhanging top at the after end. Sitting on the cockpit seat, a crewman not actually doing anything could squeeze under this overhang and find some shelter from wind, seaspray and rain. No one had yet produced flush decks, with winches amidships or worked from shallow gorilla pits just abaft the mast. Nor had they visualised the crew spending perhaps a whole watch sitting up on the weather rail, catching the worst of the elements, all in the cause of advantageous weight distribution.

Those were the days when a strict two-watch system was observed. The objective was that the watch on deck, normally for three or four hours at a time, ran the boat and could do all that was necessary to sail her, only calling up the skipper, navigator or cook for a sail change or other emergency. It was almost a point of honour not to ask the off-watch, probably snug in their bunks below, for help.

Noryema III and *Quiver III* both had owner's cabins in the forepeak. During racing this was used to store sails not in use. In harbour the bagged sails could be put on deck and the forepeak shut off into a neat cabin with two bunks and complete privacy. Their layouts were perfect for anyone with racing and cruising in mind. They were heavy, stiff boats, too. Solidly built of wood to Lloyds A100 specification, which was beginning to go out of fashion, they weighed about 13 tons.

(Top) Boyer and Miller went to Sparkman and Stephens in New York for their jointly owned 'Clarion of Wight' which won the 1963 Fastnet

(Below) Designer Peter Nicholson's answer to his American rivals was 'Rocquette', a true Solent champion

Designer Rod Stephens says of the boats of this era: 'British boats used to be heavier and stronger than the American yachts, presumably as a result of building to Lloyds specification. We used to reckon they were all right in a blow, just slogging through that short chop you get in the Channel, when finesse didn't matter too much. You only had to look at the fittings (*winches, blocks, cleats, mast fittings*). They were heavy, inefficient, like something off one of the old "J" class. If you wanted decent fittings then you had to get them from the U.S.A.'

A well known Australian yachtsman described the situation more graphically: 'The idea (*in England*) then was if it didn't in some way resemble a square rigger it wasn't a yacht!'

Two owners who tried to break away from this were Derek Boyer and Dennis Miller with *Clarion of Wight*. They went to Sparkman and Stephens in New York for a highly developed hull free of all the outdated features prevalent on the British boats—also, according to Miller, because Olin was the only designer neither of them disliked! And not only did they take a place in the victorious British Admiral's Cup team of '63, but crowned the season with an overall win in the Fastnet Race.

The partnership between Miller and Boyer was a good one. They had first sailed together on *Pym*, the Robert Clark design in which Boyer notched up many successes and which brought him to the forefront of yachting. Miller, the comparative newcomer, entered the sport with more knowledge of weather and navigation than actual sailing, but he was a fast learner, as his own words show: 'The several years I spent in the Fleet Air Arm in the war gave me the rudiments of small boat handling and an idea of what went on in the weather. Flying taught me about navigation and I developed a strong leaning towards instruments. Around 1950 a small cousin frightened the life out of me with a small dinghy and I secretly went down to practise the following morning and then raced at the weekend. This put me on the yachting trail and I looked around for a boat with which to make short passages in the Solent from Christchurch to the Needles and maybe Lymington. I bought a 22 Square Metre, *Glory*, and after a season or two was coerced into buying a South Coast One Design. The small boat did a modicum of offshore work and I managed to fit in the odd Dinard Race.

'John Houghton, bosun of *Griffin II*, got me included in the crew of the R.O.R.C. boat on a Channel Race with Johnny Coote skippering. We won handsomely and from there I had many opportunities to sail with the Lloyds club boat, *Lutine*. Then I navigated on *Pym* on a Belle Île Race and we won by a tide. From then on Boyer asked me to sail as watch captain and for several years we hardly lost a race. In retrospect this was probably due to Derek's attention to detail and his kindness in allowing me to rig the boat with instruments for sailing at night—an unheard-of innovation.

'When we split up we both had a moderately unsuccessful year apart and after the '61 Fastnet jointly commiserated over our lack of a reliable second hand. So we decided to go for a new Admiral's Cupper together and from this evolved *Clarion*, Olin's first successful R.O.R.C. design.'

The Admiral's Cup selection committee of 1963 had a difficult job. Six boats, five of them newly built, were in the running after the nominated races had been sailed. They were the Lyme Bay, Southsea–Harwich, Harwich–Hook of Holland, Morgan Cup, Cowes–Dinard and two special races of 45 miles and 12 miles in the Solent. Setting the precedent for trials to come, the committee, Sir Myles Wyatt, Mike Vernon, R.O.R.C. Vice-Commodore, and Alan Paul, Secretary, observed the inshore racing from a fast motor launch. The team they announced was *Outlaw*, *Clarion of Wight* and *Noryema III*, with *Quiver III* as reserve, and they appointed Peter Green as team captain. All three yachts had masthead rigs for the first time.

The committee said *Clarion* had emerged as the most promising yacht, especially in her performance to windward. *Outlaw* also seemed fast on the wind although not so good on a broad reach, but she had done well in weather which would normally have favoured smaller boats and would match up to big boats such as *Dyna* in the American team. *Noryema* had been consistently good offshore. The two-year-old *Quiver* had not found her form until she had been fitted out with new sails, but she had shown everyone the way around the Solent buoys.

Formal selection like this was a much more professional approach. Foreign competitors weren't completely ignored, either, and for the first time an information centre for foreign yachtsmen was set up at Cowes. Germany made its debut at the Admiral's Cup, joining the United States, France, Holland, Sweden and Britain.

Sweden took a vast lead after the Channel Race with a fine Class I and overall win for *Vagabonde* and Class II win for *Staika III*. The British position came as a shock—equal last with Holland. *Noryema III* had a five per cent penalty added to her time correction factor after she had been caught in a port and starboard incident at the start by the American *Windrose*. This put her down at the bottom of the Admiral's Cup list and *Outlaw* and *Clarion* did only moderately well.

Sweden held on to her lead after the Britannia Cup thanks to a win by *Staika III*. The race turned into a small boat benefit when the leaders were becalmed in a bunch near a mark, giving the little'uns astern a chance to catch up. The American team did best as a whole and closed the gap with Sweden. Holland pulled up to third and Britain to fourth.

The New York Yacht Club Race changed Britain's fortune. A one, two, three for *Clarion*, *Outlaw* and *Noryema* put her only four points behind Sweden with America one point behind again.

Yet winning the Cup still was not plain sailing. At the start of the Fastnet Race, which now attracted 127 entrants, *Clarion* was hit by another yacht on port tack. She suffered no serious damage and sailed a good race. Afterwards both yachts protested, the other claiming she had been calling for water at the Island end of the line. If this had been upheld *Clarion* would have been out and the United States would have scored enough to take the Admiral's Cup home again. As it was, *Clarion* won the protest and the Fastnet Challenge Cup, and Britain won the team trophy.

The man who stood to win the Fastnet if *Clarion* had been disqualified was well known nautical publisher and yachtsman Adlard Coles with his *Cohoe IV*. Only two minutes separated him from *Clarion*. The owners, all good friends, spent a tense time waiting for the verdict and Dennis Miller has this to say of the incident: 'Adlard's gentleness and kindness while we waited out the protest endeared him to me more than anything. And on this occasion another friend, John Illingworth, was a worthy opponent in the protest room.'

Winning the Cup back was a great boost to those who advocated the dedicated approach, but *Noryema*'s and *Clarion*'s incidents on the start line showed how easily victory could be snatched away. Nevertheless, once more America had been the catalyst in stirring up the British and establishing the Admiral's Cup in the big international league. From now on the investment in time, skill and money would get bigger for every series and the teams competing would truly represent the best ocean-racing talent available.

In 1964 Peter Nicholson got down to his drawing-board and came up with his answer to *Clarion*. It was his own *Rocquette* and she was a deliberate attempt to build as light as possible. Her construction was way ahead of its time—light mahogany laminated frames and two skins of planking, the inner one spruce and the outer mahogany. She also had a plywood deck.

Her measurements were 41·93 ft. overall, 30·5 ft. on the waterline with a beam of 10·85 ft., giving her the highest beam/length ratio Camper and Nicholson's had yet built. With 5·5 tons of ballast and a displacement of 11·5 tons, she had a high ballast ratio (50 per cent) and her high freeboard, lack of tumblehome, and, particularly, her beam helped her stability. She was also the first in the British fleet to be built as a flush deck yacht, with a very small doghouse well aft.

Nicholson scored some notable successes with her inshore that year, winning the Round the Island Race and the Britannia and New York Yacht Club Races at Cowes. The following year she proved herself offshore, too. As *Bluejacket III*, owned by David Maw, she was always in the reckoning in the nine R.O.R.C. races she entered and finished fourth in Class II individual points for the season. As late as 1970 she was to win Class II, showing that, although a veteran, she had been part of a significant breakthrough in design.

A new breed

'On both sides of the Atlantic ocean racing has become a sport where the monied come for kudos, attempting to employ good sailors to make up for their own short-comings and swopping boats, crews, designers and friends in the struggle to get into the year book. Maybe I helped it. If so, I regret it truly for I think it is a change for the worse and I still look for the old hands who sail well in older boats, without the glamour, and enjoy it. Many of the service boats fit this category and they carry on training good crews for others to use.'

That was Dennis Miller's opinion of the sport in 1974, when he had to some extent cut himself off from the politics of the racing scene by living in Bermuda, between the two yachting powers. In 1965 he did not appear to be one of the old school. Miller, like so many successful ocean racing owners, was a talented businessman who made it to the top in a highly competitive Midlands industry. With equal determination he had brought his competitive experience to ocean racing, to-gether with a will to be the best.

The 1963 season in *Clarion* whetted his appetite but he saw that no-one in the sport was really attacking all out. With some regrets, he split a second time with Derek Boyer because he wanted to build new for '65 as *Clarion* was poor down-wind. As Peter Nicholson describes it, his attitude was: 'Right, let's not be quite so gentlemanly about it. Let's prepare ourselves and our boats to win.'

To have the best chance of winning races, you must have the fastest boat, speed related to handicap rating. The way to get this is to go to the designer who seems to be drawing the fastest boat. This may seem obvious, but it was not part of the normal thinking process of the British in the mid 1960s. Some owners had a patriotic feeling that you could not win for Britain unless you were sailing a British-designed and built boat.

To Dennis Miller it was obvious. It was only sensible to go to the best man, even if he was an overseas designer. In Miller's opinion the New York firm of Sparkman and Stephens were currently producing the most successful designs. It was a mat-ter of course, then, that when he decided to build a boat to take him into the 1965 Admiral's Cup team, he went to the Stephens brothers. The result was *Firebrand*. Rod Stephens sees her as a main turning point for the sport in Britain. 'This boat,' he says, 'showed it could be "racing".'

She had a sistership in Arthur Slater's *Prospect of Whitby* but Miller's attention to detail, his use of the new rod rigging and the first set of American Hood sails in Britain, and a fine crew—'a determined bunch of ruffians who would give up all else for a season's racing', says Dennis—kept him ahead of his rival.

Firebrand was built at Clare Lallow's yard in Cowes. She was the designers' idea of an out-and-out racer to fit the R.O.R.C. rule. Light and strong with the aim of reducing weight and increasing ballast/weight ratio, her 43 ft. hull had a flush deck with a small coachroof. The halyard and main genoa winches placed just aft of the mast kept crew weight out of the cockpit amidships, where it could do least harm.

Miller was navigator as well as owner, skipper and number one helmsman. His crew equalled him in his reputation as a man who raced hard and played hard. If there was a noisy party ashore before or after a race you could be sure *Firebrand*'s crew were there. They were a breakaway from tradition because they were younger than other ocean racing crews. They caused some raised eyebrows among the Establishment of the R.O.R.C. but with the same exuberance and enthusiasm they proved themselves and the boat capable of winning in light or heavy airs.

Several other boats were built especially with a place in that year's Admiral's Cup in mind. Among them were *Quiver IV* and *Noryema IV*, again from Nicholson's drawing-board. The typical Nicholson layout below was their only concession to the past and the two new boats were both direct developments of *Rocquette*. *Noryema IV* was an almost exact scale-up of the *Rocquette* lines. She was 45 ft. 4 in. overall with a 33 ft. waterline, 11 ft. 9 in. beam and 7·24 ft. draught. Her ballast ratio was 47·2 per cent. Ren Clarke's *Quiver IV* was slightly bigger all round but proportionately longer on the waterline with 35 ft. for an overall length of 46 ft. 1 in. and her ballast ratio was higher at 48 per cent.

Big advances were also made in the area of sails, sail plans, rigging and masts in 1965. One of the factors which had restricted the development of the large foretriangle/small mainsail rig was getting the forestay tight. Wooden masts and wire rigging made this very difficult. The only way to get anything near a reasonably tight forestay seemed to be to keep the stay short of the top of the mast and brace it up with backstays tensioned by highfield levers. Mainsail area was comparatively cheap, rating-wise, and although the large foretriangle rig looked preferable, to stick to a seven-eighths rig and a large main provided an easy solution. Rating formula amendments were to change that.

The ever-changing rating rule is by necessity frequently in the position of catching up on wheezes discovered by clever designers and owners to gain advantages. Mainsails over a certain size were beginning to attract handicap. It became an advantage in rating terms to keep the mainsail as small as possible. The necessary sail area had to be made up somewhere and the foretriangle was the only place. Also, in the opinion of leading designers and certainly in the S. and S. camp, the big genoa/small mainsail rig looked more efficient for going to windward and permitted a much larger spinnaker downwind.

Firebrand had gone for this configuration in a big way, but it was only possible thanks to American sailmaker Ted Hood, the first sailmaker to produce a success-

Trouble aloft as Dennis Miller's 'Firebrand' glides under spinnaker through the Solent during the 1965 Britannia Cup Race

ful masthead genoa, and the simultaneous availability of rod rigging. Rod rigging on metal masts made it possible to get a forestay tight enough to drive a yacht with a large genoa and small main to windward efficiently.

The success of *Firebrand*'s rig led a whole host of owners to the conclusion that Hood sails were a number one priority in the search for speed. Unlike the British fleet of the '50s, owners now rushed to copy winning boats, regardless of cost. The era had arrived when you needed money as well as talent to stay in the top class. The 1965 team was the first to be fully equipped with Hood sails.

Miller also paid great attention to setting sails. For the mainsail he used a bendy boom with the mainsheet running through a series of blocks positioned at intervals along the boom, running to the deck in between, from aft end to mast end, to control the bend. The idea was that the sail can be flattened for fresher breezes by grinding down on the mainsheet, and conversely made fuller for light weather. He also had more than one track for his genoa lead—the trend was for genoa tracks to come more inboard—and he used barberhauls on the clews to change the slot.

The new Hood sails had a rope 'stretchy' luff instead of wire. This made it possible to alter the shape of the sail according to the wind strength by hauling up or easing off on the halyard, the same principle as with the bendy boom. The fair-lead position and the halyard had to be altered as a pair. Constant adjustment is needed to get the most out of the sail as the wind rises and falls and as the point of sailing varies from hard on the wind to reaching.

To pick the British Admiral's Cup team, the selectors were going to take into account four offshore races plus a weekend of specially run races in the Solent.

The season began with a real blow for the Lyme Bay Race. In bad visibility *Firebrand*, which had been unbeatable in her first three Solent passage races, spent about five hours looking for the elusive Lyme Bay buoy which pushed her down to 19th in Class II. Topping the list in that class was *Bluejacket III* (the old *Roc-quette*) with *Noryema IV* second. *Quiver IV* was fourth in Class I. The race was won, incidentally, by *Bloodhound*, which the Queen and Prince Philip had bought from Myles Wyatt in 1962, showing that an old timer of her calibre could still show the new ones a thing or two in heavy weather.

The Southsea to Harwich Race was completely the opposite, with fluky winds and calms to test competitors. This was the race which traditionally brought the south coast yachts around to the east coast, a feeder for the Whitsuntide outing to Rotterdam in Holland, the Harwich–Hook or North Sea Race.

Noryema won Class II, beating *Firebrand* by one and a half hours. Third in that class was the irrepressible John Illingworth, sailing *Monk of Malham* for a French owner. Class I was won by *Outlaw* with *Quiver IV* second and Geoff Pattinson's *Fanfare*, another team hopeful, third. Class III, too small for Admiral's Cup, was won by Sammy Sampson's *Golden Samphire*, one of a new breed of One Tonners which were soon to make their mark.

A pattern was beginning to emerge, as the results of the painstakingly slow North Sea Race were to show. *Bluejacket*, *Noryema* and *Firebrand* were one, two and three in Class II. The Dutch boat *Zwerver* won Class I but runner-up to her was *Quiver IV* followed by *Fanfare*, *Musketeer* and *Outlaw*.

In Class III a new boat, built in Holland of steel, was entered, designed and owned by a shy American businessman called Dick Carter. The boat was *Rabbit* and would have been placed second in her class if she had not been disqualified because her lifelines did not extend right round the deck in the legal fashion. But we were to hear a lot more of *Rabbit* and her owner, who had crossed the Atlantic because Britain could provide some 'hard sailing' and because he admired the British yachts' uncluttered interior layouts.

The same names were in the front again for the fourth nominated trial race, the Morgan Cup, back on the south coast. After a hard thrash across the Channel, this race again produced infuriating calms, but the overall victory went to *Firebrand*, her seventh win of the season. *Clarion* was second in Class II and

Every yachtsman's goal—the Fastnet Rock. 'Noryema IV' reaches the turning point during the 1965 Fastnet

Noryema IV third. *Quiver IV* won Class I with *Fanfare* second and *Musketeer* third.

Firebrand continued her winning run by taking overall honours in that year's Round the Island Race, the annual jolly around the Isle of Wight. Even so, it was no mean feat to beat 322 other craft.

By the inshore trials weekend early in July, the British Admiral's Cup team seemed a foregone conclusion, but it was still important to test the skill of helmsmen and crew around the buoys, in full view of the selectors. More light breezes played havoc with setting courses and yacht handling, but *Quiver IV*'s consistent performance ensured her a place as top scorer for all the trial races; *Noryema IV* and *Firebrand*, with her superior windward ability, completed the trio and *Bluejacket* was nominated reserve. This was a team to give the Americans and the Australians, challenging for the first time, something to think about.

The Australians, like the Americans, were to have a marked effect on future developments and attitudes in British yachting. Their impact at the Admiral's Cup was immediate. They impressed everyone with the businesslike fashion in which they approached the whole affair.

When Geoff Pattinson had taken *Zarabanda* to the Sydney–Hobart Race in 1960, he reported back that 90 per cent of the starters were potential winners of the race as they spared no effort to get their boats in tip-top condition and did most of the work themselves. They all wanted to win. That was the sort of reputation the Australians had. They were hard, ambitious offshore sailors and the thought of their competition was awesome. Perhaps, though, the degree of awe was directly proportional to the lack of real knowledge of exactly how good or how tough they were when it came to competing in waters the other side of the world.

Anyway, the fact that they were coming at all, with the tremendous complications and costs of shipping boats, plus the expense of flying crews over, confirmed that the Admiral's Cup was held in high international esteem. It was now being raced for by the world's best and was, therefore, worth winning, whatever the price. Australian team supporters had donated £20,000 for their effort.

The American teams had always sailed their yachts across the Atlantic, a long voyage but logistically simple compared with shipping yachts as delicate deck cargo. It was also that much more straightforward for the Americans because they were still selecting their team from boats that were coming over anyway.

The Australian challenge was a revelation in the northern hemisphere. The crews arrived almost a month before the Channel Race, just in time to watch the British team being selected. They settled down all together in the same lodgings in Cowes, and were hoping to discover something about the quirks of European tidal waters by taking part in the Cowes to Dinard race. They were prevented from doing this because a dock strike in Sydney delayed their yachts. Still, once their boats were unloaded and rigged the crews got down to three weeks of intensive sailing practice, the likes of which had never been seen in the British fleet.

The same applied to their crew-training programme which was very regular and professional, although running to Gurnard from Cowes didn't quite match up to Bondi beach! Some individual British owners had organised the odd training

Baron de Rothschild's enormous 'Gitana IV' from France broke the
Fastnet course record by over 11 hours in 1965

'Ease the sheets!' 'Quiver IV' about to go into an uncontrollable
broach as she passes Cowes

session at the beginning of the season, but no more than a few hours spread over two or three weekends. Training was left until crews were actually on board, racing in the Solent and Lymington to Poole early season passage races and, of course, the offshore races themselves.

Nor did the British set aside much time for sail evaluation outside the races and if any was done it was usually done alone. Without the benefit of a pace-making partner, proper evaluation of sail efficiency was impossible.

The Australians went out sailing together, helped one another to tune their boats and studied Solent tides on the water and at Southampton University. They took part in the programmed races at the weekends, won popularity all round and instilled an even greater feeling of apprehension into the British fleet.

In their team was *Freya*, launched the November before and winner of the last Sydney to Hobart classic, designed, built and owned by Trygve and Magnus Halvorsen. Then there was *Camille of Seaforth*, canoe-sterned like *Freya*, which had some notable wins back home, and *Caprice of Huon*, the 45 ft. cruiser/racer designed by Robert Clark. Thirteen years old, her sail number was 13, too, but this was certainly not unlucky for her owner Gordon Ingate, an Olympic gold medallist. Stripped out for racing, she did the double at Cowes, winning both the Britannia Cup and the New York Yacht Club Cup. Ingate and his crew brought to their racing a dedication the British still had to learn and the brilliant boat handling on *Caprice* contributed more than anything to her victories. Sir Myles Wyatt may have been gleeful over her performance but it was the new boats, the specialised machines, which finally carried off the most important prize.

Eight nations were entered that year: Holland with a strong team; France, led by Eric Tabarly who had become a national hero the year before when he won the Singlehanded Transatlantic Race in *Pen Duick II*, now rerigged as a schooner; Sweden with a new *Staika IV*, a Stephens design called *Honey* and *Vagabonde*; Ireland making its debut, her team including *Myth of Malham* now owned by David and Bridget Livingston (Bridget had made quite a name for herself as an offshore skipper in the early days of racing after the war); Germany, Britain, Australia and America.

Only 21 team yachts joined 95 others for the start of the Channel Race because the German team was delayed, held up by bad weather at Calais.

In fluky wind conditions, it turned out to be a small boats' race with Class III producing the first three overall. But Britain and Australia made an exciting contest of the Admiral's Cup with only four points between them after this race. *Quiver IV* won Class I with *Firebrand* and *Noryema IV* second and third in Class II. *Caprice* won Class II with *Freya* seventh in that class, while *Camille* was fourth in Class III.

Caprice's class win spurred her on. In the 33½-mile Britannia Cup, she made a good start against the tide and employed the right tactics throughout the race to take first place. Her team mates weren't so lucky, however, and at the end of the first round *Freya* and *Camille* failed to pass a mark correctly. *Freya* realised her mistake and lost half an hour returning to correct it. *Camille* had finished the race before she discovered she hadn't read the small print in the instructions properly—this is vital, as all visitors to Cowes discover sooner or later, usually to their cost. But the tenacity of the Australians once they had come 13,000 miles to sail was remarkable. Rather than be disqualified, *Camille* set off and sailed the course again, correctly, and so gained six points.

Britain streaked ahead with second, third and fifth in the Admiral's Cup fleet for *Noryema*, *Quiver* and *Firebrand*. She had 193 points to Australia's 165. But the New York Yacht Club Race produced an upset when *Firebrand* withdrew after hitting a buoy. Australia narrowed the gap down to 14 points with another win for *Caprice*.

The Fastnet was an easy race—too easy, said the Australians, used to more rugged stuff. Baron de Rothschild's enormous yawl *Gitana IV*, where dressing for dinner served by stewards was the form, even during a race, covered the course over 11 hours faster than any yacht had ever done, to finish first. Overall winner of the Fastnet Challenge Cup, however, was that little boat *Rabbit* owned by Dick Carter, who was quietly working his way into the forefront of yachting.

Quiver IV was second overall, beating all other Admiral's Cup yachts and this, backed up by a fourth from *Noryema IV* and 19th from *Firebrand*, gave Britain the Cup by a healthy 44 points.

Despite their defeat, the Australians were sufficiently encouraged by their own performance to announce immediately that they would be back next time. And then the story would be different. The lessons in professionalism the British should have learnt from the Australian challenge were all too easily pushed aside. The British did not exactly sit back, but they did not add anything to their effort.

Nevertheless, the mid '60s had seen the introduction of the notion that to get anywhere near selection it was vital to have a new boat built before each series, a notion that has been followed more avidly in Britain than anywhere else in the world.

Firebrand, *Noryema IV* and *Quiver IV* were all designed especially with the objective of a place in the team. Although *Firebrand* was destined to be selected for the following series, she was substantially altered in hull shape and on only one other occasion since then has a boat built originally for one series been successfully campaigned in the trials for the next. That was Don Parr's *Quailo III*, nominated reserve in 1971 but campaigned again, with extra sail area, for the '73 trials when she won her place in the team.

What is not determinable, of course, is how much selection depends on the owner and the crew and how much on the boat. It may be that some owners would have won a team place with their former yachts, but it was a risk they couldn't afford to take, especially as the next six years were to see the most rapid changes in hull design ever. They were also to produce a major rule change, plus a change, in Britain at least, in the method of calculating corrected time, which ultimately determines the winner. Faced with all this, the idea that a boat would be out of date within two years seemed highly credible.

One Ton influence

An event happened in France in 1965 which was an important step for yachting all over the world. Monsieur Jean Peytel of the Cercle de la Voile de Paris resurrected the huge silver trophy known as the One Ton Cup. This had first been presented in 1899 for races between yachts with a keel weight of one ton and from 1907 the Six Metre class raced for it for many years until their demise in the early '60s. After the 1962 event it had lain dormant.

Jean Peytel's idea was for competition between level-rating boats. That is, no handicap was involved. The yacht which finished first won. The rating set for One Tonners, as these yachts came to be called, was 22 ft. under the old R.O.R.C. rule, too small to be eligible for Admiral's Cup races, and the significance of their emergence with regard to the bigger boats was not at first realised. But One Tonners raced offshore and, like Dick Carter's *Rabbit*, fitted into the middle of R.O.R.C. Class III where, given the right conditions, they could make a clean sweep on handicap. All around 35 ft. overall, they were miniature versions of their 40, 50 or 60 ft. sisters. In fact, they may well have become the largest, most realistic and most expensive tank-test models for full-scale ocean racers yet produced!

The One Ton Cup was to be sailed rather like an Admiral's Cup series, with countries sending teams of up to three boats. Only this time it was not a team which won but the individual yacht which scored highest points. In the old days races were sailed until one yacht had won three races, with any yacht which had not had a first place in the first five races being eliminated. Now there would be two inshore races of about 30 miles and a 200-mile offshore event (these have since been increased to three short and two long races).

The first of the new One Ton Cup series at Le Havre was won by the Danish Stephens design *Diana III*, and all the 14 crews competing declared that Jean Peytel had shown a flash of brilliance by introducing level rating racing to the offshore scene. Britain had a fairly makeshift team then but the following year interest was aroused. Some prominent names in the offshore world got down to building new boats especially to have a go at this much discussed new type of racing. Names such as Sir Max Aitken, Derek Boyer, and Owen Aisher whose *Yeoman XIV* was designed and sailed by Peter Nicholson.

(Opposite, top) Derek Boyer's One Tonner, 'Clarionet'. The use of a trapeze as demonstrated here was very quickly banned on this size of boat

(Opposite, below) Another One Tonner, Max Aitken's 'Roundabout'

Aitken and his partner, Bobby Lowein, and Derek Boyer went to Sparkman and Stephens for their One Tonners and came away with *Roundabout* and *Clarionet*, the terrible twins. There was little to choose between them in the trials. *Clarionet* gained two firsts and two seconds; *Roundabout* two firsts, one second and a third. But although they dominated British waters, they were to find that man Carter again in Copenhagen sailing *Tina*, his first design commission, for Ed Stettinius of the United States. *Tina* won the Cup and *Clarionet* and *Roundabout* had to be content with fifth and sixth.

Nevertheless, *Clarionet*, painted *Clarion* blue, and the varnished *Roundabout* are worthy of detailed description as they marked a major turning point in yacht design in the British offshore fleet.

They featured big headsail and minimum-sized mainsail rigs following the *Firebrand* style. But of more importance was their underwater shape. The keel was short and the rudder was separated, hung on a skeg right at the after end of the waterline. A closer inspection of the hull revealed that the configuration of the trailing after third of the underwater hull was not of the normal fair line. The shape had fullness drawn unnaturally aft. The 'bustle' had arrived in Britain.

Clarionet was a development of Denmark's *Diana III*, winner in 1965, but with a 'long keel' design. The underwater profile had been cut back so that the forward leading edge was scooped out, the keel was a 'shark's fin' and the rudder was hung right at the end of the waterline, as far aft as possible and totally separate from the keel with absolutely nothing in between. There was a slight knuckle in the forefront of the bow in the hope of giving her better handling characteristics in a seaway.

Roundabout was a new design rather than a direct development of previous designs. The forward entry shape was quite different, a long, fair and gentle curve, very flat at and after the waterline, until the diminutive keel began. Her dimensions were almost identical with *Clarionet*'s, but her displacement was around 2,000 lb. higher. Both boats had the engine sited right in the middle of the hull, just aft of the mast.

Rod Stephens remembers them well. 'They were good boats,' he says. 'Dick Carter said to me when he saw one of them out of the water, "These are going to frighten a few people," and they did. They certainly ruffled the British ocean racing fleet.'

They were so much faster than anything else. They were launched in early June, just in time to take Class III honours in the Morgan Cup. One Tonners from home and abroad took the first 10 places in Class III. In Solent races run under R.O.R.C. handicap ratings they won easily. They were boat-for-boat sometimes faster than Class I yachts. The owners of the larger yachts were dismayed.

Something drastic had to be done for the big boats, so they picked on the most obvious difference between them and the One Tonners: the split of the rudder away from the keel. One of the first to be altered successfully was *Firebrand*, originally adapted while she was in America to sail in the 1966 Southern Ocean Racing Conference races. A temporary alteration was made, the main rudder

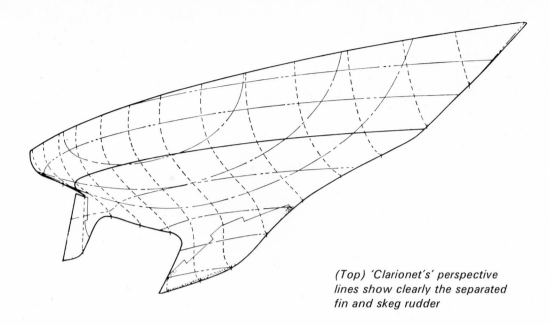

(Top) 'Clarionet's' perspective
lines show clearly the separated
fin and skeg rudder

(Below) The cross section and accommodation
plans of 'Roundabout'. Everything is concentrated
amidships to keep the ends as light as possible

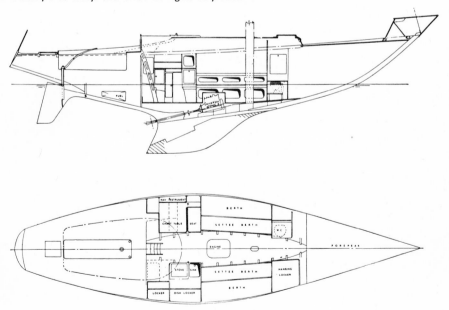

locked and a skeg literally stuck on the stern. Then she sailed in a team with Ron Amey's *Noryema IV* and Mike Vernon's *Assegai II* which won the 1966 Onion Patch series in North America. On the tough Transatlantic Race back to Denmark, the temporary skeg fell off. Proper alterations, with the old main rudder taken away completely and trailing edge fared in, were made in the winter of '66/'67, before the next Admiral's Cup.

Being a Stephens design, *Firebrand* had many modern features in her hull shape when she was originally built, before the One Tonners made their impact. Of her alteration Rod Stephens says: 'We at S. and S. were always keen on cutting down wetted surface area. Maybe this was what gave many of our designs the edge over other boats.

'For this reason we designed *Firebrand* with a very small keel. The rudder was on the back of the keel as usual, but we found downwind sailing very hard, too hard, in fact, and no fun at all. So this led us to design for her a separate rudder configuration, for us always on a skeg. *Prospect of Whitby* was also altered for Arthur Slater. This started a whole new trend.'

It did indeed, and when the One Tonners confirmed the advantages of the fin and skeg, the day of the long keel with integral rudder was over.

Nine contenders wanted to try for a place in the '67 Admiral's Cup team. But they hadn't all reacted quickly enough to the new trends that were emerging.

Obviously the separate rudder and keel configuration was superior. It cut down wetted surface area and provided the necessary control. The fin and skeg had been proved and was not just in an experimental stage. Although some hopefuls for the foremost ocean racing championship were loathe to break with tradition, the competition was now too hot for conservative attitudes to remain.

In addition to *Firebrand*, two other 'old' boats had been altered underwater. They were *Quiver IV* and *Prospect of Whitby*. *Prospect*'s owner, Yorkshireman Arthur Slater, had lost a leg driving in a Monte Carlo car rally some years before and gave up sailing Dragons for something more comfortable. He was going to instil some invigorating Yorkshire blood into the big boat arena.

Four new boats were built and two of them, from Camper and Nicholson's, had a fin keel and separate rudder mounted on a skeg. They were 44 ft. sisterships *Noryema V* for Ron Amey and *Border Law* for John Boardman. The other two, whose design featured the rudder on the keel in the conventional fashion, were *Musette*, a Holman and Pye design somewhat reminiscent of Geoff Pattinson's *Fanfare*, and *Breakaway of Parkstone*, designed by Fred Parker for toy millionaire Leslie Smith. *Breakaway*'s racing career was cut short for that year when she was run down by a coaster during the Morgan Cup Race, but she had been building for three years and was already overweight and outdated.

The other two trialists were *Clarion of Wight*, then in the hands of Sir Maurice Laing, and *Zest of Hamble* owned by Eric Haddon. Both maintained the traditional keel.

It soon became clear that the radicals had done the right thing. The one exception was *Quiver IV*. 'Looking back now,' Peter Nicholson says, 'it was a mistake

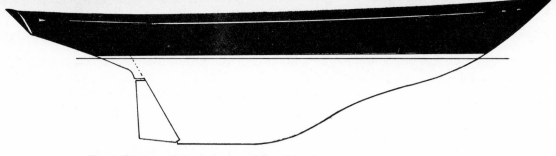

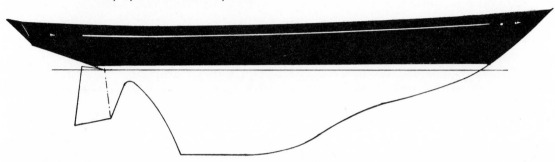

(Top) 'Firebrand's' original traditional keel.
(Below) Her hull with the separate rudder configuration designed for
her by Sparkman and Stephens

to alter her. The Australian *Balandra*, which was an exact sistership, was un-altered and she went faster.' There was clearly more to the new hull designs than simply splitting the rudder away from the keel. The S. and S. boats had those extra qualities already there.

As usual, the trial races were to be four offshore races—instead of the Lyme Bay Race the first race was the Bassurelle Race, around the lightship of that name off France—and a special inshore weekend. This time the team was chosen on a points system.

The selection committee had always preferred a system of 'selection' rather than points because, contrary to the opinion of critics, this seemed fairer to them. The trials take place before the end of June and the Admiral's Cup itself is in August when the weather pattern is very different. Because of this, they maintain they must choose the team most likely to do well in August rather than a team which has done well up until June.

If the team they select wins the Cup ultimately, their method of selection is presumably vindicated in most people's eyes. But the nature of the Admiral's Cup is such that there are bound to be some who say, 'You should have chosen so-and-so instead.' At the time this was inevitable as the Admiral's Cup was unique in that boats which did not make the team could still take part in the actual races, in the same conditions as the team boats. This way they had an opportunity to prove the selectors wrong by doing better than the boats chosen.

The situation has changed these days with the introduction of two entirely separate inshore races during Cowes Week which do not clash with the Britannia and New York Yacht Club Cups. In addition, the Admiral's Cup yachts now have a separate start in the Channel and Fastnet races, but here there is still room for accurate comparison in overall results.

In 1967 there was an attempt to placate the advocators of a straightforward points system. The points table compiled showed clearly who the three leaders were—*Noryema V*, *Firebrand* and *Prospect of Whitby*, with *Clarion of Wight* fourth, some way behind. The selection of the first three gave the other camp a chance to air their feelings: that *Quiver*'s consistency had not been taken into account, nor her skipper's Admiral's Cup experience which could be relied upon when the heat was on . . . that *Zest* had yet to reach her peak because she had a second and third in the inshore trials. . . .

But the selectors, Sir Myles Wyatt, Peter Green and Mike Vernon, stuck to their guns and their points chart. In the event *Noryema V* and *Firebrand* were outstandingly superior and there was little to choose between the results of *Quiver* and *Prospect*. In future years the selectors went back to the 'selection' method and in 1973 steadfastly resisted a particularly strong lobby from some of the Olympic-trained helmsmen and some owners for selection to be on a strict points system like an Olympic regatta.

The results of the 1967 trials seemed to point in favour of the new underwater configuration. However, *Firebrand*'s performance was not simply due to her hull shape. Nor was it because she had only the best and latest go-fast fittings on board. The determination of Dennis Miller and his crew made them win. They had the same aggressive attitude as the Australians and they pushed *Firebrand* harder than other British crews were accustomed to sail their boats.

Although they were divided into two watches, *Firebrand*'s crew was one of the first to break away from the 'when I'm off I stay off' rule. The whole crew was called on deck for every sail change, whereas on other yachts this was only done in bad weather or emergencies. On *Firebrand* the aim was to race the boat offshore with the same intensity as she was raced around the buoys. Obviously sleep was essential on a race lasting longer than a day, but the off-watch crew slept when and where they could and were always ready to come quickly on deck. In a race such as the Fastnet, this was more efficient and, perhaps even more important, more frequent sail changing was possible.

Top racing yachts were then carrying around 19 headsails. Each one was carefully picked as the right size, shape and weight of cloth for different specific strengths of wind. If you have special sails to suit special conditions, you don't benefit from them unless you hoist them as soon as those conditions occur. This is where *Firebrand*'s crew scored. They didn't waste time thinking about it. They were ready to put up a new headsail as soon as their electrical apparent-wind-speed indicator had moved up or down enough to warrant it. The wind is rarely steady for long, so frequent, efficient sail changing counts a lot. On other boats it was still usual to 'wait a few more minutes to see if the wind pipes up/eases off again!'

All this did not have the immediate impact it should have had on other crews and they were soon to find there was more to winning than even revolutionary designs could do for them. The Australians were going to show them.

The Australians arrived in England with three boats all of conventional design underwater. *Caprice of Huon*, now 15 years old, was back. The 46 ft. *Balandra*, sistership to *Quiver IV* and built in 1965, had her original long keel. The newest boat was *Mercedes III*, a 40-footer built in 1966, designed, owned and skippered by Ted Kaufman. She had a long keel with integral rudder, but her construction was seen as radical.

In an article for 'Offshore', the magazine of the Cruising Yacht Club of Australia, Ted Kaufman recalls: 'When we went to England in 1967 they regarded it as a stripped out boat, which it wasn't. A guy came up and asked how we tied the boat up as there were no cleats. I told him there were plenty of winches to tie something to, but that wasn't traditional.

'In England we did extremely well. *Mercedes* won the overall Admiral's Cup points score and the R.O.R.C. points score (*Class III championship*). We were new and we did things that according to tradition we had no right to do.'

To the Australians, the rating rules were there to be exploited in the cause of winning. Another skipper who realised this was Eric Tabarly, the most famous of all French yachtsmen. He had designed his 59 ft. *Pen Duick III* for the 1968 Single-handed Transatlantic Race but in the meantime he was representing France in the Admiral's Cup.

Pen Duick III, launched in June 1967, was one of the first successful ocean racers built in aluminium. She is best described as a wishbone ketch. The mainmast and the foremast were identical in height. The sail set between the masts, technically a foresail, had a wishbone gaff which held it out almost horizontally from the mast to fill the gap completely. The mainsail was small and accounted for a very small percentage of the total sail area.

Under the R.O.R.C. rule at that time, the wishbone sail was not penalised which meant about 25 per cent of *Pen Duick*'s total sail area was free. An extremely fast boat anyway, she was rated very favourably which naturally helped her handicap performance. That year she won the Class I championship with an unprecedented 100 per cent score, taking overall the Morgan Cup, the Channel, Plymouth–La Rochelle and Fastnet races, and class honours in the Round Gotland and La Rochelle–Benodet races. She didn't perform so well in the Solent where close manoeuvring round the buoys, short tacking and fast sail changing mean so much more.

The Australians once more presented the most organised team front for their Admiral's Cup challenge. Again they stayed together in the same house, trained together, had well prepared boats and a keen winning spirit.

Gordon Reynolds, who was skippering *Caprice of Huon* in the absence of owner Ingate, says: 'We had learned a tremendous amount in 1965 and were able to get down to sensible team work and management for the 1967 challenge. We went to Southampton University again and inspected the huge tidal model of the Solent they have there. It's a wonderful method of becoming instantly familiar with the Solent tides. One of the navigators, Bill Fesq, already knew the waters from his wartime experiences. He has done a great deal, with the help of other navigators, to build a large bank of information on tidal conditions and weather patterns on the Solent and the Channel.'

This splendid efficiency was facing teams from eight other nations, Finland being the newcomer. In the Channel Race a period of calm near the French coast dissipated the efforts of most of the teams. But the Australians' tenacity carried them on and, despite their differences in size, all three yachts finished among the first 18 boats home, out of a fleet totalling over a hundred. In Admiral's Cup positions, *Balandra* was second, *Mercedes* third and *Caprice* ninth. This gave them a total of 140 points, 26 ahead of the British team. *Prospect of Whitby* had had the misfortune to break her steering gear.

The two inshore races were close fights. The first, the Britannia Cup, produced some shocks for several team members.

Pen Duick III, which finished first, was considered a non-finisher as Tabarly forgot to sign the declaration form which must be done after a race. Dick Carter, who had been placed overall winner on handicap with *Rabbit II*, withdrew after a protest by another French yacht, *Oryx*, that he had passed the wrong side of a mark boat. The protest was actually dismissed by the Royal Yacht Squadron protest committee because *Oryx* had not flown a protest flag. Even so, Carter stepped down. Finally, the Dutch *Tonnerre de Breskens* dropped out of the race after the first 20-mile round because she misread the flag signals and thought the course had been shortened. So many details . . . That's racing at Cowes!

Tonnerre's owner, Peter Vroon, has long been a popular visitor in British waters and it is surprising that he slipped up. He originally came over to race with the Junior Offshore Group. He's turned up ever since, lately as joint owner of *Standfast* with designer Frans Maas, and reckons he has taken part in more Admiral's Cups than anyone else.

The result of that eventful race was a first in the Admiral's Cup list for *Mercedes III*, third for *Caprice* and seventh for *Balandra*. The British scored a second for *Firebrand*, fourth for *Noryema* and sixth for *Prospect*. There was only one point between the two teams, in Australia's favour.

Blustery, squally conditions for the New York Yacht Club Race did a good deal of damage to sails and called for skilled crew work—a chance for the well practised Aussies to demonstrate what it was all about. *Rabbit II* won in no uncertain way this time, but Australia produced the classic team performance of adjacent placings: third for *Mercedes III*, fourth for *Caprice* and fifth for *Balandra*. *Firebrand*'s second confirmed her strength, but her team mates slumped to 11th, *Prospect*, and 16th, *Noryema*. The Australians went a further 19 points ahead. They set off on the Fastnet Race knowing they were in a position to win the Admiral's Cup if they could keep up this form. They could and they did.

Mercedes III placed third out of the Cup yachts. *Balandra* was fourth and *Caprice* seventh. This showed remarkable consistency again because the weather pattern on the race was variable. After such a high standard of sailing, the Aussies deserved the accolade they received at the prize-giving in Plymouth. They took the Cup with 495 points; Britain trailed with 388. *Firebrand* had come out best of the British trio which took eighth, 10th and 17th.

At this time sponsorship was still a controversial word in British yachting.

4 *'Morning Cloud': after being in the 1973 British Admiral's Cup team, she was wrecked with tragic consequences during bad weather in September 1974*

5 *'Pen Duick III' raised her two masts to the R.O.R.C. rule in 1967 and as a result raced to overall honours in four R.O.R.C. races*

6 Dennis Miller (standing) on his second 'Firebrand', a Swan 43, while racing in the Onion Patch series in 1970. With him is Graham Newland, a well known Australian yachtie, and, at the wheel, Ian Nichols from the United States

7 In the early 1960s, Peter Nicholson, here at the wheel of 'Noryema', designed 'Quiver III' and 'Noryema III' with his father

8 Sir Myles Wyatt, one of the instigators of the Admiral's Cup, handling 'Bloodhound' in the big seas on the run back from the Fastnet Rock in 1957

9 Steering 'Prospect of Whitby', Yorkshireman Arthur Slater looks quite at home in Sydney harbour

There were those who thought it could lower the tone or some such nonsense. Not so in Australia, whose Admiral's Cup team had been supported by a number of commercial sponsors. To bring a team of three boats, plus around 30 crew, from Australia, was a massive undertaking, greater than any other nation had ever attempted in the field of yachting. There had already been some pessimistic speculation as to whether it would be possible to raise the money again. The Australian victory meant they had done well for their sponsors and ensured their appearance in the next series to defend the Cup.

Had Australia pulled out after only two visits, the Admiral's Cup would have jogged on at a more easy-going pace. Their popular win signified that not only would they return, but that it was worthwhile for other overseas nations to have a go. They could not use the excuse that they did not stand a chance because it was held in British waters or under British management.

The 1967 season therefore saw the recognition of three major factors: the positive, professional approach to executing a campaign was effective; building boats to the limit of the rating rule, even exploiting it, made sense; crewing boats required utter involvement and this spelt the end of an entirely separate two-watch system. It also showed that a combination of all these was necessary.

It was ironic, therefore, that in 1969 a team from the United States, still chosen on the principle of 'three boats that are going over anyway', won the trophy. But this was merely a hiccup in the steady line of progress. As time has shown since then, it is doubtful that such a fluke could happen again. The Australians had set what is now the norm when it comes to mounting a full-scale challenge.

A worrying footnote to the '67 season—worrying to the 'big boat' owners, that is—was that the One Tonners were still way ahead in terms of boat speed. *Roundabout* and *Clarionet* had been joined by *Sunmaid V*, the newest of the S. and S. designs, owned by Guy Bowles. The One Ton trials were held at the same time as the Admiral's Cup Solent trials and the One Tonners outshone the bigger boat fleet. Their starts were always much tighter, sail handling was far better and the racing itself closer. The attitude of the crews showed that they really thought seconds were worth saving. In a level rating fleet this is more apparent and the British Admiral's Cup crews needed to be convinced.

On one occasion both fleets were given the same course. All the Admiral's Cup boats misjudged the tide strength in the light airs and were nowhere near the starting line when the gun fired. The One Tonners, starting 15 minutes later, were all on their way before any of the others had cut the line. In another race over a course shortened to six and a half miles, the elapsed time for *Firebrand*, which won her second overall, was almost identical to *Sunmaid*'s and she rated 3 ft. less.

One report at the time commented that nothing raises standards better than level competition. Close, if not level, competition was to come later in the Admiral's Cup and this would play its part in improving standards. In the meantime the One Tonners were keeping owners on their toes and the style of their crews was an example worth copying.

The professional approach

To Britain's cost, she had been shown by Australia the way a challenge should be mounted. The 1969 season would reveal the details which would keep the Admiral's Cup on top of the big league. It had become the central theme around which the British offshore fleet revolved. Every owner was after a racing machine to a greater or lesser degree. Because of this competition, development of equipment and sails was spurred on and ideas became more refined.

The arrival of the Starcut spinnaker as an essential part of the sail wardrobe was one example. This was developed by the Bruce Banks sailmaking firm under the guidance of Ken Rose. Crews had to learn new handling and setting techniques for these highly effective sails which made it possible to reach under spinnaker with the apparent wind as much as 45 degrees ahead of the beam if the wind was not too strong. This gave rise to the adage that when racing you were either on the wind or under spinnaker.

The Starcut was a specialised sail for shy reaching and at its most potent with the wind ahead of the beam. When the wind crept more than 90 degrees off it was necessary to change to a spinnaker cut for running. Spinnaker changes, therefore, became more frequent and needed as skilled crew techniques and practice as changing a headsail. To have no spinnaker at all for the few moments it takes, or should take, to change from one to another would slow the boat down, so a new method was developed. It became the custom to have two spinnaker halyards and to hoist the new spinnaker while the old one was still drawing. When the old one was released from the guy the new one could immediately fill. This technique of 'peeling' was soon established in Britain and other countries followed suit, a new dimension born by invention.

One of the most radical new boats was Ron Amey's seventh *Noryema*, actually named *Noryema VGX* which stood for Variable Geometry Experiment. Amey's favourite of all the *Noryemas*, before and after, this was later abbreviated to VG when she was no longer experimental—Very Good. She was, indeed, a fast boat.

The hull and sail plan came from Dick Carter and, in his particular style, were like those of a 51 ft. dinghy. She had beautifully sleek lines, a flush deck and a small Carter-style squared-off doghouse, a tall rig, 170 per cent genoas and penalty poles for the spinnaker. She was built in steel by Frans Maas at Breskens in Holland

Since the sailmaking firm of Bruce Banks dreamt up the Starcut spinnaker in the late 1960s it has been copied by sailmakers all over the world. Compare yachts astern with Germany's 'Saudade' in this 1973 Admiral's Cup Race, and see just how close to the wind she's sailing under spinnaker

and her interior layout was the brainchild of Butch Dalrymple-Smith. Butch sailed with Amey for several years and then, as ever since, when he has been globe-trotting, built up an international reputation as one of the world's best-liked yachtsmen.

Noryema VGX could not have a conventional interior because of her most unusual feature—a lifting keel. This was a dimensional dynamically shaped construction, as distinct from a plane plate used for a centreboard, and was designed by Amey on a full-size model of the hull in his own workshops in Oxfordshire. The lift was arranged by a hydraulic ram as used for tip-up trucks, but working in reverse. The pressure was provided by the crew working seven manual short-stroke pumps located in the housing at deck level. The whole keel could be completely retracted into the hull for downwind sailing and its encasing divided the downstairs accommodation into two.

Some conservatives expressed doubts about the yacht's safety. They said with the keel completely up her self-righting ability was below par. However, experience, including her fair share of broaching knockdowns and over three full racing seasons with two Fastnets, proved her to be safe and seaworthy as well as fast. But she did not fare well under the rating rule and rated up with 55-footers. Also she was too tender on a shy spinnaker reach and in those conditions found it hard to stay with the larger ones and save her time. She was an interesting attempt at something new in design but only made reserve for the '69 team.

The list of official Admiral's Cup trialists numbered 21, and 12 of these were newly built. (In 1967 nine boats had hoped to get into the team.) By the final inshore trials the fleet had shrunk, but it was clear right from the start that this team was going to be the most hotly contested yet.

Even before the sailing season got under way, the crew of Geoff Pattinson's 51 ft. *Phantom*, built the year before and declared Ocean Racer of the Year with three R.O.R.C. overall wins under her belt, decided they would follow the Australians' example and in January began intensive, supervised physical training. By Easter they were out sailing, practising manoeuvres against the clock. Sometimes they did dry practice in *Phantom*'s marina berth at Camper and Nicholson's in Gosport, all to get timing right and save those odd seconds which can be the difference between winning and losing.

Pattinson, by now getting on in years, had not been in an Admiral's Cup team since he sailed *Jocasta* in the first series in 1957 as one of the founders of the trophy. Now, with the same determination that put his crew through their paces in the gym twice a week, he applied himself to the preparation and upkeep of his boat. For three days each week, she was taken out of the water to have her underwater hull finish prepared. This consisted mainly of meticulously rubbing down by hand the cover of antifouling, the comparatively new Graphspeed which had first been used on racing dinghies to produce a faster finish. The yard men used chamois leathers as 600 wet and dry paper was too coarse to give the required smoothness—quite a task.

The crew had guaranteed their availability to sail every weekend from Easter to the end of the Fastnet Race, and that included some Fridays, too, as the off-shore races start on Friday evenings. Just as an athlete sacrifices his personal life for his sport, so the crew had to put the boat before anything else.

Not all the 21 trialists followed such a rigorous programme, but there was a general feeling that if the British were to beat the Australians they would have to join them, at least in their methods.

The 12 yachts which took part in the final weekend of inshore trials were observed very closely by the selection committee. There were more contenders than ever before, so the selectors had to be careful they picked the best three. As far as possible they had sailed in all the R.O.R.C. offshore races which counted as trials so they could better assess performances in conditions they had experienced themselves. Then, during the inshore trials, each boat had to carry a selector in at least one of the races so he could observe the drill standard of the crew at close quarters.

Although selection was not linked directly to results and points, in the end the team more or less selected itself on results. The standard of racing had obviously improved. In 1967 the One Tonners had shown up the heavies. Two years later columnist Jack Knights wrote in 'Yachts and Yachting' magazine: 'The improvement in the general standard of the Admiral's Cup trialists . . . was unmistakable and encouraging. Starts were something like class starts, spinnaker hoists and gybes would not suffer too much in comparison with America's Cup trials.'

The transition from racing yachts offshore to offshore yacht racing seemed to have been made.

One personality now noticeably missing from the English racing scene was Dennis Miller who had gone to live in Bermuda. Since his first successful season with *Firebrand* in 1965 he had been tempted by warm-water sailing such as the Southern Ocean Racing Conference around Florida and the Bahamas and alternated this and other overseas races with sailing in Britain in Fastnet years. He was in the British Onion Patch team in '68 and '70 but when he next took part in the Admiral's Cup it was as a Bermudian representative. Definitely a long-race man, he says the Fastnet remains closest to his heart (after it come the St. Petersburg–Fort Lauderdale Race, the Australian Sydney–Hobart 'without the start and finish', the Bermuda Race, and the Transatlantic). British yachting would miss his good company and hard sailing, but other names were emerging.

The 1969 team was announced and showed that the dedication of Geoff Pattinson and his crew paid off. *Phantom*, the wooden Nicholson boat, was selected and her crew commended for fine sail handling. The other two yachts named were both S. and S. designs. One was a new *Prospect of Whitby*, her smart dark blue hull built in Holland in steel, which gained favourable help from the rating rule. The third boat was constructed of yet another material. She was *Casse Tete III*, owned by business partners Dave Johnson and Mike Hurrell, and she was a glass fibre production boat, a Swan 43, identical to others coming out of the same mould in Finland. *Casse Tete*'s inclusion in the team was refreshing and significant.

It had now become a firm adage that to make the grade in this game you had to have a one-off designed, custom-built boat and that glass fibre was only suitable for easy-upkeep family cruisers. Dave Johnson wanted to prove this was not necessarily so, and he was backed up by three other glass fibre production boats in the final bunch of trialists. His selection made his point, and two sisterships of *Casse Tete III* represented Finland in the Cup that year. They shared relative position honours and the difference in speed between these and other yachts of their size was small. Glass fibre has certainly come into its own since then and gained world-wide respect. The Mexican *Sayula*, winner of the 1973/74 Round the World Race with the ubiquitous Dalrymple-Smith on board, is a standard glass fibre production yacht.

The appointment of a non-sailing team manager that year was another indication of the growing attention being paid to shore-based organisation. The Australians certainly thought it worthwhile to have one. Now, in England, Ken Wylie was given the job and his duties were to take care of anything involving the whole team, from sailing practice to cocktail parties ashore, and from arranging moorings to sail repairs. He also had to ensure that team skippers and navigators attended briefing sessions, had the latest weather information and were generally free to race their boats without worrying about shore-side responsibilities. All subsequent teams have had such a manager.

Then there was the introduction of commercial sponsorship in a big way, two words which suddenly became mentionable—at least, for most people. The R.O.R.C. followed again the example of the Australians and accepted the commercial help of the Dunhill cigarette and tobacco company, who were already involved in dinghy racing events in other parts of the country. Some stalwarts were against such a revolutionary move, but the harsh reality was that the Admiral's Cup needed at least as much organisation as an Olympic regatta, and on a bigger, more costly scale. If interest continued to grow as rapidly as it had been, then it was automatically going to become more expensive and complicated to handle.

The R.O.R.C. were fortunate in finding a sponsor who already had experience in backing yachting and who was sensitive to the genuine desire to preserve the amateur status of the event, run for the benefit of the participants rather than the company's own ends.

Dunhill's first moves were modest. Their services included the setting up of an Admiral's Cup results board. It might seem a small thing, but until then interested spectators and crews had to either bother race officers or wait for the morning papers to see how teams were faring. They also provided a smart power launch, the *Virginia Queen*, which took the Press and VIP spectators out on the water to watch the races, fast outboard rubber dinghies for ferrying team crews, taking

(Opposite, top) Dave Johnson's and Mike Hurrell's 'Casse Tete III' was the first glass fibre boat to be selected for the British team

(Opposite, below) The crew of Geoffrey Pattinson's 'Phantom' worked hard to earn their place in the 1969 Admiral's Cup team

messages or carrying sails ashore for repair, and a generous supply of their product to all British yachts. The experiment was a success and Dunhill's involvement with the Admiral's Cup, and Cowes Week in general, continued and expanded, adding considerably to the enjoyment of the series and helping to ease the R.O.R.C.'s organisational load, until they had to pull out from the major sponsorship for financial reasons in 1975.

For its part, the R.O.R.C. decided they should have an Admiral's Cup office base at Cowes and they set up a caravan which was manned all day and well into the evening. This proved so successful that a year later a caravan was purchased to be used regularly as their out-of-town headquarters and it's now to be seen at all R.O.R.C. events.

The Australian team which came to defend the Cup indicated that they, too, were making it the main objective on their calendar. Ted Kaufman's *Mercedes III* was back, and she was joined by two brand new boats built with the event specially in mind. These were *Koomooloo*, owned by Dennis O'Neill and designed by Kaufman, and a new S. and S. design with much of the flair of the 1966–67 breed of Stephens One Tonners, *Ragamuffin*, owned by Syd Fischer.

The trials back in Sydney had been tough and they were not inclined to let the Cup go easily. They also had the added advantage of a whole season's racing behind them, when they could get their boats into top tune before coming to England.

They brought with them the same organisation and determined racing attitude, exploiting wherever possible the sailing rules. The British fleet had come a long way but not far enough. They had to learn that gamesmanship was not enough if they wanted to win. They had to be ruthless. Offshore yachtsmen were notorious compared with their dinghy sailing friends for their lack of detailed knowledge of the racing rules. The same applied to their reluctance to claim their rights, let alone deliberately making them work to their advantage. Protests were rarely put in.

If a skipper had been wronged, the usual redress was through instant verbal abuse rather than an appeal to the race committee for disqualification. In a tight situation when several boats were rounding a mark together, it was easier to keep out of trouble, partly because damage from a collision costs money but mainly because most people were never quite sure how far they could push their own rights or get others to respond.

The Australians were brought up in a different school. They were everybody's friends ashore, but on the water they were out for themselves. When they protested *Phantom* in a warm-up race before the series, and won, the British knew the fight was on. But they still behaved like ostriches. It was not until two years later, when a British boat was put out of an Admiral's Cup inshore race by *Koomooloo*, that this lesson was taken to heart properly. Nevertheless by then all the crews had been warned to learn the rules and watch the Aussies!

The Admiral's Cup fleet numbered 31, made up of nine countries with three-boat teams and two with two-boat teams. Two boats had no chance of winning the

Cup, but such was the attraction of racing against the best ocean racers in the world that the individual owners concerned, from Bermuda and Spain, sought entry and were granted team status. (In 1973 the committee ruled that all teams must have three boats.) Italy and Argentina were newcomers.

Following some criticism from participants, the R.O.R.C. introduced separate starts for Admiral's Cup yachts in the Channel and Fastnet races. It had been argued that non-team boats could affect the results, especially if they were in the same stretch of water at starts and on spinnaker runs.

The Admiral's Cup fleet started first in the Channel Race. The weather was variable but when it blew up *Ragamuffin* and the eventual winner, the New Zealand *Rainbow II*, fresh from One Ton victory in Heligoland, were in their element wearing heavy-weather twin-headsail rigs. The British fleet have often admired the efficiency of this rig, particularly *Ragamuffin*'s, but even now they have never been able to copy it with any great success.

Ragamuffin won Class I from *Phantom*. Dick Carter's new 41 ft. centreboarder *Red Rooster* won Class IIa for the United States with *Prospect of Whitby* second. The One Tonners, as usual, dominated Class III. From this race onwards, it is significant that no major trophies in Classes I and II have ever been won by yachts other than Admiral's Cup team members or trialists. A clear split had grown up between them and the also-rans, a sad state of affairs for those who have the enthusiasm but not the money to keep up.

The Australians made a great start to the series. With a first in the Admiral's Cup fleet for *Ragamuffin*, fourth for *Mercedes III* and seventh for *Koomooloo*, they gained a total of 168 points. Italy went into second place with a sixth, ninth and 16th to score 130 points. This was fairly unexpected and they owed it to poor all-round team placings by the two other seeded nations, Britain and America.

Casse Tete III had made a bad tactical error by hanging on to a Starcut spinnaker over by the French coast for far too long as the wind shifted. She had to beat against the tide to the Le Havre mark and dropped to 28th place. *Prospect* was third and *Phantom* fifth, to give Britain 120 points equal with the Americans. *Red Rooster*, the 'big dinghy' with the two-ton lead centreboard, had gained a creditable second and *Carina* eighth, but *Palawan*, a big boat not really up to modern racing, could only manage 26th.

The two inshore races were very even. The British team won the first, thanks mainly to *Prospect* which took the Britannia Cup. *Red Rooster* won the second and the New York Yacht Club Cup for the United States but *Palawan*, finishing well in the bottom half of the fleet, pulled down their score. Australia scored highest points for the two races and had a healthy overall lead of 54 points over Britain with the Americans a further 29 points after that.

There was just the Fastnet Race to come which, carrying treble points, can easily alter the whole course of the results. This was the case in 1969, although Mother Nature played a greater hand in the results than the competitors and organisers would have liked.

The Admiral's Cup fleet was last away at the start on the Royal Yacht Squadron line at Cowes. True to form, the big boats, most of them non-Admiral's Cup, led at the Fastnet Rock, *American Eagle*, the converted Twelve Metre owned by Ted Turner of the United States, *Kialoa*, also of the United States, Max Aitken's 62 ft. cutter *Crusade*, *Palawan* and *Fortuna* of Italy. They had a fast run back to the finish, with the *Eagle* taking line honours only four minutes ahead of *Kialoa* in the early hours of Tuesday morning. *Crusade* finished not long after, but these three had devoured the last of the breeze.

During the day the wind began to drop as the bulk of the Admiral's Cup fleet were approaching the Scilly Isles. By Wednesday morning, 160 boats were left wallowing between the Fastnet Rock and Plymouth.

Palawan, the first Admiral's Cup boat home, followed *Fortuna* in on Tuesday evening. The next to finish was *Ragamuffin*, raising Australia's hopes of retaining the Cup. But *Red Rooster* slid in very early on Wednesday morning, Dick Carter chasing his second Fastnet win.

By dawn, 17 yachts had finished, 13 of which were team boats. America was lucky. All three of her team were in. Australia and Britain had only one each, *Ragamuffin* and *Phantom*, and the wind still had not piped up in the Channel. This weather pattern favoured the bigger boats and for once *Palawan* came good. She was eighth in the Admiral's Cup fleet, *Carina* was third and *Red Rooster* first, to give the United States the trophy. The IBM computer also calculated that *Rooster* was the overall winner.

Rating only 25·68 ft., *Red Rooster* had proved the dark horse in a big boats' race. But although she was certainly first boat in Admiral's Cup placings, there was some doubt about her first place overall. *Crusade*, according to the computer, was only 68 seconds behind *Rooster* on corrected time, but there were rumblings about the accuracy of the finishing times taken by the lighthouse keepers on the end of Plymouth breakwater.

Yachts take their own times as well and the times recorded by *Rooster* and *Crusade* and entered on their race declarations would have given first overall to *Crusade*. Sir Max Aitken put in an official protest which, after lengthy deliberation, was dismissed by the committee who preferred to stick by the times taken at the lighthouse.

No team could have been more justified in claiming 'we was robbed' than the Australians. To be cheated by the weather, they felt, was an anti-climax to two weeks of good racing. They had had the Cup in the bag until the bitter end.

No-one was more surprised than the American selectors. The result was almost entirely due to the second, third, first and first record of *Red Rooster* for the series. Nobody, least of all the selectors, had seen her in action before then as she was completed at the Berthon Boatyard, in Lymington, Hampshire, only days before the Channel Race. Carter had done it again.

Nevertheless, the confusion with *Rooster*'s and *Crusade*'s times had left a nasty taste. The incident highlighted a serious flaw in the R.O.R.C. organisation. The weakness had already been spotted, but it took something dramatic to get anything done.

R.O.R.C. races had always been started on a transit line, usually shore-based and therefore absolutely accurate. There was always a spot-on count-down in seconds to the firing of guns and anyone over the line who failed to return and recross correctly was, in those days, automatically disqualified. This was later amended to a five per cent penalty on the corrected time, and it is still applied very strictly.

Now this may all sound very reasonable and, indeed, it is. It is all credit to the race officer and his hawk-eyed helpers that they see any yacht that is the merest inch over the starting line. But a premature start may make only a second or two's difference on a long race and so much can happen that its effect can be more than nullified.

It is at the finish that seconds count even more and by 1969 races were being won and lost by seconds. Yet there was not nearly the same accuracy in seconds and inches at the finish as there was at the start. It was even quite usual for competitors to take their own times which were taken as official. It was a luxury to have someone on the line to do the job, as in the Fastnet, but it was still hit and miss.

This state of affairs was far too amateurish for the sport as a whole and the Admiral's Cup in particular. People had travelled across the world for it and during the summer European yachts came to practise in R.O.R.C. events rather than stay in their local waters. Everyone who spends a lot of money and time to take part must be fully confident that the seconds they save or lose on a course will be accurately recorded when the computer calculates corrected times. Otherwise they would stop bothering to come.

Action was taken in 1970, not only to solve the finishing time problem but also to put the whole organisation of the racing on to the sophisticated basis the sport demanded if it was to continue to develop. The R.O.R.C. appointed Alan Green as Assistant Secretary (Racing) to take the brunt of this side of things from Secretary Alan Paul and his assistant Hope Kirkpatrick, who had been in charge for many years. (Both are now retired.) They would stick to the administrative side.

The first thing Alan did was find finishing equipment which is more sophisticated and accurate than any used anywhere else in the world. Its heart is a £200 electric chronometer which combines, with radar, night vision equipment and remote control finishing guns. A permanent finishing site was established on top of Horse Sand Fort off the entrance to Portsmouth Harbour where most races finish. Here, transit marks for a finishing line were put up, illuminated at night and linked to the remote control finishing guns. Timing for finishes no longer relied on the naked eye so it became more accurate than starting. Every two years this equipment is transported to Plymouth for the Fastnet Race. There is no worry that any boat may be cheated of even one second again.

Enter Mr Heath

There is no doubt that, by choosing sailing as his sport, Ted Heath helped to put ocean racing on the map. His superb planning and single-mindedness have been an example to all yachtsmen, but at first his influence was not so much on the sport itself as on the general public's awareness of ocean racing. It was given a new stature when a man as well known as the Leader of the Opposition, and later Prime Minister, became involved successfully. People were interested and suddenly the news media sat up and took note.

Ocean racing had always been a very introverted sport. Only a small percentage of the thousands of people who enjoy sailing ever go on an ocean race or even understand the compulsion behind it. To the rest it is a complete mystery. In the '6os, unless you happened to read yachting magazines you would not pick up much from the odd inch or two the newspapers carried. Sports editors did not rate sailing very highly, but news editors were very interested in the leisure-time activities of prominent politicians.

When the Leader of the Opposition went to Australia in 1969 and won the Sydney–Hobart Race, one of the classic ocean races in the world, he became front-page news. The 630-mile Hobart Race has a reputation for being a tough, foul-weather race and lived up to it that year. Heath was the first Englishman to win it since John Illingworth instituted and won the first race in 1945. Like him, Heath had one of the smallest boats in the fleet and sailed through a storm. The Australian papers brought out banner headlines such as 'Britannia Rules the Waves— Again' and Heath became a hero to millions.

They already knew he enjoyed sailing. He had begun his waterborne career at the age of 49 in dinghies on the east coast, progressing to a racy Fireball. He took up sailing for the sake of his health. Heath prides himself on his physical fitness. He used to play squash, enjoys swimming and had regular workouts with the late Len Hines, former trainer at London's Grosvenor Hotel gymnasium. When he took on the extra duties of Leader of the Opposition, his doctor advised him to sail in order to keep fit.

He had his first taste offshore when Sir Maurice Laing took him on a Cowes–Dinard Race in *Clarion of Wight*. He was hooked. 'I think this appealed to him rather more than the Fireball,' Heath's ex-navigator Anthony Churchill, formerly of *Phantom*, says. 'This long distance get-away-from-it-all atmosphere where he can relax, away from politics.'

'Work is the curse of the sailing classes,' said Mr. Heath, heady from his Hobart win at his champagne victory party after the race. In an interview later that month, this son of a builder and carpenter said: 'I am determined

The boat that started it all—Mr. Heath's first 'Morning Cloud', a production glass fibre yacht. The owner is at the helm

There are times when a can of cold beer are the only reward a man wants in life, especially when you've just won the Sydney—Hobart. 'Morning Cloud's' crew in 1969, from the left: Anthony Churchill, Owen Parker, Sammy Sampson, Jean Berger, Ted Heath, Duncan Kay

to keep time for sailing. I think it is essential that you should keep yourself fresh.

'There is a terrible danger of politicians going stale. I think people are making a big mistake if they vote for you and then expect you for seven days a week. All you get is people who are tired and stale and overworked and then you get bad government.'

Morning Cloud was a 34 ft. glass fibre production boat from a Rochester firm on the River Medway. The mould for these S. and S. 34s, as they were called, had been taken from *Morningtown*, a one-off Stephens design built in wood for the 1968 One Ton Cup. *Morningtown*'s crew included Owen Parker, who was to become Ted Heath's number one on successive *Morning Clouds*.

Owen left school at 14 and was a professional yachtsman until he was 27. 'Then I gave up. There was no future in it.' He regained his amateur status, skippered the Twelve Metre *Kurrewa V* that was beaten by *Sovereign*, and sailed as tactician and sail trimmer on Guy Bowles' One Tonner *Sunmaid* before joining Duncan Kay on the foredeck of *Morning Cloud*. Ted Heath was a customer at the marine supplies firm in Southampton where Owen was working, which is how he came to sail for him.

Morningtown and her Italian sistership *Kerkyra II* were fourth and third respectively at the One Ton Cup, confirming the design was a good one. *Morning Cloud* was the first one out of the mould. Another notable owner to have one was well known east-coast skipper Rodney Hill who names his *Morning After*.

Right from the start there was intense rivalry between *Cloud* and *After*. Rodney Hill's experience carried off most of the early races for *Morning After*. But Ted Heath learnt quickly. He applied the same determination to his racing that had brought him to the top in politics and by the end of the season the honours were more or less equal. *Morning After* won the R.O.R.C. Class IIIb (One Tonners were in IIIa) championship 16 points ahead of *Cloud*, but *Cloud* won the East Anglian series on the east coast by just one point.

Then in August, after the Fastnet Race, a selection had to be made between the two for a place in the team to go to Australia for the Southern Cross Trophy.

The R.O.R.C. selectors had made it clear that a place in the Admiral's Cup team did not guarantee a place in the Southern Cross team and the selection races for Australia would be, to all intents and purposes, the Admiral's Cup races. Also the bottom size limit for the Southern Cross was lower than for the Admiral's Cup, low enough to embrace One Tonners and S. and S. 34s. *Prospect of Whitby* was chosen as a middle-size boat, and *Crusade*, which had done so well in the Fastnet, was picked to provide cover at the bigger end of the size scale if the notorious Hobart turned out to be a big boats' race. The best small boats keen to go and available to cover the other end of the scale were *Cloud* and *After*. It was a difficult choice for the selectors as *Morning Cloud* was improving all the time. In the end they put Rodney Hill's experience first and chose *Morning After* but nominated *Morning Cloud* as reserve to travel with the team.

To send *Morning Cloud* as an official member of the team was an important decision. There had been little success up to the time of selection in finding sponsors to support the representation down-under and owners offering themselves for selection had to take the gamble that they might have to carry most costs themselves. Although the team was selected on performance there was, therefore, a certain element of 'whoever's prepared to go and pay their way' included in it, too. Arthur Slater spearheaded the money-raising activities. It had to come from outside the Club as it was felt any money raised by members shouldn't be used to help a few yachts go to Australia when the Club premises and Club yacht needed finance.

Slater persuaded Qantas Airlines to help with air fares for the crews but this still left the enormous shipping costs for boats. At the eleventh hour Dunhill's stepped in with cash support of around £5,000. Their involvement with yachting was growing and it was a logical step for them to move in and help with the Southern Cross. But the fact that Mr. Heath was a member of the team must have made their decision easier. His inclusion meant that the event would receive publicity in the mass news media, the thing that sponsors of any event are always looking for. Whether Dunhill's would have come in anyway is open to conjecture, but it is a fact that the first name mentioned in their Press release announcing their connection with the British Southern Cross effort—they called it 'throwing the life-belt'—was Mr. Heath and his yacht.

So, in one easy move and almost without a shudder, the R.O.R.C. had accepted the principle of substantial cash sponsorship. The precedent set, similar support has since been gratefully received. The 1973 team which went to Australia was backed by cash from Barclay's Bank and the 1974 One Ton Cup series run by the R.O.R.C. again saw Dunhill's providing a substantial amount of cash as well as Press office and Press boats, just as they had done for Cowes Week.

The results in Australia for the first Southern Cross challenge were good

Newspaper cartoonists had a heyday after the 1970 general election

enough to keep sponsors and the R.O.R.C. happy. The British conceded the team trophy to New South Wales, but in the final race, the Sydney–Hobart, Britain captured nearly all the silverware. *Crusade* took line honours, reserve *Morning Cloud* won the race outright, and her division; *Prospect of Whitby* was second overall, winning her division (Arthur Slater says it was the hardest race he's ever done with the last two days cold and hard on the wind); and *Morning After* was third in Division III.

No longer was Mr. Heath 'all at sea', just one of the permutations of the endless puns journalists and cartoonists found in his seagoing activities. On December 31st, 'The Times' and 'The Daily Telegraph' in Britain both carried full reports and photographs on their front pages, and as soon as Mr. Heath was back in England receptions and parties were given in his honour.

There would have been nowhere near the same amount of coverage of the Southern Cross series, let alone front-page space for it, had the Leader of the Opposition not been involved. The fact that he was expected to make a strong fight at the general election only months away was the icing on the cake which made his victory all the more meaningful. Mr. Heath was a difficult personality to write about. He was a politician who played the organ. Now he was a top participant in a rugged sport, a man who had restored some of Britain's seafaring pride. Even the Australians were proud of the 'Pommy' win.

How had the new boy scored such a success? 'Before we went to Australia we had a number of meetings at his flat,' says Anthony Churchill, 'and because he's not an absolutely brilliant social talker he's willing to let other people have their say, and he makes up his mind in the end. He does a lot less talking and a lot more listening than the rest of us. By the end of that season he'd mastered techniques that at the beginning of the year he knew nothing about.

'The great point about Heath is that the man is a doer. He's got fantastic stamina.' The crew soon discovered this when they were called to discuss boat business with him at breakfast parties and later, when he was ensconced at No. 10 Downing Street, in the small hours of the morning. Whatever other urgent matters of state he had on his mind, he put them aside and was often the most alert person there.

His crew included the best available, another factor in Heath's favour. As well as Churchill and Parker, he had brought Jean Berger, owner of the Swiss One Tonner *Joran*, to his team and Duncan Kay who had sailed on *Joran* and *Rabbit II*. Second helmsman and in command in Heath's absence was Sammy Sampson, a top-class skipper in his own right.

Six months after the Hobart Race, Heath became Prime Minister which gave even more scope to the 'Heath at the helm' type journalism. Still, a new interest was created with more inches on the sports pages for all yachting events, plus more television coverage. Yacht racing will never be much of a spectator sport, but Southern TV regularly has programmes on Cowes Week and the Admiral's Cup. What is more important to crew members, their bosses now know what they are talking about when they ask for Friday afternoon off to go racing!

An excellent way to get politics out of your system—yell at the foredeck crew!

Encouraged by his success, Mr. Heath, 1970 Yachtsman of the Year, announced he was building again with the '71 Admiral's Cup in mind. He set about this in a manner befitting a Prime Minister. He went to Stephens for a design (the fact that he did not choose a British designer was not lost on the Press) and she was built in wood at Clare Lallow's yard at Cowes. A tight security blanket was thrown around the new boat and no-one was allowed to see her until she was launched, again by his stepmother.

In the meantime, Heath had again recruited a crew of 'stars' to sail with him, just as a Prime Minister would pick his cabinet ministers. He added Peter Holt and Peter Dove, from the Hood sailmaking company, to his band of blue-oilskinned yachtsmen while Berger dropped out. Some pundits reckoned there were too many experts and not enough workers for them to get on together and sail as a team. But Mr. Heath's leadership qualities were equal to the challenge and *Morning Cloud* was perfectly campaigned in the trials.

Sailing *Morning Cloud* was often hindered by motor launches which followed him at close quarters to take photographs. They made concentration difficult for the crew and sometimes physically interfered with the progress of the yacht by blanketing the wind or disturbing the water with their wash, and the noise was infuriating. Despite these annoyances, *Morning Cloud*'s performance was exemplary and it was no surprise when she was selected for the 1971 team and Mr. Heath was invited to captain that team.

It was an even bigger boost to British yachting when the Cup was won back under his leadership. National and international press and TV coverage was greater for the Admiral's Cup than ever before, the main interest being Prime Minister Heath.

'Of course we'll win,' he said confidently before the series. 'If you get yourself a first-class boat it really is a bloody good investment,' was how he justified the whole thing to the left-wing 'Daily Mirror'. During the build-up to the series he had been accused by Labour leader Harold Wilson of being a part-time Prime Minister. During Cowes Week and the Admiral's Cup itself, the troubles in Ireland were going through a particularly violent phase, but Heath still went off on the Fastnet Race in the face of much criticism. *Morning Cloud* was equipped with a hotline to Whitehall and a helicopter was standing by to lift him off if necessary.

Somehow things had turned a little sour on the Hobart Race hero, as critics looked more closely into his sailing activities. These days the problem has reached the stage where public opinion so begrudges him his private, leisure activities that he has to think twice about getting a new boat when he wants one. But in 1971 he was not going to be bothered by public opinion. Being Prime Minister did not interfere with sailing 'except in extreme circumstances' said the man who had been given special permission by the Queen to sail in the Morgan Cup Race, an Admiral's Cup trial, instead of attending the annual Trooping the Colour ceremony—unprecedented for a British Prime Minister.

'Aboard, I never think of politics. I come back from a day's racing refreshed. I go straight to a meeting with a member of the cabinet completely relaxed.' His physical fitness and energy must help in both walks of his life because, as he says, during a race 'you get to sleep when you can, make the most of it and are prepared to go a long time without it if you have to'—not much different from the lot of a politician.

He sees a similarity himself. 'Everything on the boat is done by a process of discussion. You get a momentary impression of a Cabinet meeting discussing whether a turn to port—or left—would be the right thing to do. Eventually somebody has to take a decision.' He was the man to make the decision—as skipper or P.M.

Heath's presence also helped to improve the efficiency of running races, as a columnist pointed out in 'Yachts and Yachting' in 1971: 'Over the past two years, ocean racing people have been getting used to the publicity that Ted Heath's participating in the sport has produced, brought to its peak ever since he has been Prime Minister. Not everybody welcomes all the effects of this but there are undoubtedly some advantages.

'For example, after his overall win in the Seine Bay Race, which he finished not long before midday on Sunday, the results were calculated quickly enough for his victory to be announced on the 5 p.m. news that afternoon.' Before such attention from the news media, it could take until the Tuesday after a weekend's race for the final results to be calculated.

Mr. Heath built new again for the 1973 series, the same *Morning Cloud* which sank so tragically in gales in September 1974. S. and S. and Cowes-built again, she proved to be very consistent in all wind strengths. Everything about her reflected the thorough planning and smart execution that went into sailing her and the *Morning Cloud* team were again selected to sail for Britain. Even though Britain failed to retain the Cup, and Heath himself *was* absent for part of the time, he left his legacy of publicity.

Many purists found the extra attention distasteful and were equally unhappy about the potential growth of commercialism in the sport, not only from sponsors.

Winning became much more important than just participating because winners would get their names in the papers. Designers, builders, sparmakers, sailmakers, winchmakers, paintmakers could all gain from the publicity. A winning boat will sell sails and equipment and the yachting trade will readily supply expert yacht crews from their staff to give owners on-the-spot benefit of their knowledge and help them along to victory. This leads to cries of 'Professionalism'.

It is a thin dividing line between who is a 'Professional' yachtsman and who has the professional attitude to racing and finds it easier to take part in it by getting a job in the industry rather than, say, being an accountant in London. The line is thinnest in the case of a builder who might own and skipper his own prototype for a production model. If he wins races then he will get publicity and in turn this will mean orders for the book. Winning or losing could mean for him the difference between commercial and financial success and failure and this is what upset the opponents of publicity. In fact, such an area of professionalism already existed, although the publicity was less dramatically confined to word of mouth in the club bars and in the yachting magazines. There is no way of stopping it, short of stating that anyone who is in the trade cannot race with his own products, which would be a ludicrous state of affairs.

Nowhere is the commercial pressure higher than in the One Ton Cup, but this does not affect the sportsmanship of the participants. As long as ocean racing remains a non-spectator sport and prize money is nil or negligible, the game is unlikely to be taken over by individuals more interested in personal gain, publicity or no publicity.

The diehards remain but, in general, increased publicity for offshore racing and continued sponsorship help to maintain the high standards demanded by any international sporting competition. It has attracted new blood from other fields of sailing. There are now several former Olympic medallists from the smaller classes who are keenly involved because the Admiral's Cup presented another challenge. One of them is the 1973 British team captain, Robin Aisher, who took on the job with an unremitting competitiveness that even outshone Heath's own.

All this has helped improve standards in racing. Heath, a respected owner and skipper, showed that careful pre-planning and strong purpose of mind were yet another formula for winning. I am sure that he would rather have the effect of his participating in the sport remembered for this than for any transient glamour he may have generated.

Rules and regulations

The years from 1971 to 1973 saw a consolidation of the advances already made in boat design and crewing. The major changes were being made off the water, the most significant being a new rating rule, followed a year later by a new time allowance system. Reactions to them were mixed.

The '71 series was the first Admiral's Cup and, indeed, the first international competition of importance, to be raced under the new International Offshore Rating rule (I.O.R.), rather than the R.O.R.C. rule. The limits for Admiral's Cup boats were altered to 60 ft. maximum and 29 ft. minimum rating instead of 60 ft. and 25 ft. which had been the case in 1969. (Before then, the limits had been 60 ft. and 30 ft. waterline length.) This change was to take account of the formula producing slightly different figures rating-wise. It preserved the lower limits, though reduced the upper a little, thus allowing roughly the same size of boats as before.

The limit is set quite deliberately to exclude One Tonners which, under I.O.R., have to rate 27.5 ft. maximum. The new I.O.R. ratings were expected to come out very similar to waterline length and this turned out to be more or less true.

The earliest Admiral's Cup contender to be launched in '71 in Britain was *Cervantes IV* for Bob Watson, the first of four new Stephens' boats being built in Cowes. Following her into the water were *Prospect of Whitby*, Arthur Slater's new one, *Morning Cloud* (the second) and *Carillion* for Derek Boyer, previous owner of *Clarionet* and *Clarion of Wight*.

Cervantes IV was a small boat with a 30 ft. waterline. Her I.O.R. rating came out at 29.5 ft. She sported the new Stephens feature, a blister deck. This gave a flush-deck type of clear working surface for the crew and provided reasonable headroom below without requiring too high a freeboard. The entire Cowes quartet incorporated this feature, although the camber of the blister varied according to the overall size of the boat—the bigger the yacht, the less pronounced the blister had to be.

Three other administrative alterations were made for the series. Firstly, the R.O.R.C. took the plunge over the inshore races during Cowes Week. They decided the Admiral's Cup 30-milers would be sailed on the Monday and Wednesday, quite distinct from the rest of the cruiser racing. This created a new élite, but also meant Admiral's Cup yachts could take part in the Britannia and New York Yacht Club Cups, the races the R.O.R.C. had always said foreign visitors came to Cowes Week for anyway. Arthur Slater himself says he gets his greatest racing thrill whenever he wins the Britannia Cup.

In order to make sure, as far as it is ever possible to allow for the weather, that the Admiral's Cup fleet were back in plenty of time for Monday's race, the start of the Channel Race was moved from Friday evening to Friday late morning.

It was made compulsory for all Admiral's Cup boats to arrive at the Gosport marina by 9 a.m. the day before the race so there would be ample time for the measurers to remeasure any yacht whose rating certificate looked in the slightest way doubtful. Failure to be there by the deadline would mean disqualification. This was an important step as there had been too little observation and checking of ratings in the offshore handicap classes. Verifying measurements was an idea borrowed from dinghy classes and meant no-one would slip through illegally.

The first to suffer under this rule was the French team. Eric Tabarly arrived too late with *Pen Duick IV* and was not allowed to compete in the Channel Race. France's hopes were further destroyed when the Carter-designed *Gitana V*, having been provisionally placed first overall, retired from the race after agreeing that by mistake she had rounded the wrong mark off the French coast. The third boat in the team was placed last but one. Later, in the second inshore race, *Gitana V* retired again and *Pen Duick* was disqualified. There was no hope for the thoroughly unhappy French team, and Tabarly did not bother to compete in the Fastnet. The Admiral's Cup no longer held any chance for a team which could not co-ordinate itself for a 100 per cent performance.

The British fleet was certainly taking the series extremely seriously. The list of contenders for a place in the team totalled 27 and 15 of these were new boats, although during the season the number of possibles was reduced to 23.

The R.O.R.C. selectors were also being very conscientious and issued a series of notices to contenders exhorting them to make thorough preparations. In previous years, they felt, crews had not experimented enough when tuning up their yachts.

The answer to this from the owners was that they felt they were being constantly scrutinised and one failure might ruin their chance of selection. They did not dare experiment too rashly in case it was not a success and they turned in a bad result. So the selectors made a point of stating categorically that early races in the season would not be taken into consideration.

There were to be no selection races prior to June 5th but seven races in May were strongly recommended for practice. These included three races open only to Admiral's Cup possibles over the Spring Bank Holiday weekend. The selection races proper were in June: two R.O.R.C. offshore races and two inshore weekends.

The selection was not easy and the choice did not please everybody, mainly because it was a 'small boat' team. This meant that if either of the major offshore races turned out to be in the larger boats' favour, the British team could be in trouble. They were all S. and S. designs. The largest of the trio was *Prospect of Whitby*, Arthur Slater making selection for the third time running. She was right at the bottom of Class I, rating 33 ft. dead. *Morning Cloud* rating 30·7 ft. and *Cervantes IV* at 29·5 ft. were both in the lower half of Class II with *Cervantes* only just large enough for Admiral's Cup inclusion. Many people were disappointed that the Nicholson 55 *Quailo III*, owned by Don Parr, only made reserve. At 40·9 ft.

she was the highest-rating boat in the list of possibles and sailed well enough, they felt, to be selected.

Seventeen countries entered teams. Of these, New Zealand and Austria had only one boat and although Poland entered a full team none of them turned up. The dismal effort by the French team reduced competition still further, but there were still more countries represented than ever before.

The Channel Race was sailed in ideal conditions with the wind never dropping below Force 3. There were some changes in its direction, but fortunately the British boats were in the right position to take advantage of them.

At the finish the new electronic finishing equipment was used and there were no complaints about the result. *Prospect* won overall and *Morning Cloud* won Class II from *Cervantes*, altogether a result to bolster the selectors' confidence. On Admiral's Cup positions it was almost too good to be true, a first, third and fifth. The only regret was that the wind shifts had turned the race into a 'big boat benefit' and if *Quailo*, second overall, had been in the team the British card would have read first, second and third.

Nevertheless, it was a fine start. There was still a long way to go and the challenge from both the United States and Australia looked very strong. The first inshore race confirmed this and also that the Australians meant serious business. The British were taken unawares and caught by the rule-book tactics they had been warned about.

Starting at Cowes is always difficult in a large fleet. *Cervantes* was playing safe on the Monday Admiral's Cup Race but not so the Australian *Koomooloo*. With some aggressive start-line manoeuvres she taught the British boat a lesson that should have made an impression after previous Australian visits. With little steerage way, *Cervantes* found herself the underdog in a port and starboard situation only 15 seconds before the start. *Koomooloo* put up her protest flag, having quite intentionally set out to trap the British boat.

The $33\frac{1}{2}$ mile course set consisted of two west-about triangles. The American *Yankee Girl*, with Rod and Olin Stephens sharing the driving, led throughout and won the race in fresh reaching and beating conditions. *Prospect* was only 58 seconds behind, *Morning Cloud* came fourth and *Cervantes* was placed provisionally 11th.

After four hours of deliberation at the protest meeting, the race committee upheld *Koomooloo*'s protest and *Cervantes* was disqualified. This could have spelt complete disaster but the Americans and Australians had not had much luck. Somehow Britain managed to stay in the lead by a slim nine points over the United States and 37 ahead of Australia. Team mates to *Yankee Girl*, both large boats, *Carina* and *Bay Bea*, could only scrape up 10th and 16th and the Australians had a bad day with seventh for *Ragamuffin*, ninth for *Koomooloo* and 21st for Arthur Byrne's *Salacia*, younger sister to *Rago*. She had been delayed by a fouled genoa sheet just before the start.

The other places in the first ten were well spread around, which again helped preserve Britain's lead. Holland's *Standfast* was third. Argentina's *Matrero* was

'Prospect of Whitby' overhauls the South African 'Omuramba' at
the start of the 1971 Fastnet

fifth. Dennis Miller took sixth place in *Firebrand II* for Bermuda and Italy's
Mabelle was eighth. None of these individual efforts was backed up by reasonable
results from their other team members.

In the second inshore race the wind was blowing Force 6 to 7 from the west and,
because the tide was running strongly against the wind for the first three hours,
quite a sea was running.

The Australians lived up to their reputation of enjoying a good thrash and
skilfully kept their boats going fast in rugged conditions. The course set was the
same as for Monday's race and once again the fleet leader was *Yankee Girl*. *Salacia*
was only 10 seconds astern with *Ragamuffin* one minute later. *Koomooloo* was well
up with *Prospect*, but both *Morning Cloud* and *Cervantes* were suffering from poor
starts.

After the second round, when most boats further reduced sail, *Yankee Girl*
sailed home first and would have taken second overall had she correctly complied
with the complicated Cowes Week sailing instructions. She had cut through the
starting line on her run eastwards instead of passing outside the limit buoy, and

was disqualified. The 46 points she lost were going to prove critical when it came to totting up the final points.

Australia won the day. *Salacia*, *Ragamuffin* and *Koomooloo* in second, third and fourth places scored 135 points to Britain's 120. This meant that Britain entered the Fastnet Race still on top, 22 points ahead of the Australians and 61 ahead of the United States. But no-one was going to forget the '69 series, when the Australians started the Fastnet in the lead and were dislodged by the Americans. The British team could not afford to be over confident. Nevertheless, morale was high.

The Admiral's Cup fleet started last in the 605-mile classic, at noon, in a fresh Force 4 westerly which freshened to Force 5 before the fleet left the Solent. The leaders reached the Fastnet Rock on Monday evening. *Ragamuffin* was among them although the computer gave the unofficial lead on handicap to *Cervantes*.

The run back from the Rock was a testing time for all crews as a north-easter of up to 40 knots was blowing. The larger boats all averaged over 10 knots. It was on this run that *Koomooloo* gybed and in the process carried away her rudder. She had to accept assistance and retired, dashing Australian chances. They knew nothing of this on *Ragamuffin*, of course, and she continued at a hair-raising pace.

First boat home was *American Eagle*, in 3 days, 7 hours, 12 minutes, a new record by over two hours. *Yankee Girl* was the first Admiral's Cup yacht to finish but only two minutes astern of her was *Ragamuffin*, with the British reserve boat *Quailo* one hour later. All eyes strained to catch sight of *Cervantes*, but the wind died on the last leg from the Lizard and she eventually placed third overall, second in Admiral's Cup placings.

Ragamuffin was a popular overall winner and *Quailo* was runner-up. The British support for *Cervantes* was poor, *Prospect* 12th and *Morning Cloud* 14th, but they stayed ahead of the Americans who actually scored most points for the race. *Bay Bea* had at last found conditions to suit her and gained a fifth in Admiral's Cup places, to join *Yankee Girl*'s third and *Carina*'s disappointing 15th. *Salacia* finished 13 hours after *Ragamuffin* and still took eighth. But with *Koomooloo* out there was no chance for the Australians.

The fact that Britain won the trophy back would seem to justify the selectors' choice. However, the winning margin of 46 points depended heavily on misfortunes suffered by main rivals Australia and America, *Koomooloo*'s rudder and *Yankee Girl*'s disqualification. *Koomooloo* had been well placed ahead of *Prospect* and *Morning Cloud* when she dropped out. She needed only to finish in 11th place, one place ahead of *Prospect*, for Australia to have snatched victory. Still, you have to finish the race to score points and you get nothing for pushing your boat fastest for half the race. Britain had the Cup again.

In retrospect, had *Quailo* been included she would have scored more points than any of the team members, but things could have gone the other way for her. Luck counts a lot—on the other hand, the best boats seem to have the most luck!

The British did not fare so well in Australia that year. The selectors decided to endorse their Admiral's Cup winning team and the same three boats went to the

(Right) Intense concentration from owner/skipper Max Aitken steering 'Crusade' during the 1971 Fastnet

(Below) Ocean racing is a tough demanding sport but there's always time for a good party. The late Uffa Fox (standing), entertains Prince Charles (on his left), Sir Max Aitken (centre) and Prince Philip (on Sir Max's right) in an after-dinner speech on the eve of the 1971 Fastnet

Southern Cross, with no reserve this time. There they performed with mixed fortunes and had to be content with a second again.

The same thing happened the following year when Britain sent a team to compete in the Onion Patch series, the American four-race series. *Noryema VIII*, *Crusade* and Dick Thirlby's *Maverick* were placed second. But there was some consolation in *Noryema*'s overall win of the Bermuda Race, the first non-American boat to win it. This was certainly a boost for British offshore sailors and Teddy Hicks, skippering her in the absence of owner Ron Amey, was made Yachtsman of the Year to acknowledge his services to yachting over many years and in many *Noryema*'s.

All eyes were now on the 1973 Admiral's Cup, including those of the R.O.R.C. who started a controversy by announcing they were adopting a new time allowance system. It came as something of a shock to prospective competitors, at home and overseas.

When an owner is building a racing boat, an important factor he must consider is where he is going to race and what weather and sea conditions he can expect there. The sort of boats that are successful in the English Channel may not necessarily win races in America or Australia.

He must also consider the method used for calculating the corrected time of yachts in a race. In America this is done by a time allowance directly related to the length of the race, usually referred to as time on distance. This tends to favour bigger boats, and, as American races are often almost straight-line courses or made up of very long legs, they are comparatively unaffected by tide and involve very little short tacking. Time on distance means that, whether it is a fast race or slow race, a boat that is bigger in rating has to allow a smaller boat the same amount of time, regardless of distance.

In Britain the system used was time on time. In other words, a yacht's elapsed time was multiplied by a time correction factor, which was constant and based on rating, to produce the corrected time. The amount of time a high-rating yacht had to allow a smaller one therefore varied according to whether it was a fast or slow race. If a race sailed under this system starts with a period of calm, or is sailed in light breezes, then calculations favour the smaller boats. If it is a fast race in fresh conditions, the reverse is true.

Both methods of calculating results have their champions and critics and obviously these factors play an important part in determining size of boat and the relation of sail area to hull weight and rating. The weaknesses in both systems are also acknowledged and the ideal method of working out times is constantly being sought. In 1972 the R.O.R.C. reckoned they had found the best method, known as the Performance Factor system.

The idea was that it took into account three factors instead of just one pair or the other—that is, the yacht's time over the course, the course distance and the yacht's rating which is used to calculate the time correction factor. This has become known, not strictly accurately, as time on time on distance. It was claimed this system was more flexible and would maintain fair competition in average conditions and permit any size of yacht to win in extreme conditions. Ratings and the I.O.R. Mark III method of calculating them would not be affected.

The reaction to this was not favourable. The new system was an unknown quantity in the tricky formula of winning a R.O.R.C. race. For the overseas Admiral's Cup aspirants it added yet another problem to the selection of team yachts. It was one which had never been tried and therefore there was no guiding evidence from the past for it.

This made things difficult, particularly for the Australians whose boats were all built and team selected many months before any race would actually be sailed under the P.F. system the following season in Britain. They already realised that their selection trials in Sydney merely produced the best boats in Australian waters and not necessarily the boats most capable of winning in European weather, wave and tidal conditions. Now there was something new with no yardstick to help them gauge which boats would fare best by it.

Many argued that the new system should certainly not be used for the first time in an Admiral's Cup year. The R.O.R.C. were not to be swayed and on December 8th, only eight months before the next Admiral's Cup and well into the Australian summer sailing season, the Admiral's Cup management committee announced that the P.F. system would be used for all races in the series. The same announcement had to admit, though, that all other handicap racing during Cowes Week, including the Britannia Cup and the New York Yacht Club Cup, would be raced on the old time-on-time formula.

The Solent clubs decided not to change for their Solent Points series whereas R.O.R.C. races would be sailed under the new system, which meant that British Admiral's Cup hopefuls would be racing and tuning up under two different methods of calculating results. This seemed hardly a ready acceptance of the new system.

The supporters of the P.F. system claimed that both other methods had disadvantages in exceptional weather conditions and that the P.F. overcame this. So it did, provided that a race was all calm and slow, or all fresh and fast.

In reality, the main reason why small or large boats are favoured in different conditions is quite simple. Big boats finish in actual time before small boats and if the weather conditions change, as they frequently do, between the time of the first boats finishing and the smaller ones coming in then, depending on what the weather change is, that will decide which boats are favoured. The change need not necessarily be in wind strength. Even minor directional changes can make the difference between beating and fetching or reaching and running. Then there may be tidal changes. The P.F. exponents made the error of assuming that conditions, whatever they are, will be experienced uniformly by all yachts, fast or slow.

After the 1973 Fastnet the P.F. system was defended by one official on the grounds that the Fastnet winner and Admiral's Cup winning team would have been the same if the old system had been used and only a handful of boats would have had a different individual position. This viewpoint seemed hardly positive, especially when, just over a year later, the R.O.R.C. announced it was abandoning the P.F. and adopting a new formula time-on-time system.

The Germans succeed

Thirty-two owners presented their boats for the 1973 trials in Britain. The smallest rated 29 ft., exactly on the minimum, and the largest 43·3 ft., the maximum allowed being 45 ft. Twenty of the boats rated between 30 ft. and 33·9 ft. This shows clearly the concensus of opinion was that the best size for English conditions and the P.F. system, was on the small side, in the top two-thirds of Class II or at the very bottom of Class I. Twenty-four of the boats were built for this series and the search for design improvement was intense.

Twenty-three of the trialists were S. and S. designed, eight of which were Swan 44 production series boats first built in 1972. There were three designs by American Dick Carter. There were three from Camper and Nicholson's, and one each from Angus Primrose and Britton Chance. Van de Stadt of Holland completed the list.

Sir Max Aitken's centreboarder *Perseverance* was one attempt to try a new approach to design. A Britton Chance design, she was a sistership to the American *Gannet* and a scaled-down version of the successful American campaigner *Equation*, but she was finished late, and never got into her stride.

The clutch of S. and S. designs, production and one-offs, all sported the basic flush deck feature with or without a small doghouse blister, and all had minor variations in hull shape or weight distribution, although the duck's tail shape of the after overhang was dubbed the '73 Stephens feature. Except for the Swan 44s, none of the yachts seemed significantly different.

The most adventurous of the S. and S. owners was Arthur Slater. In his search for something better, he tried a seven-eighths foretriangle on his new *Prospect of Whitby*. The idea was to get the same sail area for a lower rating. The experiment failed, *Prospect* did not go well under that rig and for the first time since 1967 there was no *Prospect of Whitby* in the team. After the trials her rig was changed to the more conventional masthead. She suddenly came alive, was placed fourth and eighth in Class I in the Channel and Fastnet Races, and then went to Australia where she helped Britain to win the Southern Cross Cup for the first time.

In retrospect, the other one-off designs must be judged a decline for S. and S. as they seemed to have developed too far in the direction of excess beam. The problem that faces all designers is that if they have a successful design, they cannot stay with it because owners buying new expect something even more advanced the next time. The end result can be slower than the so-called 'old' design. Pundits have commented that later Stephens designs look more like their successful

'Frigate's' crew sit 'birds-on-a-branch' style on the windward deck as she approaches a Solent race buoy during the 1973 Admiral's Cup series

hulls of a few years ago. Certainly in the '74 America's Cup trials, the Twelve Metre *Courageous* found it hard to overcome *Intrepid* which had first defended the Cup in 1967. This would suggest that the S. and S. firm reached a design peak in the late '60s, a barrier it is finding hard to break through. No other designer has found the breakthrough either, but others may have caught up some.

In the area of sails there was little advancement. North sails were being used more, breaking the virtual Hood monopoly. North is an American company which had established a new loft in Britain at the beginning of the season. No doubt the fact that Britain's Flying Dutchman Olympic gold medallist, Iain Macdonald-Smith, was working for North and crewing on *Frigate*, the hot favourite, helped stir up interest in this new brand.

Various systems had been invented which made it possible to hoist a new genoa while the other was still up. The methods fell into two broad types. The first was simply an extension of the Hood Sea-Stay (which was a rod forestay with a C-shape groove on the back edge into which the bolt rope on the luff of the genoa was fed as it was hoisted, in the same way as a mainsail is hoisted up the mast in a luff groove). The refinement was the Twin Stay, which, as its name implies, was two grooves side by side. Another type had the grooves opposite.

The second method was to have a vaguely U-shaped plastic shield which fitted over the normal forestay with the open end facing aft. It worked in the same way as a single luff groove. Then it was discovered that if the bolt ropes on the genoa luffs were made small enough, two sails could fit in the groove at the same time. This proved best of all.

There were more experiments with winches. In the past, conventional geared winches had been used by most people and only a few tried a cross-linked system or the upright two-man coffee grinder winches to haul in the genoa as speedily as possible. Now coffee grinders appeared on several yachts and cross-linked winches with remote drive linked mole-hills became the norm for the rest. Such equipment was very expensive, but pennies weren't being spared.

The R.O.R.C. Admiral's Cup committee, in a determined effort to defend the Cup, decreed more trial races than ever before. The races covered five weekends over June and into July. Although only two R.O.R.C. offshore races were included, an extra night race was added to the trials programme. This was the result of suggestions by the trialists themselves who were concerned about the predominance of inshore round-the-buoys racing.

The selection committee, led by David Edwards, maintained that they observed inshore races to watch crew-work and handling of the boat rather than actual results. It was impossible, he said, for selectors to go offshore on the yachts themselves, although they sailed on other boats in those races to get first-hand knowledge of the conditions.

Not convinced, the owners and crews wanted to be sure they had plenty of opportunity to show their strength in the more important area of offshore. Okay, said the selectors, and suggested a special 100-mile race to start in the evening after a normal Saturday 30-miler. This would mean the crews would do a hard day race and then set off again an hour or so after finishing. Presenting it in such an unattractive way, they seemed somewhat surprised at the enthusiasm which greeted their idea. The crews really wanted to sail offshore, especially overnight when races can be won or lost. That was what the boats were built for and the crews trained for. That was where stamina counted. They were following in the tradition of such people as Illingworth and Miller.

The committee responded splendidly to this attitude and in their enthusiasm went even further themselves. In addition to selecting a team, they nominated three reserves, matched to the size of the team yachts. They also arranged practice sessions during the lull before the competition proper. These included starting tactics, sail evaluation tests and team tactic talks led by the team captain, Robin Aisher.

Aisher was the skipper of the most outstanding boat in the British fleet, *Frigate*. This was not so much from a design point of view, although she represented the latest thinking from Dick Carter, but more from the whole campaign surrounding her.

The boat was a joint venture between Tony Boyden, who had owned Twelve Metres *Sceptre* and *Sovereign* and a Nicholson 55 offshore racer, and Robin Aisher, a highly respected Olympic medallist in the 5·5 Metre class and son of Sir Owen Aisher, the incumbent Admiral of the R.O.R.C.

As far as Aisher was concerned, his only reason for taking up ocean racing was the challenge of winning a place in the Admiral's Cup team. That was the prime objective for the boat. If that objective was achieved, then helping the team to retain the Cup was the next. In building *Frigate* there was no consideration beyond this. She would be redundant after the series and there was no business investment involved. The designer, Dick Carter, was told to worry about nothing other than winning.

Crew selection, training and racing of the boat were equally intense. On board life was spartan and often extremely wet. Everything was planned to help the boat go faster. Before the race, sails were packed in tight bricks which were shifted around the boat to alter trim or add weight to windward. After they had been used, it was impossible to repack them into bricks on board, so, particularly in heavy weather, the inside of the boat was gradually filled up with a mass of wet sails, among which the crew often found themselves sleeping rather than in the bunks.

On a beat to windward, any crew below was woken up on each tack and moved to windward bunks. If on deck, they sat birds-on-a-branch style, facing outwards with their feet dangling over the weather side—although with their torsos in the strictly legal position *inside* the lifelines. There was no time to enjoy this business of sailing.

The crew stayed ashore rather than on board during inshore weekends and were ferried to *Frigate* by a smart motor tender which also took unwanted gear.

Aisher was not impressed by the way traditional offshore skippers raced their boats. He thought crew-work was slack and helmsmen were line-shy at starts.

He raised a few eyebrows when he advocated putting the opposition out of a race by using the rules rather than allowing them to get through by pulling punches, still an attitude reckoned 'not British'. But within the context of the *Frigate* campaign that attitude was logical and pleased the rest of the dinghy-trained blood in the offshore fleet.

The sceptics said it wouldn't work. But *Frigate*, one of the smallest in the fleet, won her Admiral's Cup place, was top points scorer in the British team and third highest scorer in the whole Admiral's Cup fleet, won Class II handsomely, won the Alan Paul Trophy for the most consistent performer of the year and was Ocean Racer of the Year. How's that for an object lesson? To build and campaign she cost an estimated £50,000 and was put on the market for £40,000.

Major General Bill Woods, the team captain for 1973, is quoted as saying that he expected a handful of yachts to emerge ahead of the others after only a few trial races. The conflicting results of the first two showed this to be an optimistic assumption.

In the first trial, a 30-mile course around the Solent, *Morning Cloud* won from *Quailo III*, *Superstar*, *Noryema IX*, *Winsome*, *Frigate* and then the rest. The race was sailed on a perfect Solent day and the course set by the Royal Thames Yacht Club was a true test, including 12 miles of windward work.

The second trial, which was the innovated overnight 100-miler, started at 8.30 p.m. the same evening. The course was east to the Owers light vessel, then west to the Shambles and back again to Cowes, giving the fleet a practice run over the first part of the Fastnet course. Just in time, after some hints from the crews, the R.O.R.C. hurriedly added that the Isle of Wight should be left to starboard between the Owers and the Shambles.

It was a disappointing race, spoilt by the undue influence of the tide which bunched the fleet at St. Catherine's Point. The result was that sailmaker Bruce Banks' *Northwind*, the smallest boat in the fleet, won from *Marionette*, *Frigate*, *Chandanna* (Colin Fenn) and *Morning Cloud*. *Noryema IX*, which finished first, and *Quailo III*, the largest boats in the fleet and therefore taking more than their fair share of adverse effect from the tide, were 28th and 29th respectively.

Only three yachts were in the first 10 in both races: *Frigate*, *Morning Cloud* and David May's *Winsome* which was eighth in the second race. The P.F. system almost produced one of its 'freak' events. *Northwind*, rating 29 ft. dead, the minimum, averaged 7·2 knots while *Noryema IX*, about 10 ft. longer and rating 10·5 ft. more, had averaged only 7·7 knots.

The third trial, the Le Havre–Royal Sovereign offshore race, began off Southsea with about four hours of very light breezes. Once the fleet was around the Nab Tower, the pace increased and on this occasion the P.F. system saved the bigger boats from the fate they normally meet after a calm at the start. *Perseverance*, on her first outing, was first from *Quailo*, Rodney Hill's *Morningtown* (a Tartan 41), *Noryema*, *Morning Cloud*, *Superstar* and *Battlecry* (both Swan 44s), and *Frigate*.

At the end of the next three inshore trials only two yachts had helped to justify their claims for a team place: *Frigate* with a fifth, third and sixth, and *Quailo* with a seventh, fourth and fifth. Not superb, but the inconsistency of the other contenders made them look good. *Morning Cloud* had a second, ninth and 13th; *Battlecry* a first, 16th and ninth; *Northwind*, third, 14th, 16th; *Noryema* fourth, 20th, eighth—and so on.

The way races were won and lost was not encouraging, but the committee set difficult courses. Two of the races started with windward legs of only one mile which resulted in complicated bunching at the first mark. The courses also involved a good deal of short tacking along Cowes Green, against the tide, where big boats always lose to the niftier little ones. Had it not been for the P.F. system, the bigger boats would not have had even the moderate look-in they had. In any case, each race went to the boat which had chosen the right end of the line to start and was able to wriggle clear of the pack in the first short legs.

The seventh trial was the Morgan Cup around the Channel. It was beset with calms and in these conditions the larger boats could not shake off the small ones. *Frigate* won convincingly, but the race had little significance as far as the other contenders were concerned. *Noryema* was sixth, *Quailo* eighth and *Morning Cloud* not even in the top half of the list.

The final inshore weekend was also disappointing, with both trials scheduled for Sunday abandoned due to lack of wind. Saturday's race, a Solent Points Race in which all-comers took part, was again in fickle weather which meant it was hardly satisfactory or a true indication of form. *Morning Cloud* won from *Synergy* and *Kealoha* (both Swan 44s), *Oyster*, *Quailo*, *Samphire*, *Battlecry*, with *Frigate* ninth.

The trials didn't produce a clearly outstanding team. The boats chosen were the only ones which showed any consistency at all: *Frigate*, *Morning Cloud* and three-year-old *Quailo III* which had been reserve two years before. Their success was the product of excellent crewmanship rather than exceptional boat speed and to many it looked a mediocre team. It was interesting that the three boats were all from different design boards, Carter, Stephens and Nicholson.

A second interesting point which emerged, perhaps contrary to a logical expectation, was that the massive increase in trialists, 32 compared with 17 two years before, had not improved the competition. Because of the extra number of yachts, trained offshore talent was spread too thinly over the fleet or concentrated on too few boats. Other owners had been forced to recruit crew members who were less than world-beating standard. *Quailo*'s and *Morning Cloud*'s crews had remained substantially intact since 1971 and *Frigate*'s was exceptionally organised. This was the decisive factor in the selection. Even the concentration of the fleet within a small range of sizes, producing close boat for boat racing (especially among the Swan 44s), did not raise the standard as it should have done.

The British team had their first look at the opposition in the Cowes–Dinard Race and were trounced by Australian boats. Two new Bob Miller designs, *Ginkgo* and *Apollo*, had joined *Ragamuffin* in the team and looked like world beaters. So far the Cup had only ever been won by Britain, Australia and the United States, but before the series began one or two were tipping the strong-looking teams from Germany and Holland. The time seemed ripe for Europe to have a look-in at the silverware, or perhaps one of the South American teams.

There were 200 starters in the Channel Race, spread over five classes plus a sixth class for the Admiral's Cup boats, 16 teams in all. There was no windward beating work in the fresh conditions and the P.F. system worked against the larger boats. The overall winner came from Class V.

The first leg was a square run to the Royal Sovereign. *Quailo* was sailing as fast as she had ever gone downwind, but she could not hold *Ginkgo* which rated 4 ft. lower. A navigational error at the Le Havre buoy—arriving too far to the east, downtide—lost her more time, and she finished boat for boat astern of *Ginkgo*.

The leading boats finished with a fetch to the line, but the wind freshened and backed for the later arrivals giving a proportionately faster leg. *Frigate* paced the United States' *Lightnin'* (Ted Turner) all the way and both these small boats were well placed. *Morning Cloud* recorded a position which was above her rating position in the fleet.

However, there was one boat which managed to break the size-order finishing pattern. She was the 47 ft. *Saudade*, the German hull-sister to the failed *Prospect of Whitby* and rating 34·1 ft. She sailed a faultless race and won Class I convincingly by 10 minutes from *Ginkgo*, and was fourth in the Admiral's Cup fleet behind three tiddlers, *Revolution*, rating 29·7 ft. and representing France, *Frigate* and *Lightnin'*.

Saudade's team mates, *Rubin* and *Carina*, were also fairly large, rating 39·4 ft. and 37 ft. respectively. They placed 13th and 14th in the Admiral's Cup fleet but it was enough to take Germany into an early lead. Behind her came Holland, Italy, Australia, France and Britain (*Frigate* was second, *Morning Cloud* eighth and *Quailo* had dropped right down to 41st). The big American boats had bombed out and they were lying ninth equal with Bermuda.

The first inshore race on the Monday of Cowes Week again showed *Saudade* as the pace-setter. All other racing was cancelled that day because of rough weather, but in winds of between Force 4 and 7 the Admiral's Cup fleet enjoyed long legs to windward which suited *Quailo* down to the ground. She powered to the first mark ahead of the fleet. *Morning Cloud* and *Frigate* were well up and *Frigate* ran down the next leg in company with several much higher-rating boats. *Lightnin'* was never far away and the French *Revolution* was sailing downwind way above her rating. Had she had two more potent team mates to back her up, the French could have come right into the reckoning.

Quailo was gradually overhauled by the Brazilian *Saga* and at the leeward mark slightly crisper sail-handling on the American *Charisma* cost her another place. *Saudade* was hanging on with determination to the larger boats and she finished just ahead of *Apollo II*, which rated over 2 ft. higher.

It was a big boats' race but in the end *Saudade* showed she could outdo the big ones as she did most of the small ones in the Channel Race. She was first by six minutes, an amazing margin in a fleet of this standard. There were eight boats in the next six minutes!

Designer Frans Maas is at the helm and co-owner Peter Vroon keeps
a look-out down to leeward on the Dutch entry 'Standfast'

Germany stayed ahead, *Rubin* coming 10th and *Carina* 13th. Australia, top scoring team in this race, moved into second slot with a winning grouping of fourth, fifth and seventh. Britain pulled up to third place with *Quailo* third, *Morning Cloud* ninth and *Frigate* 15th. Two of the big three were now back in the running and the United States had recovered marginally to seventh place.

On Wednesday, a perfect, steady Force 3 westerly permitted full sail. On the long beat from Cowes to Lymington Spit, the four biggest boats, *Saga*, *Salty Goose* (U.S.A.), *Quailo* and *Safari* (Finland) pulled clear. *Quailo* and *Morning Cloud* both had spinnaker snarl-ups but sail handling on *Frigate* was immaculate.

Saudade was ninth to finish and on corrected time again won, this time by three minutes over *Morning Cloud* which was 17th boat to finish. Britain had the best team score of the day with *Frigate* fourth and *Quailo* 11th. The finish was so close that *Quailo* could have been sixth had she been only one minute quicker over the course. The spinnaker wrap at the first mark was wryly remembered. Australia was second best with a fifth, eighth and 10th for *Apollo*, *Ginkgo* and *Ragamuffin*. The German support for *Saudade* was disappointing with *Rubin* sixth and *Carina* 21st, but they managed to hold on to their team lead by seven points.

In the clubs and bars ashore, everyone was talking about the incredible *Saudade* which was sailed by Hans Beilken, former One Ton Cup champion at the helm of *Optimist*. She was almost winning the trophy alone. Could she do it again in the Fastnet?

Team fortunes could be won or lost all over again in the big race. But, despite its reputation, the Fastnet was a great anti-climax for most of the 258 entries.

The race began ominously when the start was delayed for half an hour to allow

the wind to get up from flat calm to a whisper. It freshened during Saturday and Sunday and provided an easy romping close fetch to Land's End. The beat to the Fastnet Rock was in light, fickle airs instead of the tough bash to windward the race is known for.

At the Rock the German team were in a neat team group, *Saudade* bracketed by her larger colleagues. *Quailo* was well up and ahead of her rating. *Frigate* was only an hour behind *Saudade*. *Morning Cloud* had faired poorly on this leg and was to fall even farther back.

The weather was very variable for the downwind leg to Bishop Rock, but things grew worse. The stretch from the Bishop back to Plymouth was almost a complete calm. For many the 90-odd miles from the Scillies to the finish were a nightmare. A few of the early finishers covered the distance in under 24 hours, but most took between 36 and 48 hours.

The bigger boats undoubtedly got off more lightly than the others, *Saga* from Brazil taking the prized Fastnet Challenge Cup. The heavyweight American team made a dramatic bid to steal the show with third and fourth Admiral's Cup places for *Charisma* and *Salty Goose*, but the minimum-rating *Lightnin'* only placed 17th and the Americans could not repeat their coup of 1969. The consistency of the German team, with seventh, 10th and 11th, led by *Saudade*, gave them second highest score for the race and sufficient points to win the Admiral's Cup.

Saga's overall victory was popular and well deserved, but she was backed up by only a ninth and 44th in Admiral's Cup positions from the other Brazilians. Second overall also went to South America, Argentina's *Recluta*, and with a 27th and 41st from her team mates, she had helped them into sixth place out of the 16 teams. *Recluta* was second highest individual points scorer after *Saudade* in the series. She is from Argentinian designer German Frers, who served his apprenticeship at S. and S. and he can produce more like her for new owners. A team of *Reclutas* in 1973 might have resulted in a Latin American win. The success of *Saga* and *Recluta* will have stimulated interest back home in South America and also encouraged other nations who have hitherto been classified as also rans.

On return visits the Brazilians are hardly likely to ruin their performance again by leaving marks on the wrong hand, as two of their team did in the second inshore race. *Saga* discovered her mistake and turned back, losing 26 places boat for boat and more on corrected time. *Wa-Wa-Too III* realised too late and sailed into Cowes without crossing the finishing line. Later the third member of the team, *Cangaceiro*, went aground and the Brazilian disaster was complete.

All that was made up for a week later with *Saga*'s triumph in the Fastnet Race. The buoyant Brazilians celebrated like champions, bringing colour to the dreary Plymouth docks.

Perhaps the most important thing about the 1973 Admiral's Cup is that it demonstrated that the ability and resources to win were more universally distributed. The Germans had brought a meticulously prepared team demonstrating excellent boat handling and tactics, all of which beat the seeded countries at their own game. It meant the next one could be anybody's championship.

Fifty years on

After the Admiral's Cup defeat, British offshore yachting needed a boost. It came with a Southern Cross win in Australia for *Prospect of Whitby*, *Quailo III* and Alan Graham and Dave Johnson's Swan 44 *Superstar*.

Then an even bigger surprise came in 1974 when there was a revival of interest in the One Ton Cup, which was being sailed in British waters that year. More than that, the British came out convincingly on top in a fleet of 33 yachts from 14 nations. Overall winner was *Gumboots*, a production boat built by the Lymington firm of J. C. Rogers and based on American Doug Peterson's *Ganbare* design. She was sailed by her owners, the Rogers brothers. Second was *High Tension*, owned by a former *Morning Cloud* crewman George Stead and designed by Dutchman de Ridder.

This success gave a great lift to British yachting prestige but of greater interest was the breadth of designs at the competition. Race-winning design is no longer the province of one or two firms. Up until then Stephens and Carter had shared most of the laurels between them. An observer at the Torquay series looking for a possible designer for his next Admiral's Cup boat would have needed to jot down five different names: Peterson, de Ridder, Ron Holland (designer of the fast Irish *Golden Apple*), Carter and Stephens. Add to this Frers, Maas, Hood, Miller and Cutherbertson and Cassian, all of whom were well represented at the '73 Admiral's Cup, and the choice becomes almost too wide.

What, then, can we expect of the future? Undoubtedly the Admiral's Cup will continue to dominate the offshore handicap scene, though level racing in the Ton Cups, quarter, half, one and two, will develop, especially as a proving ground for hulls, sails and equipment. Financial situations around the world will tend to keep the boats small. The Admiral's Cup management committee has already made the size range for Admiral's Cup eligibility smaller, 29 ft. rating up to 42 ft., thus further forcing the trend.

It is only since '70 or '71 that quick changes seem to have given way to consolidation and refinement. A new era is now getting under way of 'find a good one and keep working on her to squeeze more and more out of her.' This has certainly been the case in the U.S. and, since the British always seem to follow suit, it is not unreasonable to speculate that the same trend will appear here.

British yachts in the States for the '74 Southern Ocean Racing Conference and the Onion Patch series saw another trend which over there seemed to bring good results. It was simplicity of construction and especially deck layout, proved admirably by the Frers-designed *Scaramouche* which wiped the board in nearly all the races.

More development can be expected in sails, particularly more versatile sails. There is a move to limit the number of sails carried by yachts. If this ever transpires, it would bring about the rapid development of sails to cover more than a narrow range of wind strengths. The idea of the 'Compensator', thought up by the Australian firm of Miller and Whitworth, will be copied by others.

Winches and other fittings will be further refined and crewing, honed by closely sailed Ton Cupping, will improve. With so many designers drawing boats of near equal speed potential, crewing and sailing tactics will be at a premium.

Offshore racing has come a long way in the years since the war. From a friendly weekend pastime it is now big business, with sophisticated boats and organisation, with amateur crews putting in dedication, training practice and investment of time worthy of professional sportsmen, and with a small though growing band of actual professionals who are as valuable assets as a new winch or sail.

Arthur Slater sees a big difference in crews since 1965: 'Now they are all experts,' he says. Certainly this will continue and men will specialise in being crews, with no ambitions of ownership. Guy Shackles, Slater's number-one hand since the first *Prospect of Whitby*, has tried being an 'owner', in Quarter Ton proportions, but has decided he prefers being a crew, with the thrill of being on a powerful big machine and being part of a co-ordinated team. 'If I did own a big boat I think I would share a cruising boat with someone else but I'd still like to race on other people's boats,' says Guy.

'I've always sailed with Arthur, though I have occasionally done the odd race with other owners when *Prospect* has been laid up. *Prospect* has always been a very happy ship. If Arthur stopped racing I think I would give ocean racing a rest for a while, and put in some time at the office (*in Yorkshire*) which has been sadly lacking for the last ten years!'

Does Slater foresee a time or circumstances when he would give up? 'No, not really, except for one thing—the taxman!'

Nevertheless, more young owners are somehow finding the cash and joining the circus, mainly thanks to the good glass fibre yachts being produced. The day of the one-off has not disappeared but the day of the production boat of race-winning potential has firmly arrived. Future Admiral's Cup fleets will see more of this type of boat from a variety of designers.

There is a band of new designers coming up behind the Stephens brothers and Dick Carter. At the moment they are all designing boats with broadly similar lines. But a design breakthrough such as the 1965–66 S. and S. advance is what they are all searching for and it may not be far away. The Admiral's Cup owners, slightly less cautious and with the Ton Cups fresh in their minds, are giving the new boys a chance. Already, Frers, Bob Miller, Peterson and Stephen Jones designs are certain to be included in the 1975 British trials,

The 1973 'Prospect of Whitby' didn't go well at first. But in Australia that year team captain Arthur Slater (standing by the helmsman, looking up) led the British to Southern Cross victory

although S. and S. boats are still likely to be the most numerous from any one designer.

Winning the Admiral's Cup is now within the reach of virtually all countries who hold organised offshore racing. New Zealand, for instance, which has never had a full team before, put 14 or 15 hopefuls in the water for trials and Dunhill's are sponsoring their hotly organised, official 1975 challenge.

Appropriately, 1975 is the 50th anniversary of the R.O.R.C. The first Fastnet Race was sailed 50 years ago. So this is a special year, when budding talent will burst on to the Admiral's Cup stage like the final starshell of the Cowes Week fireworks.

It is not the end. It is the beginning of another 50 years of investment, invention, work and closely fought competition. As long as the Admiral's Cup remains, people will come for the challenge and the honour of winning the world crown of ocean racing.

Yet in the final reckoning it is not just the winning that counts. Now he has had time to look back at his racing career from across the ocean, Dennis Miller, who has by no means given up yet, says: 'In retrospect it was not winning but the people. In Bermuda they all sail through at some time and the yarns and a few drinks below are the high points. My other enjoyment is to see the many young people who have sailed with me, who today are experts. I have always refused to pay crew but it is always a compliment when another owner offers them a full salary to race on his boat!'

PART TWO

The Southern Cross Cup

Sydney to Hobart

There is a story going around Britain that Australian yachts carry shotguns to blow holes in their heavyweight storm spinnakers when running with them becomes too dangerous. This is not true, as far as I know, but there are any number of instances of skippers running on in extreme weather until the spinnaker has blown itself out rather than risking crewmen on the foredeck to take it down.

Flying spinnakers to destruction point has long been accepted as part of the price of winning in Australia. Racing in a weather system forged between the Roaring Forties to the south and tropical cyclones to the north, Australians have had to get used to strong winds and big seas.

Captain John Illingworth, the English yachtsman and designer, first showed the Australians it was possible to race small yachts hard through bad weather with his win in the very first Sydney–Hobart Race in 1945.

While the Australians' familiarity with strong winds has earned them reputations as good heavy-weather sailors, the successes of Australian yachts in international competition reflects another British influence. The entry of Australia in the Admiral's Cup in 1965, its continuous participation since, and the introduction of its own Southern Cross Cup series have developed all-round yachting skills in Australian offshore yachtsmen. The round-the-buoys inshore races of these series demand a good appreciation of tactics and rules, while the close racing on the 30-mile courses develops slick crew work, attention to sail trim and an awareness of tuning.

Once, the ocean-racing sailors of Australia were a breed apart from the rest, with little cross-flow from the dinghy or one-design keelboat classes. The main qualification for a crewman used to be the ability to hang on in a Force 8 blow. Now the offshore crewman is expected to know about sail trim, rig tuning and have some appreciation of tactics. Most of the successful boats have a specialist tactician aboard and many carry a sailmaker as well. There is much more movement of top one-design sailors into ocean racing. The 1973 Admiral's Cup team included eight crewmen who had represented Australia in the Olympics.

The Australians have their problems and their weaknesses. The money to fund big yachts and the talent to man them is thinly spread. There is a lack of patience with light winds. But each year the prospect of international competition, especially in the Admiral's Cup, steadily draws new owners to the sport of ocean

'Rani', the 34 ft. 9 in. cutter Illingworth sailed to victory in the first Sydney–Hobart in 1945

(Inset) Captain John Illingworth

racing and attracts good sailors from the Olympic, international and skiff classes. After a lean period in the late 1960s, when Sparkman and Stephens designs dominated Australian racing, local designers have regained respect at home and won commissions, mainly through the successes of Bob Miller's designs. And Australia has all the sailmaking and rigging skills needed to stay with the leaders in international ocean racing.

The first offshore race was sailed from Sydney Cove to Botany Bay and back as part of the Anniversary regatta of 1861.

The first long distance race, of 140 miles from Sydney to Newcastle and back, was a portent of future ocean racing patterns on the Australian coastline. Charles Parbury, owner of the 30-tonner *Xarifa*, designed with identical symmetrical lines forward and aft by the Australian Richard Harnett (inspired by a mackerel he caught in Woolloomooloo Bay), challenged William Walker, Commodore of the newly formed Royal Sydney Yacht Squadron and owner of a 71-ton iron-hulled barque *Chance*, to a match race.

Parbury staked £100 to Commodore Walker's £150, and the two yachts set off in a southerly gale. The bigger *Chance* soon ran ahead out of sight of *Xarifa* which lost more ground when she broke her topmast, causing the crew to reef heavily. But this rig was ideal for the thrash back to Sydney Harbour and *Chance*, skippered for Commodore Walker by a supremely confident professional recorded in history only as 'Sandy the Scot', did not reef before turning at Newcastle, broached while recklessly gybing, then lost the lead to *Chance* as the crew struggled to tie in a reef. *Xarifa* won easily.

Little more is recorded of offshore racing in Australia until 1907 when four yachts sailed the 196-mile course from Port Phillip Heads to Low Head at the mouth of the Tamar River in Northern Tasmania for a cup presented by the American magazine 'Rudder'. The winner was *Thistle*, a 48 ft. yawl owned by E. Newland. The race began with calms and ended in a gale. The wife of *Thistle*'s owner, who was aboard for the race, was so shaken by the experience that she refused to give up the Rudder Cup, which was to have been a perpetual trophy, saying she wanted to spare others the miseries of ocean racing.

The race was revived, as the Bass Strait Race, in 1929 by E. J. ('Doc') Bennell of the Royal St. Kilda Yacht Club (now Royal Melbourne Yacht Squadron), beating five other yachts with his 42 ft. ketch *Oimara*. The following year Bennell cruised to New Zealand and tossed out a challenge for a race back across the Tasman Sea to Australia, and the Norwegian yachtsman, Erling Tambs, took him on. Tambs was on a world cruise with his wife aboard the pilot cutter *Teddy*, a 40-footer designed by Colin Archer. A third entry was the 38 ft. Auckland yacht *Rangi*, originally built as a fishing boat.

Tambs, who signed on a crew of four local Auckland yachtsmen for the race, won easily with the help of a generous 96-hour handicap allowance for the 1,200-mile race. *Oimara* was first to Sydney by 48 hours, in 11 days, 20 hours. *Teddy*

The Sydney–Hobart Race course

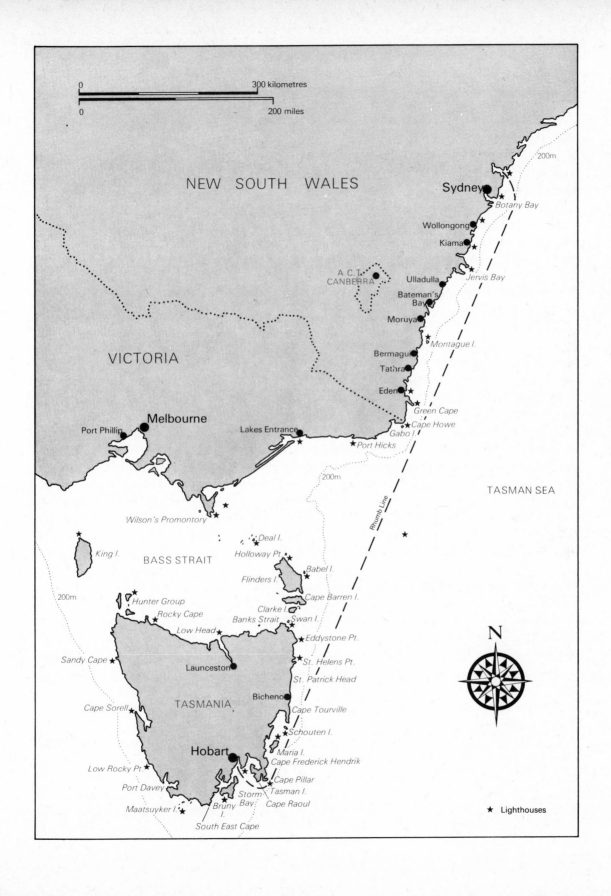

0   300 kilometres

0   200 miles

NEW SOUTH WALES

Sydney

Botany Bay

Wollongong

Kiama

A.C.T.
CANBERRA

Ulladulla

Jervis Bay

Bateman's
Bay

Moruya

Montague I.

Bermagui

Tathra

Eden

Green Cape

Cape Howe

Gabo I.

VICTORIA

Melbourne

Port Phillip

Lakes Entrance

Port Hicks

200m

TASMAN SEA

Rhumb Line

Wilson's Promontory

Deal I.

Holloway Pt.

Babel I.

King I.

BASS STRAIT

Flinders I.

Cape Barren I.

200m

Hunter Group

Rocky Cape

Clarke I.

Banks Strait

Swan I.

Low Head

Eddystone Pt.

Sandy Cape

St. Helens Pt.

Launceston

St. Patrick Head

TASMANIA

Bicheno

Cape Tourville

Cape Sorell

Schouten I.

Maria I.

Hobart

Cape Frederick Hendrik

Cape Pillar

Low Rocky Pt.

Tasman I.

Port Davey

*Storm
Bay*

Cape Raoul

Maatsuyker I.

*Bruny
I.*

★ Lighthouses

South East Cape

N

was faster than her beamy shape suggested. She had quite fine underwater lines. *Rangi* finished eight days behind *Oimara*. She had been hurriedly prepared for the race, left without accurate navigation instruments, and was slowed by calms.

Doc Bennell's son Frank skippered *Oimara* to win the next Bass Strait Race held in 1934 to coincide with the Melbourne centenary celebrations, and the Royal Yacht Club of Victoria again revived the 198-mile race in 1946. It has been held annually, at Christmas, since 1950, over a course from Queenscliff, just inside Port Phillip Heads, to Devonport, on the north-west coast of Tasmania, but it is overshadowed by Australia's deep-water classic, the Sydney–Hobart.

From its inception, the Sydney–Hobart Race became Australia's premier offshore event. Held every year, starting on Boxing Day, it is sailed over a 630-mile course which takes the yachts down the New South Wales coast, usually before following north-east breezes, then across the exposed, eastern approaches of Bass Strait. Here, icy blasts spinning off from the Roaring Forties pose a constant threat of high sou'westerly headwinds with big seas. Then the yachts close the eastern coast of Tasmania, where unreliable winds are often experienced. They round the sheer rock cliffs of Tasman Island, marking the south-east tip of Tasmania, and finish up the Derwent River, right in Hobart's heart.

The course is a challenging one, usually providing a full range of winds, from calms to gales, and is complicated by currents and tides. Tremendous public interest is created, with the start in the confined waters of Sydney Harbour being crowded by hundreds of spectator craft, and the Battery Point finishing line is a grandstand for thousands of Hobart people. Three-times-a-day radio reports of the yachts' positions create a great 'running' story for newspapers and radio. No other race in the world, not even the Fastnet, has such an audience.

The race was born in 1945. The previous year a few yachtsmen in reserved civilian occupations who, during the war, had formed the Naval Auxiliary Patrol, held a race from Sydney northwards to Broken Bay, for ten bob in, winner take all. As the yachtsmen got together in The Basin, a sheltered corner of Pittwater, just outside Sydney, the idea of regular ocean races was kicked around. Soon afterwards they formed a club, the Cruising Yacht Club of Australia.

At that time Captain John Illingworth, a committee member of the R.O.R.C. in Britain, was stationed in Sydney as Engineer Commander of the Garden Island dockyard. He was invited along to a club meeting, held in the photographic studio of the secretary, Peter Luke, to give a talk. Afterwards, Luke said he and two other members, Jack Earl and Bert Walker, were going to cruise to Hobart at Christmas. 'Why don't you come along?'

'I will, if you make a race of it,' Illingworth replied.

(Top) The beautiful Fife design, 'Astor', racing to Hobart in 1964, shows that the 'big boy' is nothing new. She was built in 1924 of Burma teak for Sydney surgeon Sir Alexander McCormick

(Below) Vic Meyer's 'Solo' was the most noteworthy design of Alan Payne in the 1950s. She won the Sydney–Hobart twice, in 1956 and 1962

He then bought himself a yacht, a small, 34 ft. 9 in. overall cutter called *Rani*. Designed by A. C. Barber of Sydney, she was the light displacement type which Illingworth as a designer himself, favoured.

In his classic book on ocean racing, *Offshore*, Illingworth says *Rani* was a 'brilliant design' with a 'very easily driven hull that was fast and sea-kindly under all conditions.'

Illingworth gave the cruising men a racing lesson in that first Sydney–Hobart Race, and it set the pattern for the whole future attitude of Australians to ocean racing. A gale from the south-west hit the fleet off the New South Wales coast on the second night out. While the eight other yachts in the race hove-to or ran for shelter, as prudent cruising seamen did in those days, Illingworth pressed on. The little *Rani* nearly foundered off Montagu Island but when the crew suggested they reduce sail, Illingworth replied: 'No. We'll only have to put it all up again.' While *Rani* pressed on, one of her competitors sheltered behind Gabo Island, and to pass the time, the crew went ashore and shot rabbits!

There was no radio contact with the yachts in those days. After the storm clouds cleared, *Rani* could not be found although spotter planes located all the others. Anxiety mounted ashore. Then, after being missing for four days, she re-appeared dramatically out of squalls and mist near Tasman Island. Although her time was slow by today's standards, 6 days, 38 hours, 22 minutes, she finished 17 hours ahead of the next yacht, the Tasmanian 52 ft. cutter *Winston Churchill*, and on corrected time was winner by a clear day and five hours. *Rani*'s mainsail had been ripped and she blew out a jib. The crew spent 24 hours stitching the mainsail. Captain Illingworth, with British penchant for understatement, told newspapermen: 'Apart from the storm, the voyage was uneventful.'

The Illingworth lesson was that quite small yachts can be sailed hard through atrocious weather, night and day, providing their crews are tough enough to urge them along, through hours and days of living in cramped cabins, wet blankets, often without proper food and a minimum of sleep. This capacity to keep their boats driving hard in bad weather, beyond the normal limits of physical endurance and to the point where sails blow out, has become the greatest attribute of the Australian offshore yachtsman.

Through the 1950s, yachts especially designed for ocean racing gradually took over from the mixture of heavy cruising boats and converted harbour racers that dominated the early Sydney–Hobart race fleets. A young Sydney naval architect, Alan Payne, designed a 36 ft. class, the Tasman Seabird, especially for Australian conditions. The Seabird was fast, supremely seaworthy, and, above all, designed to handicap well under the R.O.R.C.'s rule of measurement, and a Tasman Seabird, *Cherana* (Russ Williams), won the 1959 Sydney–Hobart.

Payne's most famous design of the 1950s was *Solo*, built and owned by Vic

'Kurrewa IV', formerly 'Morna', was owned by Frank and John Livingston. She won Hobart line honours four times but rated too high to do any good on corrected time

Meyer, a renowned, tough skipper. *Solo*, a 57 ft. steel cutter, had a remarkable record. She won the 1956 and 1962 Sydney–Hobart races and took the fastest-time prizes in 1958 and 1959. She won the 350-mile Montagu Island Race, next to the Sydney–Hobart the principal New South Wales race, five times in five starts. In 1961 she set a new record in winning the Trans-Tasman Race, from Auckland to Sydney, in 7 days, 21 hours, 12 minutes.

Her 1962 Sydney–Hobart victory was over *Ondine*, the 57 ft. yacht owned by American Huey Long. *Ondine* set a new race record of 3 days, 3 hours, 46 minutes and 16 seconds that year, which stood until 1973. She had a great photo finish in the Derwent with Peter Water's *Astor*, a beautiful old Fife-designed 73 ft. schooner. But, snapping across the line 43 minutes behind *Ondine* came the shark-like bow of *Solo*. She won on corrected time by 39 minutes.

Vic Meyer, an engineer born in Switzerland, moved in his forties from motor-boating to sailing. But he quickly became a complete yachtsman who could handle most jobs aboard better than his crew. He was the first 'dean' of the rip-or-bust school. Vic would hang on to a spinnaker in a gale until it blew out. Only then did he consider it was time to hoist a smaller one. Following his 1962 win, he converted *Solo* from cutter to yawl rig and took up long-distance cruising, sometimes with all-girl crews.

Into the 1960s Australian designs dominated the Sydney–Hobart Race, and the nature of the race itself had a profound influence on local design and ocean-racing techniques. Under the spur of competition, skills were developed and courage hardened by familiarity with bad weather and, especially, crews learnt to cope with the more difficult point of heavy-weather sailing—downwind. Boats had to be able to run hard and straight under spinnakers of cloth that would not blow out in a gale. Australian yachts carry storm spinnakers of heavy cloth—three ounce to five ounce—specially cut with narrow shoulders and short foot to be strapped down solidly to the deck, offering little movement in the head to reduce the dreaded rhythmic rolling that almost inevitably leads to the out-of-control broach or gybe-broach. The boats also needed to be designed to take punishment on the nose, bashing to windward through Bass Strait's sou'westers and big seas.

Other local designers challenged Payne. One of the outstanding ones was Ron Swanson. He began ocean racing with Sydney yachtsman Graham Newland in the 35 ft. *Siandra* which won the Sydney–Hobart in 1958 and 1960. Swanson, a Sydney boatbuilder, soon began designing his own yachts and racing them with his brothers Jim and Ken. With *Camille*, he won a place in the first Admiral's Cup team to visit Britain in 1965, and *Cadence*, a 30 ft. double-ender he built and partly designed (Wally Ward originated the shape), won the 1966 Sydney–Hobart Race. *Cadence*, and others of this type (known as 'Mickey Mouse' boats), made life miserable for the bigger, heavier yachts in light weather. Then Ron Swanson designed and began building the Swanson 36, the first Australian glass-fibre stock production ocean racer. He followed this with the Swanson 27 and Swanson 32.

The masters of Australian offshore racing in the 1960s were the Halvorsen brothers, Magnus and Trygve, who won the Sydney–Hobart four times in yachts they designed and built. They won with *Anitra* in 1957, and then three times in a row with *Freya*, in 1963, 1964, and 1965. Members of a Norwegian boat-building family with long seafaring traditions, the Halvorsens were complete seamen: Magnus, big, bluff, strong; Tryg, quiet and withdrawn, a perfectionist in boat preparation and maintenance. Both had vast practical experience in yachts at sea, both were expert long-distance tacticians, and both had the ability to keep their yachts moving at night when the concentration of others fell away.

They had good men with them. Stan Darling brought a more exacting precision to the art of navigation in Australian ocean racing. Trevor Gowland added muscle as well as sailing ability. But they always believed, too, in having one or two less experienced young yachtsmen aboard to 'break in' for future races.

While corrected time victory for the Tattersall's Cup continued to be the main objective of yachtsmen and designers, the race to be first to Hobart, regardless of handicap, became an event of its own.

Free of time-correction complexities, this is the part of the race the Australian public readily understands, and to yachtsmen, and the owners who can afford them, there is a special magic in sailing really big, fast yachts. Some of them, especially in the days before powerful winches, were 'slave' ships, carrying crews of 15 to 20 tough men.

The first of these was *Morna*, a 65 ft. Fife-designed cutter that had been built as a Twelve Metre in 1913. Owned by Sir Claude Plowman, she took fastest time in the 1946, 1947 and 1948 Sydney–Hobart races. In 1948 she set a record of 4 days, 5 hours, 1 minute and 21 seconds.

Morna re-appeared in the 1954 race as *Kurrewa IV*, in the hands of Frank and John Livingston. These two were irrepressible gentlemen playboys who first appeared in the Sydney–Hobart in 1946 after purchasing the 58 ft. *Kurrewa III* from the Commonwealth Disposals Commission at Thursday Island. She was not a fast boat and had little racing success. But with *Kurrewa IV*, the Livingstons had speed enough to be first to Hobart in 1954, 1956, 1957 and 1960. She had a hopelessly high handicap rating, which kept her out of the corrected-time placings, but they didn't care.

In 1957 they broke the record with a time of 3 days, 18 hours and 39 seconds, the fastest until *Ondine*'s run of 1972. But *Kurrewa IV* was showing her age, and she had to withdraw from the 1959 race, leaking badly. She had one last fling in 1960, with Tasman boat builder Jock Muir as skipper, beating *Astor* and *Solo* in a close race for line honours, and that was it. *Kurrewa IV* still swings on a mooring in Neutral Bay, Sydney Harbour. John Livingston won't sell her, and talks of giving her a Viking's funeral.

When Vic Meyer retired *Solo* to cruising, Australia was without a really big, high performance yacht, and the next five Sydney–Hobart race fleets were headed home by overseas entries. Line honours in 1965 went to the lightweight South African 73 ft. plywood ketch *Stormvogel* (Cornelius Bruynzeel), and in 1966 a skinny 61 ft. harbour racer, *Fidelis*, skippered by Jim Davern, was first to Hobart and he became the first New Zealander to feature in the prize list.

International challenge

The 1967 Sydney–Hobart Race distinctly marked the ending of a stage in the story of Australian ocean racing. It introduced the new and current period of striving for all-round excellence as well as driving boats hard, and it introduced as winner of the race that year, Chris Bouzaid, a young New Zealander who was to have a significant influence later on the sport in Australia and internationally.

This was the first year of the Southern Cross Cup and experiences flowing from the first entry into the Admiral's Cup in 1965 were by now having their effect. Yachtsmen coming home from this and other international competitions brought with them fresh ideas that helped accelerate the change.

One of those yachtsmen, Richard Hammond, who sailed his first Sydney–Hobart Race in 1952 aboard an old schooner, skippered by two brothers both more than 70 years old, is today one of Australia's best offshore navigators. His experiences span both the drive-to-destruction era of Australian ocean racing and its more refined modern period. He says international experience has vastly improved the standard of Australian yachtsmen in recent years: 'I noticed it when we returned to Sydney with *Mercedes III* after the Admiral's Cup series in 1967.

'Now, there are so many boats and crewmen doing the international bit that local fleets almost have divisions within divisions—the experienced international types vying for more international honours; and those who race solely for the recreation and friendly competition.

'The difference sailing with these worldly-experienced crews is very noticeable. There seems to be a lot more opportunity in Australia now for people to make a living out of boats (making sails, designing, building, rigging and so on) and able to spend a lot of time around boats and on the water. Professional isn't the right word to describe them, as very few people, if any, actually make money out of just sailing on boats. However, the day of the paid hand is with us. Jobs like scrubbing down, provisioning, fitting out, which used to be shared by the entire crew, are often the responsibility of one hand these days.'

The Australian Admiral's Cup challenge of 1965 changed Australia's whole way of ocean racing. The decision to challenge had been reached after the Sydney–Hobart Race the previous year by yacht owners Bill Psaltis, Norman Rydge Jr. and Tryg Halvorsen. The idea, as so many good ones are, was hatched over a few beers around the cockpit of a yacht moored at the race's end in the hospitable haven of Constitution Dock, but none of the three could have realised then that they were leading Australia into a significant period of change in both design and racing attitudes.

Until 1965, the Sydney–Hobart Race set the styles for offshore-racing tech-

The Halvorsen brothers' 'Freya', Sydney—Hobart winner in 1963,
1964, and 1965, was in the first Australian team to go to Britain for
the Admiral's Cup series

Ron Swanson's 'Camille' (MH 111) and Gordon Ingate's 'Caprice'
were selected for the 1965 Admiral's Cup team

niques and design in Australia, and winning the Sydney–Hobart was the major achievement in ocean racing. To do this, a yacht had first of all to be able to run hard, carrying spinnaker and full mainsail in big seas to capitalise on the northeast wind pattern down the coast of New South Wales. It then had to be powerful enough to drive hard to windward through the strong sou'westers of Bass Strait and the Tasmanian coast, spinning off from the Roaring Forties to the far south. So rigs tended to be squat, and hull design slanted heavily towards downwind and strong wind performance. Two of the boats in the 1965 Admiral's Cup challenge, *Freya* and *Camille*, were of this type.

The selection trials were sailed in strong to gale force winds. *Freya* and *Camille* were the first two choices, and just scraping in by one point from Arthur Byrne's more modern *Salacia* for third place in the team was Gordon Ingate's *Caprice of Huon*. This boat, then 13 years old, turned out to be Australia's outstanding boat in the 1965 Admiral's Cup races. The lighter winds and flat water suited her fine, metre yacht lines and her skipper, a graduate from close one-design racing in Dragons and 5·5 Metre yachts, was right at home in the big fleets in England.

Camille and *Freya* were not at home in English conditions but sailed well enough for Australia to have had a chance of taking the Cup when it came to the Fastnet Race and their second place bred a determination to challenge again in 1967.

In the build-up for 1967 the transformation began, from the rugged downwind Hobart flier to the high-pointing windward performer suited to round-the-buoys racing.

Sir Robert Crichton-Brown built a new 46-footer, *Balandra*, to the same Camper and Nicholson design as *Quiver IV*, Britain's top performer in the 1965 Admiral's Cup. She proved to be the fastest yacht of her size to windward seen in Australia up to that time, and she had little difficulty making the Admiral's Cup team.

The other newcomer to the team was a remarkable 40-footer, *Mercedes III*, designed by her owner Ted Kaufman in collaboration with Bob Miller—then with several successful dinghy designs to his credit but, with *Mercedes III*, stepping out for the first time into the problems of offshore yachts. Ten years before, a very youthful Miller had crewed for Ted aboard a Star, the first *Mercedes*.

Ted is an engineer, and, with the experience of a steel-hulled offshore yacht *Mercedes II* behind him, put a lot of time and thought into selecting the construction method for *Mercedes III*. He found a builder, Cec Quilkey, who was designing and building high-speed motor cruisers with more pride in the finish and standard of workmanship of the final result than concern for money.

For *Mercedes III* they decided on the cold-moulding technique already well known and refined in sailing dinghy construction but not widely employed for big yachts. Laminates of thin oregon skins were glued and fastened together with thousands of monel staples while the glue set. *Mercedes III* was a plain but simple boat with an extremely strong, light hull, relatively shallow in form with a tight turn at the garboards to a thin keel.

Kaufman was mainly interested in a very light boat. He found this hard to

When Bob Crichton-Brown launched his Nicholson designed 'Balandra' she was the fastest hull to windward for her size ever seen in Australian waters. On this occasion, however, the problem is to keep going downwind at optimum speed

achieve under the existing R.O.R.C. rating rule because of scantling specifications. However, he calculated that by using cold-moulded wood construction he could save half a ton in the weight of fastenings.

From launching, *Mercedes III* was a winner. In her first 14 starts in Australia she scored nine wins, a second, two thirds and a fourth.

The third yacht of the 1967 team was the veteran *Caprice of Huon* again. Between them they clinched the Admiral's Cup.

The same year the Cruising Yacht Club of Australia instituted the Southern Cross Cup, to be held every second year after the Admiral's Cup and the Los Angeles–Honolulu (Transpac) Race. The idea was to stimulate overseas interest in the Sydney–Hobart Race (which, unlike the Fastnet, is held every year) by offering extra races beforehand in Southern Cross years. A team championship, it has the same points scoring system and similar race format to the Admiral's Cup and consists of four races: a 180-miler for the Royal Sydney Yacht Squadron Cup, a 30-miler for the Royal Prince Alfred Yacht Club Bowl, another 30-miler for the Middle Harbour Yacht Club Cup, and finally the 630-mile Sydney–Hobart.

Unfortunately, the same dock strike in Britain which prevented the proposed entry by a British team for the first Southern Cross series also stopped the return of *Balandra* and *Caprice of Huon* in time for the first race of the series on December 15th.

International spice was added by the entry of Eric Tabarly's *Pen Duick III* from France, winner of the Fastnet Race and R.O.R.C. Class I Championship for that year. Tabarly, then 36, brought with him a crew of nine, mainly young Frenchmen but including his 64-year-old father as ship's cook and sail repairer. Navigator Gerard Petipas, who has since remained in the Tabarly 'club' of crewmen, said of his skipper when they arrived in Australia: 'The boats may have changed but not Tabarly himself. Victories have not turned his head. Nor is he the "sit back" type of skipper. He will leave the helm to climb the mast, do the navigation or the dishes. He never raises his voice or shows any sign of temper with his crew, and if there is anything wrong, he rushes to see to it himself.'

In Australia Eric certainly had an absolutely iron-grip control over his crew. At the end of the 1967 Sydney–Hobart Race, *Pen Duick III* was moored up alongside the 61 ft. New Zealand yacht *Fidelis* in Constitution Dock when a party began aboard *Fidelis*. The young Frenchmen aboard *Pen Duick III* brought out their bottles of wine and joined in. It developed to the point where Olivier de Kersauson of Tabarly's crew, having won a mast-climbing competition, was sitting at the first crosstrees of *Pen Duick III*, blowing a hideous noise from a battered old bugle to the cheers of the dockside crowd. Suddenly he sighted Eric Tabarly and his father walking towards the dock after a sightseeing trip. Olivier slid down the mast and, in seconds, there was not a Frenchman or a wine bottle to be seen above *Pen Duick III*'s clean flush deck!

The Southern Cross Cup of 1967 encouraged the strongest entry of New Zealand yachts, in quantity and quality, ever seen in the Sydney–Hobart race fleet. Up to that time, the New Zealand competitors had tended to be heavy cruising boats that failed to make the top sector of the result sheet although *Fidelis*, a harbour racer converted to ocean racer, had scored a fine line honours win in the 1966 race.

Among the nine New Zealand yachts which sailed the 1,200 miles across the Tasman for the Southern Cross Cup was a Sparkman and Stephens One Tonner called *Rainbow II* owned by Auckland sailmaker Chris Bouzaid. She was well prepared and sailed by a keen, young and experienced crew. The previous season they had won the Whangarei to Noumea race.

The Southern Cross Cup 180-miler rounds Bird Island and Tom Thumb Islet or Flinders Islet. Olympic courses outside Sydney Heads were adopted for the 30-milers in 1973

(Top inset) Typical inshore courses for the Southern Cross Cup up to 1971

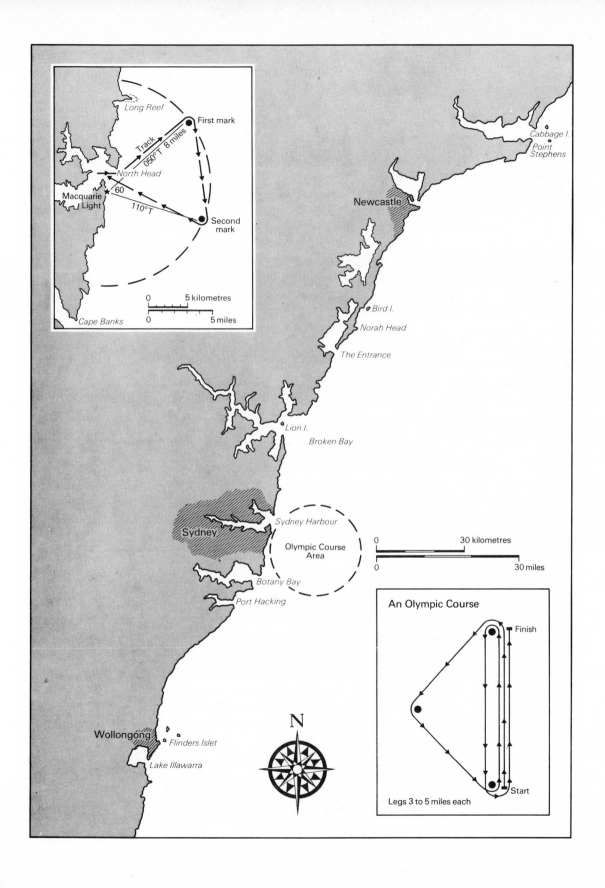

Long Reef

First mark

Track

050°T 8 miles

North Head

Macquarie Light

60

110°T

Second mark

Cape Banks

0   5 kilometres

0   5 miles

Cabbage I.

Point Stephens

Newcastle

Bird I.

Norah Head

The Entrance

Lion I.

Broken Bay

Sydney Harbour

Sydney

Olympic Course Area

0   30 kilometres

0   30 miles

Botany Bay

Port Hacking

N

Wollongong

Flinders Islet

Lake Illawarra

An Olympic Course

Finish

Start

Legs 3 to 5 miles each

New Zealand's Southern Cross Cup team besides *Rainbow II* consisted of *Satanita*, Ron Wilkie's 43 ft. Sparkman and Stephens design, and *Castanet*, a 31 ft. Carmen class, owned by Lyn Carmichael, of the same Ron Swanson design as *Cadence*, the 1966 Sydney–Hobart winner.

The New South Wales team was strong with *Mercedes III* back from the Admiral's Cup in time to compete, joined by two very well sailed Swanson designs, the Swanson 36 *Moonbird*, owned by Norm Brooker with a crew that included skiff-class graduate Hugh Treharne, and the Carmen class *Calliope*, owned and skippered by Charlie Middleton.

At the time, both the Swanson 36s and the Carmens were popular and successful performers in Sydney, with enough of them competing to virtually provide class racing within offshore race fleets.

Sydney sailor Phil Deaton, whose 50 ft. steel sloop *Bacchus D* missed out on selection for the N.S.W. team, rushed off to join a Canberra yacht club and form a team representing the Australian Capital Territory whose sole sailing water is Lake Burley Griffin, a small man-made waterway suited only to dinghies and small keel boats. (This device, at that time legal within Southern Cross Cup rules, has since been outlawed.) The States of Tasmania, Victoria and Queensland were also represented.

The early races of the series were sailed mainly in hard breezes which suited the home team. New South Wales held a handy 47-point lead before going into the Hobart race.

The first race, a 200-miler for the Royal Sydney Yacht Squadron Trophy, began in a solid 25-knot nor'easter. *Bacchus D* loved it and led *Mercedes III* through Sydney Heads bound for Bird Island, 45 miles to the north. The New Zealander, *Satanita*, was next but New Zealand's *Castanet* was last through the Heads. She looked extremely tender, with her leeward gunwale buried in green water. Launched only 10 weeks beforehand, her crew had had little experience with her in fresh winds.

But by 11 p.m., six hours after the start, the north-easter had died, as it so often does off the N.S.W. coast. By daylight, *Castanet* had worked through to fifth place, level with the two well campaigned Sydney Carmens, *Calliope* and *Cavalier*. From there these three little 'Mickey Mouse boats' sailed the race in sight of each other, and only 20 minutes separated them when they crossed the finishing line.

Bacchus D died when the wind dropped off Tuggerah and *Mercedes III* took the lead to round Bird Island first ahead of *Odin*, Lou Abrahams' steel version of *Freya*, representing Victoria.

The north-easter, the N.S.W. coastline's sea breeze, generated again the following day and, as it reached 15 knots, *Bacchus D* stirred again and finally headed the fleet home, but only 6 minutes and 18 seconds ahead of *Mercedes III* and *Mercedes* won with a corrected time of 33 hours, 31 minutes and 36 seconds from *Calliope* and *Castanet*. New South Wales earned 96 points from the race, New Zealand 78 and the A.C.T. 62.

Race two for the Royal Prince Alfred Yacht Club Bowl, around a 30-mile offshore course, was full of incidents and upsets. A punishing sea and a fresh 25-knot south-easterly blew out many a spinnaker and blew away one of the rounding marks. *Rainbow II* was disqualified from second place following a converging incident at the start between *Huon Lass* (Hedley Calvert, Tasmania) and *Cavalier*, a non-team member owned by John Roche and skippered by E. C. 'Boy' Messenger.

The windward rounding buoy at Coogee broke free and washed on to the rocks soon after the leaders rounded, and the 35-footer *Maria Van Diemen*, an individual entry from Sydney, lost her life raft soon after rounding the Coogee mark. Several yachts behind her mistook the inflated life raft for the orange buoy and chased it instead of heading for the official boat that moved in to act as the mark.

Rainbow II blew out two spinnakers on consecutive runs before being blown out of the race in the protest room.

The race was a triumph for the N.S.W. team with *Moonbird* first on corrected time 6 minutes and 46 seconds ahead of *Mercedes III*, with *Calliope* fifth. *Huon Lass* was third. The race was a bad one for the New Zealanders. On top of *Rainbow II*'s disqualification, *Satanita* and *Castanet* only managed to make 10th and 12th place respectively.

The wind continued to blow strongly from the south and the Cruising Yacht Club decided to hold the second short race of the series, for the Middle Harbour Yacht Club Cup, over the 26-mile storm course inside Sydney Harbour. They did not want to risk damage to the fleet only a few days before the Sydney–Hobart.

The entry of three line honours favourites for the Sydney–Hobart—*Fidelis* and *Kahurangi* of New Zealand and *Pen Duick III* from France—aroused tremendous public interest in the race and headland vantage points such as Bradley's Head and Nielsen's Park were packed with spectators.

The race, in the strong winds and within the confines of the harbour, was a thriller. *Fidelis* shot away from the down-wind start and Jim Davern called for a big spinnaker. The cigar-shaped *Fidelis* rolled madly the length of Sydney Harbour to Manly but her crew held on and built a line-honours winning lead.

Pen Duick, the boat Davern was gunning for, started cautiously, but under small mainsail and big spinnaker overhauled boat after boat. Her crew work was indifferent and she continually lost ground through slow headsail sheeting. As a final indignity, a small ship flying the tricolor of France, outward bound for New Caledonia, crossed her path at a vital stage of the race and pushed her right off course.

Bacchus D was in her element and sailed a faultless tactical race to be third across the line, behind *Kahurangi*, and winner by 15 seconds over *Rainbow II* on corrected time.

But the consistent *Moonbird* was third, only 10 seconds behind *Rainbow*. *Mercedes III* was fifth and *Calliope* came in 13th. This gave the N.S.W. team a total 186 points, 47 points clear from New Zealand with 139. A.C.T. collected 117 points, Tasmania 87, Queensland 74 and Victoria 55.

The Sydney–Hobart Race that year was even more sensational than the preliminary races of the Southern Cross Cup. It ended with the 37 ft. One Tonner *Rainbow* snatching victory by 58 minutes on corrected time from *Pen Duick III* which lost at least an hour through being becalmed in the Derwent River, 12 miles from the finish.

The start was the wildest mixture of competitors and spectator craft ever seen on Sydney Harbour. On Boxing Day in Sydney it is a tradition for the whole boating community to climb aboard their yachts, power cruisers, dinghies, canoes and surfboards to soak up some sunshine and farewell the Hobart fleet. The start is a great spectacle but the ever-present problem is keeping the spectator fleet in some sort of order, ensuring a clear passage for the yachts to the open sea.

In 1967, to help spectator-fleet control, the yachts were required to round a buoy between the 500 ft. high cliffs of North Head and South Head at the entrance to Sydney Harbour. The buoy was laid four hours before the start. Sometime in between, the crew of a wandering trimaran moored on to it.

The weight of the moored boat was too much for the anchor rode, a piece of hard-drawn eight-gauge stainless steel. About the same time the starting gun was fired, the anchor rode broke. With 67 yachts charging down on it from an offwind start, the buoy began to wander away.

Olivier de Kersauson aboard *Pen Duick* summed it up beautifully: 'This chase developed into something resembling the hunt for the wild boar.' The fleet suddenly found it had to dive into the spectator fleet, lined up around a well-marshalled lane, to chase the buoy. There were scores of minor collisions and some extremely dangerous situations as the yachts manoeuvred to avoid competitors and the completely bemused spectator fleet.

Later that day, Royal Yacht Club of Tasmania Rear Commodore Alan Goodfellow and Cruising Yacht Club of Australia secretary Merv Davey sent this statement to skippers from the Caltex radio-relay vessel *Bali Hai*: 'Any skipper who considers his yacht's position was unduly prejudiced because of the South Head marker buoy drifting out of position should enter a protest under Rule 12. The race will not be cancelled or abandoned and the race committee will make such arrangements as it deems equitable. So carry on and have a good race. There is a long way to go.'

Afterwards, about 10 skippers claimed from 40 minutes to an hour for time lost in locating the missing buoy. The sailing committee of the R.Y.C.T. and C.Y.C.A., however, decided that no yacht's position was materially prejudiced.

Kahurangi, Lawrence Nathan's 62 ft. cruising Twelve Metre from New Zealand, pulled through from the middle of the line to be first to the South Reef gas buoy and hauled on the wind to begin the hunt for the orange marker buoy, which

(Above) A spot of kite bother here but hanging on to her spinnaker in broaching conditions helped Chris Bouzaid sail 'Rainbow II' to victory in the 1967 Sydney–Hobart

(Below) 'Mercedes III', Admiral's Cup boat and twice in a victorious Southern Cross Cup team. Designed by her owner Ted Kaufman in collaboration with Bob Miller, she's of cold-moulded construction built at Cec Quilkey's

should have been to windward, 600 yards north-east of the Hornby Light on South Head. *Bacchus D* was the first to spot the missing buoy, at least half a mile to leeward of its station and drifting steadily towards the rocks of Dobroyd Point. Some boats rounded the buoy; some didn't bother and headed out to sea. Down the coast the fleet split—half standing well out in search of the south-bound current that sometimes runs at up to two knots, sometimes not at all, the others moving inshore hoping to find a breeze off the land at night.

That evening, *Huon Lass* went from a brisk eight knots to a full stop when she hit a 25 ft. long whale. Someone seems to hit one every Hobart race.

After calms during the night, a north-easter generated early in the morning, favouring first the inshore group off Jervis Bay. From this group, *Mercedes III* emerged as fleet leader until the slender 61-footer *Fidelis* went by, winding up to maximum hull speed as the wind strength built to 15 knots.

Rainbow II and *Pen Duick* had both suffered by going to sea on the first day. During the second they gradually worked their way through the fleet and by nightfall *Pen Duick* was challenging *Fidelis* at the head of the fleet. *Fidelis* gybed just after dark and ran in towards Cape Howe, anticipating a forecast south-west change and trying to shake off *Pen Duick III*.

The third day of the race began badly for Eric Tabarly. At 1 a.m. the inboard end of the spinnaker pole fell on him when a control line slipped through its jamb cleat. The pole end hit him in the face. There was a lot of blood, but Eric is hard-shelled.

Pen Duick III, reaching well during the night under light spinnaker, big foresail and mainsail, passed *Fidelis* to take the lead. The sou'wester was a 'fizzer', no more than a 15–20 knot line squall, and the wind behind it was light, and headed *Fidelis* during the morning.

At the evening radio 'sked', reports from the boats meant that *Pen Duick III* held a six-mile lead over *Fidelis*, averaging nine knots for 20 hours. But by 9 p.m. the wind had dropped and headed *Pen Duick III* as well. At midnight, with the wind strengthening again, *Pen Duick III* replaced her big foresail with a fully-battened smaller one. Early in the morning of the fourth day, she handed her mainsail as well.

The fourth day was the decisive one. *Pen Duick III* averaged 10 knots, surfing before a moderate nor'wester on good seas, and *Rainbow II* picked up boat after boat.

Kahurangi broke a steering fitting at 11 p.m. She sailed the remaining 110 miles to the finish with two men wrestling the heavy yacht with an emergency tiller.

The fifth day of the race was a bad one for the Frenchmen. *Pen Duick III* lost the wind off Tasman Island and by 6 a.m. *Fidelis* had closed to within 15 miles. Then, approaching the finish, in a light nor'wester, *Pen Duick III* went the wrong way, standing across Storm Bay towards Bruny Island while *Fidelis* closed the gap to within five miles by working the eastern shore.

Near the Iron Pot Light at the mouth of the Derwent River, 12 miles from the finish, *Pen Duick III* languished in a calm. The crew made five sail changes and eventually had to anchor for three-quarters of an hour, unable to make progress against the outgoing tide, before she picked up a faint nor'wester. *Fidelis* fell into a calm, too, off Betsy Island and she finished 2 hours and 26 minutes behind *Pen Duick III*.

Outside Storm Bay, on the east coast of Tasmania, the race was still well and truly on. *Rainbow*, staggering along under her 1,050 sq. ft. biggest spinnaker on a fresh nor'westerly, broached 25 times during the day. *Mercedes III* lost her chance when she sailed into an area of calm and changeable winds near Maria Island.

That evening, a fierce sou'west change swept through the fleet, and *Pen Duick III*, despite the time she had lost languishing in the river, was looking a good prospect for a win on corrected time as well as line honours. The yachts still at sea faced a cold, tough punch into bad seas around the forbidding 800 ft. high cliffs of Tasman Island at the south-east corner of Tasmania and across Storm Bay to the Derwent.

Aboard *Rainbow*, Christ Bouzaid and his crew—Gil Littler, Fred Andrews, Mait Hilson and Steve Armitage—figured, 84 miles from the finish, they could still win if they averaged five and a half knots. So when the sou'wester struck, at about 9 p.m., they kept lumping as much sail as they dared, to keep the speedo needle swinging around six knots.

They carried full mainsail and working jib to belt across Storm Bay. In the stronger gusts, Bouzaid was 'splitting the puffs', luffing to keep the boat on its feet, driving off for speed in the lulls. It was a wet night aboard *Rainbow*. The boat was heeling so much the bilge water was sloshing up the cabin sides to deck level, out of reach of the pump.

Other boats were in trouble in the punishing 40–50 knot winds. *Odin*'s new 47 ft. aluminium mast collapsed under compression load and came crashing down as she began to beat across Storm Bay.

Rainbow slipped across the finishing line early the following morning to become the first New Zealand yacht to win the Sydney–Hobart Race and also the first overseas winner. (John Illingworth, winner of the first Sydney–Hobart Race in 1945, was an Englishman, but his yacht, *Rani*, was Australian.)

The sou'west change put an end to the chances of the smaller yachts caught farther up the Tasmanian coast. *Castanet* took six hours to round Tasman Island against the strong wind, big seas and a current.

But *Rainbow*'s win was not enough to overcome the lead of the New South Wales team in the Southern Cross Cup. *Mercedes III* placed fifth in the Hobart, *Calliope* 11th and *Moonbird* 12th against *Rainbow*'s first, *Castanet*'s eighth and *Satanita*'s 15th, and the scoreboard finally read: New South Wales 312, New Zealand 268, Tasmania 183, A. C. T. 174, Queensland 134 and Victoria 97.

Fresh blood in the fleet

In mid-1968, a tall, tough, handsome-in-a-rugged-kind-of-way character began pounding around a gymnasium floor in Sydney at the head of a group of yachtsmen that were to have a profound influence on the style of Australian ocean racing for the following four years, and maybe longer, because they are still at it.

Syd Fischer was one of half a dozen owners building new yachts that year with the intention of qualifying for the 1969 Admiral's Cup team. But he was the only one that insisted his crew be physically fit during those winter months in Sydney and no-one in that group of yachtsmen that gathered Tuesdays in the Dupain Institute of Physical Culture, an ancient gymnasium run by a shrewd old physiological master called John Craig, was fitter than Syd himself.

Syd Fischer, in his early forties at that time, had fought his way to the top with a multi-million dollar construction empire he had begun as a one-man house-building business.

Like many another millionaire who had made his pile, he looked around for a sport to enjoy with a touch of prestige, and settled on yachting. But Syd is by no means the wealthy yacht owner buying himself an Australian blazer. He is 'one of the boys' who 'plays' with his crew ashore after the big races in the same hard fashion that he drives them on the water.

He has always enjoyed tough sports. When younger, Syd Fischer was a first grade rugby league forward with the Manly club in Sydney and the sweep man— the skipper who manages the steering oar and calls the shots—in a surfboat at the North Steyne and Bilgola surf clubs. When he felt he was becoming too old for surf boats he looked around for another sport. He tried water-skiing and then he discovered ocean yacht racing.

'I found in ocean racing,' he says, 'the kind of blokes I was used to in football and surf clubs—the types who had a go and liked a bit of fun.'

Syd's yachting career began with a few sailing lessons in the late 1950s. The head of the sailing school, Jim Bruton, was crewing at the time aboard *Caprice of Huon*, then owned by Bill Northam. One day he invited Syd out for a sail on *Caprice* and Fischer was hooked for ever.

He bought an old 41-footer and spent a great deal of time renovating the hull himself, replacing the deck and making a new mast. He learned about yacht construction and he learned how to sail. In 1962 he was ready to buy a 35 ft. Arthur Robb design Lion Class sloop called *Malohi*, a sistership to Graham Newland's *Siandra*, Hobart winner in 1958 and 1960. He enjoyed moderate success with her, scoring fifth placings overall in both the 1962 and 1966 Sydney–Hobart races.

Through 1967, he began putting together the total boat and crew effort that was to become *Ragamuffin*, but he waited for the outcome of the 1967 America's Cup before choosing a designer. He wanted the best and he reasoned the best designers available to him at that time were Olin Stephens, designer of the defender *Intrepid*, and Warwick Hood, designer of the Australian challenger *Dame Pattie*. He went to Stephens.

He chose the best builder—Cec Quilkey whose cold-moulding method of construction had contributed so much to the success of *Mercedes III*. Fischer wanted a winner and insisted that he got it. He made thousands of dollars worth of telephone calls to the Sparkman and Stephens office in New York. He ruthlessly kept the builder to schedule. The boat, he reasoned, had to be ready for the Montagu Island Race, the 350-miler that traditionally opens the Sydney offshore season, and he all but forcibly removed the hull from the builder's shed to make the race. When *Ragamuffin* was launched, they found the steering gear, through haste, had been connected up back to front, and throwing the wheel to starboard sent the boat off to port.

Ragamuffin made the Montagu, just. She was full of carpenters' tools and shavings, the deck seams leaked, the stove did not work. And it was a wet, cold, hard race. Without hot food and soaking wet below, the crew had a miserable thrash home against a northerly gale that forced 10 retirements from the fleet of 34. But within the Admiral's Cup division *Ragamuffin* was second only to the well sailed veteran *Caprice of Huon*.

That hard race consolidated a tremendous crew spirit within *Ragamuffin*. Fischer put his crew together with characteristic shrewdness, choosing each man for his ability to contribute cerebration as well as muscle to a total effort. His right-hand man, 'mate', as he called him rather than sailing master, was Graham

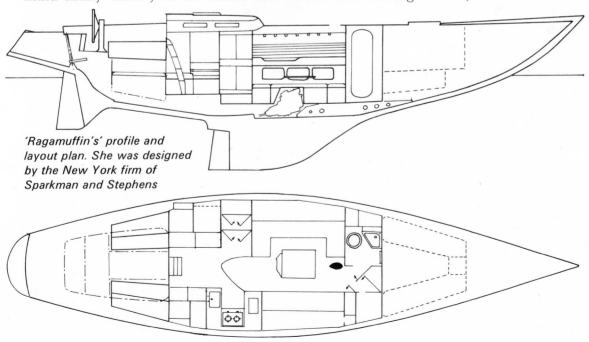

'Ragamuffin's' profile and layout plan. She was designed by the New York firm of Sparkman and Stephens

Newland. Besides winning the Sydney–Hobart Race twice with his own boat, *Siandra*, Newland was an engineer whose interest in yachting had led him into making fittings for big yachts and into an outboard marine dealership.

Newland was able to incorporate ideas in the engineering of the yacht, placing the engine, designing the mast-base support that, with thoughtful hull construction, enabled a significant improvement in the designed ballast ratio.

With Graham Newland came Doug Patterson, a big, strong man with massive shoulders who is a devoted student of every aspect of yacht racing. For big-yacht expertise, Fischer chose Tony Ellis, who had sailed on the foredeck of *Dame Pattie*, and Frank McNulty who was aboard *Gretel* in the 1962 America's Cup challenge.

Peter Hemery was recruited from *Balandra*, Admiral's Cup team member in 1967, and John Noakes from *Bacchus D*. Jim Mason, skipper of the 1966 Sydney–Hobart winner *Cadence*, was a late addition as navigator. Jack Christoffersen, who had sailed with Fischer on *Malohi*, completed the crew.

Syd's guidelines for picking his crew are these: 'I always ask myself before selecting a crewman what the man can contribute to the boat and if he will fit in. You must have blokes who can get on together under all kinds of difficult circumstances and who will be a little bit forgiving of the others' weaknesses. But they must also have the will to win. I like to have in my crew a man's man; a fellow with some courage who will work hard and who doesn't get upset if things are not going his way, and a man who will fight his way out of a corner if necessary.'

There was strong competition for places in the 1969 Admiral's Cup team through the 1968–69 Australian summer. *Koomooloo*, a bigger version of *Mercedes III*, designed by Ted Kaufman, was built by Cec Quilkey for Dennis O'Neill. She was a foot longer than *Mercedes III*, immaculately prepared and equipped, and her crew was top class. It included Richard Hammond who navigated *Mercedes III* in the 1967 Admiral's Cup. (*Koomooloo* went on to win that year's Sydney–Hobart, sailed predominantly in strong winds.)

The Admiral's Cup team, selected after a series of trials through November and December, was *Ragamuffin*, third in the Sydney–Hobart, *Koomooloo* and *Mercedes III*. But the Admiral's Cup that year was snatched from their grasp by the United States.

The following December the Southern Cross attracted a full British team: Arthur Slater's 41-footer *Prospect of Whitby*, Sir Max Aitken's cutter *Crusade* and Rodney Hill's 34-footer, *Morning After*. Edward Heath's sistership of this S. and S. 34 class, *Morning Cloud*, also came from Britain as reserve boat and sailed as a private entry with great success. But the New South Wales team, comprising *Ragamuffin*, *Mercedes III* and the Sparkman and Stephens one-tonner, *Boambillee*, owned and skippered by Vince Walsh, was a strong one, and Australia retained the Cup.

'Ragamuffin' was the bombshell Syd Fischer dropped on the Australian racing fraternity in 1968. She was a winner from the moment she left the builder's yard

(Inset) 'Ragamuffin's' almost aeroplane-like cockpit layout

The 'Morning After' incident during the 1969 Southern Cross Cup series. 'Bandit', third from left, is about to hit no. 184, the British team boat. 'Morning After' retired with a broken cap shroud and after a protest meeting the race was abandoned

All three of the shorter races preceding the Sydney–Hobart were won by the 48 ft. *Ragamuffin*. She just could not go wrong and was often right up at the head of the fleet in company with the biggest yachts. In one of the 30-milers she rounded the windward mark after a six-mile beat, neck and neck with the 62 ft. *Crusade*.

The series started with the first race being abandoned. *Morning After* successfully protested that her chances in the 30-mile Royal Prince Alfred Yacht Club Bowl had been materially prejudiced through no fault of her own when the South Australian yacht, *Bandit*, tore out *Morning After*'s cap shroud in a collision, forcing her to retire. *Bandit*, running on port gybe under South Head to round the South Reef Gas Buoy in Sydney Harbour after a windward and return leg out to sea, hooked her main boom into *Morning After*'s rigging as the British boat, on starboard tack, was heading out to sea.

This non-race was the most spectacular of the series with the yachts climbing out to sea over an unusually heavy 10 ft. swell and surfing back on the downwind legs before a 15–20 knot southerly. There were a number of collisions and near misses rounding marks. *Rebel* (New Zealand) protested *Prospect of Whitby* over a mark-rounding incident, and *Mercedes III* withdrew after hitting the Manly buoy.

The New Zealanders were unhappy with the decision to re-sail. Their team of One Tonners put up its best performance of the series with *Rebel* fourth, *Renegade* fifth and *Outrage* eighth, to take a 12 point lead over N.S.W. *Ragamuffin* won the race from *Prospect of Whitby* and *Boambillee* before the decision to re-sail was made.

So the first race of the series now became the 200-mile Royal Sydney Yacht Squadron Cup, south to Tom Thumb, north to Bird Island and return to Sydney. The race was sailed in a mixed weather pattern which tended to favour the bigger yachts by giving them more time off the wind. As the breeze freshened to 20–25 knots on the first night, the New Zealander *Roulette* lost her mast when a spreader collapsed. But generally the winds were light, and *Ragamuffin* won in conditions which did not normally suit her, with her crew working hard to keep her moving through the calm patches. At one stage off Norah Head they either used or had on every sail in the wardrobe, from nine-ounce headsail to a 'floater' half-ounce spinnaker, to handle a period of calm punctuated by 25 knot thundersqualls.

Crusade, first to finish, was second on corrected time and the new Sparkman and Stephens designed New Zealander, *Satanita II* (Ron Wilkie), in her best performance since launching, was third. *Morning After*, which revelled in the beat north on a light nor'easter, was fourth. *Apollo*, the new 57-footer Bob Miller designed for Alan Bond of Perth, showed promise that she may have the speed to overcome her heavy handicap penalty by finishing fifth. *Boambillee* was sixth, *Prospect of Whitby* eighth and *Mercedes III* 11th—she was caught on the wrong side of a south-westerly change approaching Tom Thumb and had to fight her way back from among the tailenders.

New South Wales took over the points lead in the re-sail of the Royal Prince Alfred Yacht Club Bowl. The race was sailed in a nor'easter that freshened from five knots to 20 knots and then fell dead again when a thunderstorm killed the sea breeze as the yachts began the final run home for Sydney Heads. *Ragamuffin* won, *Mercedes III* was second and *Boambillee* seventh against *Crusade*'s third, *Prospect*'s fifth and a poor 17th from *Morning After*.

The second 30-miler was a replay for the N.S.W. team which went further ahead with another win by *Ragamuffin*, second by *Mercedes III* and seventh by *Boambillee* against a third by *Prospect*, eighth by *Crusade* and 11th from *Morning After*. The race was sailed in a good, true 15-knot southerly. *Ragamuffin* and *Mercedes III* made excellent starts, but *Morning After* made a disastrous one when she failed to lay the leeward end of the line and had to return.

The Sydney–Hobart Race that year, the 25th, bore some coincidental similarities to the first. Edward Heath's yacht, *Morning Cloud*, won it and her navigator Anthony Churchill followed the advice of the very first winning skipper, John Illingworth: 'Forget the weather forecasts and stay out to sea.'

Yachts that worked east of the rhumb line did better right from the start, gaining more and better use of the moderate to fresh north-east and northerly winds which shoved the fleet along under spinnaker for the first two days. And they were better placed for the stinging 35-knot southerly change that finally headed the fleet off the Tasmanian coast.

Those yachts tempted to the west of the rhumb line by forecasts of south-westerly winds ran into calm patches along the New South Wales coast, lolloping along at less than three knots while those to sea were working the waves to boom away at maximum hull speed. And when the southerly came they were pinned down on the Tasmanian coast and had to spend more time on the wind against awkward seas.

Morning Cloud won by 52 minutes on corrected time from *Prospect of Whitby* with the N.S.W. yacht *Salacia* third. From the start, *Morning Cloud* set out to be 30 miles to windward of the rhumb line for the light to moderate running breezes of the first three days. She ran for 56 hours under the same spinnaker on the nor'-easter at an average seven knots.

When the southerly came she surprised everyone, including her crew, by her ability to windward in the 30–35 knot breeze. With her mainsail rolled down to the spreaders, and a short-hoist 12 ft. luff genoa, she still blasted along to windward at six and a half knots in the bad head sea. Having four good helmsmen alternating on the tiller helped keep her moving consistently through the last bad day and a night. They played the shifts, tacking on headers along the shore until they were nicely freed on starboard and were able to settle into a winning tack up to Tasman Island.

The wind began to ease as they approached the island. They were able to change up, first to the 17 ft. hoist intermediate genoa with two rolls in the main, and, finally, as they cleared the island for the close fetch up Storm Bay to the finish, to the 150 per cent working genoa and full main.

The little 34-footer beat many bigger yachts to the finishing line, including all of the One Tonners. It was fortunate for the N.S.W. team that *Morning Cloud* was only reserve to the British team. The N.S.W. team placings were reasonable, but *Ragamuffin* lost all chance early in the race by choosing an inshore course and finished 17th. *Mercedes III* was sixth overall and *Boambillee* seventh. The British team placings were *Prospect of Whitby* second, *Morning After* eighth and *Crusade* 30th, and the final points for the series were: N.S.W. first team 419, Britain 387, New Zealand green team 316, N.S.W. second team 269, Western Australia 205, Victoria 184, New Zealand red team 173, South Australia 137. (New Zealand and New South Wales were both allowed to enter two teams to discourage the practice of forming 'dummy' teams like the Australian Capital Territory team of 1967. Since 1969 each State has been restricted to one team.)

The line-honours battle that year had renewed interest with the building of a flat-out speedster called *Apollo* for West Australian Alan Bond. Bond comes from

Arthur Byrne had 'Salacia II' built in direct competition with 'Ragamuffin'. The two are very much alike and had some great sailing duels. But "Rago" remained the champ

Perth where the summer breezes blow steadily and strongly, encouraging yachts-men to sail high performance boats. Speed is the thing there and more glamour surrounds being first to finish than winning a handicap prize. Bond, a new million-aire from a property-developing empire, badly wanted a boat to outpace the reigning West Australian line honours champion *Siska*. This 56 ft. ketch, owned by sailmaker Rolly Tasker, was converted from an old metre yacht design. She was lean, very fast to windward in smoother water and a sight to behold downwind under her outsize spinnakers, one of them 3,500 sq. ft. in area.

Bond went to Bob Miller, the volatile Sydney sailmaker who had only just be-come known as a designer for his share in the lines of *Mercedes III*. Miller created a long, shallow, lightweight speed machine, 57 ft. 4 in. overall, with lines reminis-cent of a Flying Dutchman dinghy. She displaced 33,000 lb. and had a 19,000 lb. lead ballast keel.

Apollo was rushed into the water on an 18½ week building programme just in time for the race. She was cold-moulded in four oregon skins by H. and J. Griffin of Mona Vale, New South Wales.

For her first Hobart race *Apollo* had a real pacemaker in Max Aitken's *Crusade*, which had added some Australian muscle and local knowledge to her crew for the Hobart race.

Reasoning that in her untuned state *Apollo* had more chance for line honours than a corrected time prize, Bond had Miller make a 4,000 sq. ft. spinnaker, accepting a handicap penalty. The spinnaker blew out on the first night of the race. The sewing machine taken aboard for just such a mishap would not work and Miller spent the next six hours hand-sewing the spinnaker together again, and on the second night he had the satisfaction of feeling his creation surfing at 15 to 17 knots as she felt the full weight of the nor'easter.

When a southerly hit, *Apollo* proved to be fast upwind as well. Down to trysail and staysail only at one stage, she still blasted along at seven and a half to eight knots, and she began to overhaul *Crusade* hand over fist. Tryg Halvorsen glued himself to the helm for six hours to con her to windward through the difficult seas. 'A man had to get a bit of fun,' he explained later, 'and she is such a delight to sail. The closest thing I can compare her with is a Twelve Metre.'

Into the Derwent *Apollo* suddenly lost sight of *Crusade*'s navigation lights ahead. 'Electrical trouble' was the excuse from *Crusade*; 'deception', was the accusation from *Apollo*. But after *Crusade* beat *Apollo* across the line by 18 minutes, 44 seconds, just after 3 a.m., all was forgiven as a champagne party began with people spilling across both yachts moored alongside each other at Constitution Dock.

That race hooked Alan Bond into international yachting. It was to lead him to the United States and Britain with *Apollo* and ultimately to challenge for the America's Cup with a Bob Miller design.

But in 1970, thanks largely to the success of *Ragamuffin*, Sparkman and Stephens designs were the most sought after in Australia. Arthur Byrne, whose *Salacia* had only just been beaten for selection in the 1965 Admiral's Cup team by *Caprice of Huon*, commissioned a *Ragamuffin*-style hull from Sparkman and Stephens, up-

10 Ted Turner's 'American Eagle' threads her way among the onlookers in search of a favourable lift from the shore at the start of the 1971 Sydney–Hobart Race

11 The biggest spectator fleet in the world gathers in Sydney Harbour every Boxing Day to see yachts begin the annual race to Hobart

12 Spinnakers being dried out in the park by Rushcutters Bay, home of the C.Y.C.A.

13 After many hundreds of miles and hours of discomfort, this is the moment when crews breathe a sigh of relief as the bridge opens and they enter Constitution Dock in Hobart, Tasmania, at the end of the race

14 Evan Julian's 'Inca', of the unlucky New Zealand team which
came so near to carrying off the 1973 Southern Cross Cup

15 'Fidelis', Jim Davern's 61 ft. flyer from New Zealand, which won
line honours in the 1966 Sydney–Hobart Race

16 *(Previous page) 'Ceil III' was in the 1973 Southern Cross Cup Hong Kong team. She did them proud, winning the Sydney–Hobart Race overall*

17 *The 'floating footpath' approaches the race's end at Hobart. Dr. Tony Fisher's ferro-cement 72-footer 'Helsal' was barely completed before the start of the '73 race, but she knocked over two hours off the record*

18 *In 1971 American Huey Long was out to break the record he'd set for the Sydney–Hobart Race in 1962 with his first 'Ondine'. But this time he didn't travel quite so fast*

rated to take advantage of the International Offshore Rule which came into effect in 1970.

Byrne and Syd Fischer had more in common than two 48 ft. S. and S. yachts. Like Fischer, Byrne was a self-made millionaire. He made his money from a roll-up garage door system and relatively late in life looked around for something enjoyable and prestigious to do in his spare time. Like Syd, Arthur Byrne enjoys the emotional and physical facets of ocean racing afloat and the camaraderie and post-race fun on shore.

His decision to choose a boat just like *Ragamuffin* was a brave one. It meant he was placing his own reputation as a sailor on the line with the successful practitioner Fischer, in yachts that were near enough to being identical. But he reasoned that having *Ragamuffin* as a known constant must lead his own boat to a peak of excellence through boat-to-boat competition. He retained Graham Newland, still crewing aboard *Ragamuffin*, as a consultant to supervise the construction, organize the engineering and tuning, and this commission led Graham into a full-time business as a professional consultant on building, rigging and tuning big yachts.

The summer of 1970–71 was enlivened by the duels between *Ragamuffin* and *Salacia II*. *Rago* remained the champ but *Salacia II* was closing the gap, and they finished first and second in the selection trials for the 1971 Admiral's Cup team. Third member of the team was *Koomooloo*, purchased from Dennis O'Neill by Norman Rydge Jr. She was extremely well sailed by a crew that included 1962 and 1967 America's Cup helmsman Jock Sturrock and a shrewd alternate helmsman, Mick Morris. But the fortunes of the three on the other side of the world were very mixed.

Proud owners Vince Walsh ('Boambillee'), Syd Fischer ('Ragamuffin'), and Ted Kaufman ('Mercedes III') with the Southern Cross Cup at the Hobart prizegiving in 1969

'Rago's arse beats class'

It's dark and chilly even for England in August, this early morning in 1971, and only isolated huddles of relatives and friends are greeting yachts trickling in from the Fastnet Race. But one of the yachts at the Millbay Dock, Plymouth, is aglow with excitement in the darkness, for the crew of this plain but ruthlessly efficient 48-footer have experienced enough triumphs and disappointments in the chancy sport of ocean yacht racing to know they have done well, extremely well. And in the cabin, boat moored up and sails stowed, the beer cans are popped and the Scotch poured as with wives, girls and friends they relive the wildest downwind ride of their sailing dreams.

The cosy fug below is cut back and forth by the stabbing voices as each crewman re-lives the moment, the minute, the hour of an experience that is, perhaps, never to be repeated in a lifetime. . . .

'The boat was lying flat on its side, in a 45 knot breeze. A lot of bodies were piled up on the cockpit floor trying to reach the boom vang . . .'

'The tops were flying clean off the waves . . .'

'The bow wave was hitting the mainsail four or five feet up from the boom . . .'

And at 2 a.m. the party develops. The nine men of that great crew have long since lost track of night and day in the unrelenting effort of keeping their boat moving at its maximum speed through calm and gale, for more than 600 miles. They are too high in spirit over the achievement of boat and crew for sleep, and a party after the finish is something of a tradition aboard Australian yachts. It is daylight before fatigue catches up and finally sends them to bed.

When they wake, Syd Fischer and his crew of *Ragamuffin* are told they have won the Fastnet Race, at that time the greatest individual achievement of any Australian ocean-racing yacht.

The day after that they throw a party aboard for the other crews. Syd Fischer hands out lapel buttons he has had printed especially for the occasion: 'Rago's arse beats class'—in competition with the 'Ted's Ahead' of *Morning Cloud* and 'Slater is Greater' of *Prospect of Whitby*.

Fischer, typically, was understating. There was more than luck in *Ragamuffin*'s 1971 Fastnet win. It capped three years of intelligent planning and sheer hard work, ashore and afloat. Never before had an Australian yacht been so well prepared for ocean racing as expressed in its newly specialised form, demanding excellence in tactics, crew-work and boat-handling around the buoys as well as sheer marathon endurance on the longer offshore courses.

Ragamuffin did have her luck early in the race. On the outward leg from Cowes, she held the breeze all through the first night, and in the morning, approaching the

Lizard headland, the only yacht ahead was the converted Twelve Metre, *American Eagle*, owned and skippered by Ted Turner of the United States.

Around the Fastnet Rock, *Ragamuffin* was still well placed but then her luck ran out. When the crew tried to start the engine to generate the batteries, the solenoid jammed and shorted out and, within a second or two, the batteries were completely flat. *Ragamuffin* was left with just enough emergency power to raise a dim glow in the navigational lights, but she was deprived of her electronic wind instruments, important aids to night sailing, for the remainder of the race.

But then the wind began to blow strongly from astern, giving *Ragamuffin* a fresh chance of winning. Now it was back to the brute force of a downwind spinnaker ride using the boat- and crew-punishing techniques evolved over 25 years by the toughest and most daring of the Australian crews.

Five hours after rounding the Fastnet Rock, *Ragamuffin* was running under spinnaker before 40 knots of breeze, giving Syd Fischer the kind of ride he remembered from his younger days as sweep for the Bilgola surf boat: 'The water was shooting in a plume from the bow wave, eight feet up the mast,' he said. 'And I reckon the waves were 15 feet high from trough to crest.'

Once *Ragamuffin* lifted her 60,000 lb. bulk to perform a feat known in surfing as 'doubling the wave'—that is, surfing down the face of one wave, up the back of the wave in front and down the face of it.

With the speedometer frequently 'off the clock', speeds were difficult to estimate but the boat was certainly travelling at 12–14 knots in its surfing bursts. At the end of it all, *Ragamuffin* had logged an average of nine knots for the 106 miles between Fastnet and Bishop Rock, and that included a significant time pause while the crew unscrambled a gybe-broach disaster.

This happened at night. Without wind instruments and the boat only just under control, helming was difficult. One big wave, crushing in at an angle slightly out of pattern to the rest, screwed the bow off to leeward. Syd Fischer lost the fight with the wheel and the boat crashed into an all-standing gybe. Momentum and the weight of wind carried *Ragamuffin* on into a rounding-up broach. And there she lay, helplessly on her side for 10 full minutes, water pouring into the cockpit and spurting through a submerged ventilator, galvanising the watch below into frenzied action.

The spinnaker, of 1·5 ounce to the square yard cloth weight, took itself off in a few seconds, tearing and wrapping in shreds around the rigging. But the boat still lay on her side, pinned there by the pressure of wind in the mainsail with the mainboom held high in the air to windward by the boom vang since the involuntary gybe.

Crewman Doug Patterson warned: 'I'm going to ease the boom vang.' The crewmen, struggling from below into the cockpit, immediately scuttled back into the cabin like rabbits shooting for a burrow to avoid the heavy boom they knew would sweep across the boat with tremendous force once the vang was released.

Fischer, wedged in a corner of the cockpit, appraised the situation. 'Not yet, Doug,' he growled. 'Look where your head is.'

Patterson's head was through the falls of the mainsheet system. Had he released the vang then, he could have been decapitated and would certainly have suffered serious injury. So he re-positioned himself and carefully released the vang. The mainboom crashed down and, with the pressure of wind released from the mainsail, *Ragamuffin* struggled on to her feet again.

Ragamuffin ran on under poled-out genoa jib while the crew cleared away the shreds of spinnaker and gradually gathered courage to set another, this time the three-ounce cloth-weight storm spinnaker. The watch below heavily stopped the storm spinnaker and, concluding the wind was too strong for it, went back to their bunks. But, from the helm, Fischer insisted he did not have enough pressure and ordered the spinnaker to be set. So up it went and as it was cautiously broken from its stops the sail immediately slammed into life. 'Too much pressure; too much pressure,' Fischer yelled and *Ragamuffin* went haring off again, plunging down the waves and through the tops, water continually sweeping almost the full length of the deck.

Carrying the spinnaker was daring to the point of foolhardiness, but *Ragamuffin*'s opponents were running safely but more sedately under poled-out genoas. So hanging on to those spinnakers finally secured *Ragamuffin* her Fastnet victory.

Much of the strength behind the success of Australian yachts when they're sailing in Britain—and certainly he couldn't be blamed for their failure to win the Admiral's Cup in 1971—came from Gordon Reynolds, their team captain until 1975.

Reynolds epitomises the Australian approach to racing. They enter because they want to win. They train hard as a team to win and, unfashionable as it may seem against the increasing trend to internationalism in sport, they are proud of representing their country.

They have been criticised for playing the game too hard. After all, the Admiral's Cup began as a side issue to the Fastnet and Cowes Week, to encourage 'foreign' yachts to race in Britain. But, after the America's Cup, the Admiral's Cup has become the best publicised yachting event in Australia.

The approach, as a closely knit, well trained team, began straight after Australia's first challenge in 1965 when Reynolds sailed with Gordon Ingate on *Caprice of Huon*. In 1967 he skippered *Caprice* back into the Australian team. For the 1969 challenge he applied for the job as team captain, submitting his own interpretation of its responsibilities. The organising committee accepted him and his ideas. They were followed through in 1969, 1971 and 1973 and Reynolds took the typical Australian approach, crystallised it and polished it to its present efficient shape.

The organising committee itself is formed by the Cruising Yacht Club of Australia, the challenging club, and while the committee takes over the whole burden of organising selection trials, arranging shipping for the yachts, air travel for the crews and raising the finance, it remains answerable to the Board of the C.Y.C.A. But the training programme has been left to the team captain.

The Reynolds concept was to implement an intense group sailing programme for the three yachts in the team immediately after the selection was announced. Conveniently, except for *Apollo II* in 1973, teams have always comprised yachts based on Sydney Harbour—Sydney sailors have dominated Australian offshore racing in recent years. The training programme has usually covered a three-month period. Reynolds says: 'It involves using every hour of sailing time available from the time the team is selected to the time the yachts have to be shipped to England.

'Besides sailing in every programmed inshore and offshore race, there are intensive sessions of gear-handling and tuning on the harbour on Sundays and any spare Saturdays. A typical weekend programme would be to sail in the C.Y.C.'s Saturday race—a must to gain racing practice. Then on Sunday, starting no later than 10 a.m., we gather off Clark Island for team training in the harbour.

'This involves a series of six or eight exercises—little races over a course of one or two miles, rounding six or eight marks, with upwind starts, downwind starts and gear-handling against the stopwatch . . . spinnaker sets, gybes and headsail changes. At the end of the programmed set of exercises, if there is time, the boats

The men behind the challenge. Norman Rydge, owner of 'Koomooloo', receives a cheque from Richard Dunhill of Alfred Dunhill Ltd. who sponsored the 1971 Australian Admiral's Cup challenge. Looking on, from left to right, are Syd Fischer, Gordon Reynolds, John Stuckey of Dunhill's, and Arthur Byrne

will stay out and work on any weaknesses that showed up during the day's work. It's quite amazing the improvement a stop watch can drag out of a crew bashing around short courses this way in just a month.'

Besides the crew drill, a big proportion of these short training races were devoted to improving boat speed, and outside tuning partners are sometimes enlisted. In 1971, Syd Fischer's *Ragamuffin* and Arthur Byrne's *Salacia II*, near sisterships, were obvious partners. But as a tuning partner for Norman Rydge's 41 ft. *Koomooloo*, the 43-footer *Bacardi*, owned by sailmaker Peter Cole, entered the Sunday sessions. This also gave Cole an opportunity of evaluating sails. That year, his Hood Australia loft outfitted the whole team. Individual sails and sail combinations were tried out against the tuning partner yardsticks. Working this way, *Salacia II* and *Ragamuffin* were able to perfect the cutter rig that both used effectively in hard windward conditions in Britain.

The training did not stop when the boats returned to their berths late on Sunday. Midweek, besides the normal maintenance and think sessions by the individual crews, there were regular navigators' meetings and smaller meetings of representatives from each yacht—for instance, one committee of a man from each boat, plans the catering. Every task faced in Britain is pre-planned in Australia.

One night a week there was a compulsory training session of an hour-and-a-half at a gymnasium. Gordon Reynolds attended to check on defaulters and sometimes to have a work-out himself. The night at the gym, plus occasional dinners and get-togethers for the whole team, all helped to build a team spirit before leaving Australia.

By the time the team arrives in Britain, everything is ready for them to immediately begin sailing. The Australians usually take up the whole of the accommodation in a guest house in Cowes—in 1971 and 1973 they stayed at the very comfortable Regency Club.

'We've always arrived at Cowes as a very tightly-knit body,' Reynolds says. 'I've never allowed them to drift in one by one. We live together and we stick together. I think in that lies a lot of our strength.

'Our aim is to settle in as quickly as possible and immediately get in as much sailing as possible. I like to see a minimum of two weeks on the water, apart from the inevitable small things that go wrong and the necessary re-calibration of instruments. I think it takes 10 days of good hard sailing, training and racing in Britain to bring boats and crews to peak tune. Anyone going to Britain who cannot get that time on the water isn't giving themselves much of a chance in the Admiral's Cup.

'In Britain, the team captain's job is very much full time—under one cap the captain looks after all the managerial details and under another is responsible for organising race participation and training. I've spent six hours straight sitting by myself, stopwatch in hand, in a little dinghy out in the middle of the Solent.

'We meet each morning at Cowes—skippers and navigators—to plan the day's programme for training or the tactics for the day's racing and there's always a good exchange of ideas.'

Although he has never had to employ his ultimate disciplinary power, to send a team member home, Gordon Reynolds would not hesitate to do so if the need arose. 'It's clearly understood from the moment the team is selected that they are the official representative of Australia . . . and that the team captain's word is final in all respects,' he says.

'I believe our strength has been in our preparation. We have worked so well together before reaching Britain and become dedicated to a purpose—to win the Admiral's Cup—and nothing else. The social side comes a distant second. We go to Britain at a very great cost to our sponsors, supporters, and the sport itself in Australia. The distance travelled and the cost involved in the challenge makes everyone conscious they must do well.'

The Australian challenges would not have been possible without generous financial help from commercial sponsors, especially the cigarette makers Rothmans and, more recently, Dunhill, and Qantas, the Australian airline. While there have been owners who could pay in full to send their yachts and crews to Britain, they have tended to the view that, as part of a national team, it would be wrong to do this. So the team effort extends to helping raise the money collectively, to pay the bills.

'The Americans have never liked the sponsorship aspect,' Reynolds says, 'and the British didn't either. But the British are condoning it now and I venture to say that in time the Americans will condone it, too. We could have had the most brilliant sailor in the world, skippering a fast yacht, who just could not afford the cost of taking it to the Admiral's Cup on top of the very real cost of campaigning an Admiral's Cup sized boat.

'The 1971 challenge cost about $55,000—shipping the three yachts there and back, flying the entire team of 26 or 27 men, and handling charges in England—road haulage of some description is usually involved. The crewmen pay their own accommodation, living and internal travel expenses in Britain.

'For 1973, to cope with rising shipping costs, we budgeted for a minimum of $60,000. The owners themselves paid a very high entry fee for the 1973 trials of $250 a boat. With 17 trialists, that gave us $4,250. And with all sorts of fund-raising schemes set in motion by a special sub-committee we somehow raised the money.'

Organization apart, why have the Australians done so well in Admiral's Cup racing?

'Because we're bloody good sailors,' is Reynolds' instant retort. 'Australians play their sports hard. In Britain we have been accused of sailing too hard, in 1967 especially, which was nice after being pitied in 1965. Now, the other nations are sailing hard, too. And the tough waters off the New South Wales coast, and in Bass Strait, condition a more rugged type of seaman than in America or Britain.

'We also have some very good boats and our locally made equipment is equal to anything available overseas.'

Kiwis up front

Nineteen hundred and seventy-one was the year of an emerging nation of tough-minded sailors, the New Zealanders. They not only took the Southern Cross Cup home with their team of One Ton Cup class yachts, but made a clean sweep of the first three placings overall in the Sydney–Hobart Race.

That success story really started back in 1967 with *Rainbow II*'s Sydney–Hobart win. Encouraged by this success, Chris Bouzaid took *Rainbow II* off to Heligoland in Germany for the 1968 One Ton Cup, where she finished a good second to the German *Optimist*. She returned the following year and this time won outright, and Chris Bouzaid and his crew took the One Ton Cup back to the sailing-mad city of Auckland and a hero's welcome.

The New Zealanders went to extraordinary pains to organise the One Ton Cup in March 1971 and, although the Australians stole the bacon from them when Syd Fischer won the Cup with a last minute entry in *Stormy Petrel*, the effort that went into the build-up for the One Ton blossomed into the Southern Cross Cup win later that year and success in the 1972 One Ton Cup.

Victory in the Southern Cross was sealed with a remarkable Sydney–Hobart result. Brin Wilson's *Pathfinder* won by 58 minutes from *Runaway*, sailed by his brother-in-law, John Lidgard. Ray Walker's *Wai-Aniwa*, skippered by Bouzaid, was third, only another 11 minutes 12 seconds behind on corrected time. The Kiwi trio crossed the finishing line within an hour and 14 minutes of one another. There was no team plan dictating the closeness of the New Zealand boats, but this result was also noticeable in other races in the series.

Their success was the natural outcome of many keen races in New Zealand waters between boats of the same type. One Ton competition had brought all crews to a high but even standard and this levelled out the design differences of the boats themselves. *Pathfinder*, 38 ft. 5 in. overall, with 29 ft. 4 in. on the water-line, 11 ft. 9 in. beam and 6 ft. 6 in. draft, was designed by Sparkman and Stephens and built by her boat-builder owner. She was expected to be a champion. Dick Carter, the controversial American designer, drew *Wai-Aniwa*, complete with the usual Carter touch of exotica—this time a swivelling keel, swinging from the aluminium hull which could be adjusted to reduce leeway while sailing to wind-ward. *Wai-Aniwa* is 39 ft. 1 in. overall, has a 29 ft. waterline, 11 ft. 4 in. beam and draws 6 ft. 1 in. But the third yacht in the New Zealand team was a home-grown design by her owner, John Lidgard. Smaller than the other two with major dimensions, 36 ft. 1 in. overall, 28 ft. 6 in. waterline, 11 ft. 1 in. beam and 6 ft. 6 in. draft, but just as fast. Lidgard's wife, Heather, navigated the yacht and their son Kevin, aged 17, sailed in the crew.

The New Zealand team yachts sailed with unwavering consistency in all weathers, well crewed by predominantly young hands, and in the long races sailing to a common tactical pattern. The British team, the '71 Admiral's Cup trio of *Morning Cloud*, *Prospect of Whitby* and *Cervantes IV*, obviously offered the strongest opposition. Affairs of state kept Admiral's Cup team captain Ted Heath away—Sammy Sampson skippered the boat in his absence—but otherwise the same people who had won the Admiral's Cup were all involved.

The British did not become acclimatized to the confused sea pattern off the New South Wales coast quickly enough, and their crews were stale after a three-month lay-off following the British season. Their high-pointing techniques, so effective in smoother water during the Admiral's Cup, just did not work.

The N.S.W. team comprised the mighty *Ragamuffin*; *Pilgrim*, a One Ton Cup class (near sistership to *Pathfinder*) owned by Graham Evans; and *Polaris*, one of the local Peter Cole-designed glass fibre Cole 43s, well sailed by an experienced crew from Lake Macquarie, under Les Savage. But it lacked the consistency of the New Zealand team—*Pilgrim*, especially, suffering from some erratic performances that pushed her back to 10th place in two of the races—and the potent performance of the British team's near brand new designs. *Cervantes IV*, especially, was to show her finest form in Australia.

Three spectacular big American yachts formed a U.S. team. Their main interest was in the line-honours struggle for the Hobart race and they carried far too big a handicap load to mix it with the efficiently sailed smaller yachts. They were Huey Long's *Ondine II*, Jim Kilroy's *Kialoa II* (both 73-footers) and the converted Twelve Metre, *American Eagle*, converted for ocean racing by Ted Turner. After the first 30-mile race sailed in a 10–12 knot wind, Jim Kilroy calculated that *Kialoa II* would have had to have averaged 11·38 knots to win.

The Southern Cross Cup fleet of 21 was given a separate start, 15 minutes ahead of 20 or more boats of all shapes, sizes and speeds, sailing for the same prizes as the national teams. The bigger yachts from this second fleet sailed through the smaller boats of the Southern Cross Cup fleet, causing some interference and argument on the shorter courses.

The first race, the 180-miler for the Royal Sydney Yacht Squadron Cup, was won by the British *Cervantes IV* from *Ragamuffin* and *Polaris*. The race was sailed in a 20–30 knot southerly, up and down the coast from Sydney, around Tom Thumb Islet to the south and Bird Island to the north.

American Eagle, down to six rolls in the main and number two genoa on the long beat to Tom Thumb, lost the lead on the 90-mile run to *Ondine II* and *Kialoa II*. Her close-winded superiority won it back for her on the beat home to Sydney and she got the gun to set a new record of 24 hours, 90 minutes, 30 seconds for the 'Two Islands' course. *Kialoa II* finished 15 minutes later, followed by *Ondine II*.

The wind was made to order for *Ragamuffin*, fourth across the line and with high hopes of a corrected-time win as the breeze began to moderate at nightfall, after she finished. But *Cervantes IV*, handling the confused coastal seas well, went faster as the wind eased, enabling her to change back to full sail. A shift to the east gave her a better lay down the coast from Bird Island to Sydney, and she took the race by 5 minutes, 36 seconds on corrected time. Third, a minute and 12 seconds behind *Ragamuffin*, was *Polaris*. *Wai-Aniwa* was fourth and *Pathfinder* fifth. Earlier, it looked as though the New Zealanders would sweep home together, but *Runaway* ran into two flat spots in the moderating breeze and was eighth on corrected time behind *Prospect of Whitby* and *Morning Cloud*.

The New Zealanders showed their potency in the first 30-miler for the Royal Prince Alfred Yacht Club Centenary Bowl, sailed in a 'sick' easterly, 5–10 knots at the start, freshening to 12 outside the Heads. *Pathfinder* won by 12 seconds of corrected time from *Ragamuffin*, with *Wai-Aniwa* third and *Runaway* fourth. The New Zealanders, apart from *Runaway*, were buried at the start by the bigger yachts, but recovered well in the open sea. The British team had a bad day— *Morning Cloud* fifth, *Prospect of Whitby* seventh, *Cervantes IV* 10th. They realized after this race that their flatter sails did not give them enough power to punch through the sloppy, confused seas raised by the backwash from the ocean roll against the N.S.W. cliffs.

American Eagle again took line honours from *Kialoa II* and *Ondine II*, sailing so well on the wind that she scored a sixth on corrected time and on the first beat looked to have a chance of being higher on corrected time.

The third race of the series for the Middle Harbour Yacht Club Trophy was close, with an interesting protest sequel. In another light breeze *Wai-Aniwa* turned on her best windward performance of the series to win by six seconds from *Prospect of Whitby*, also having her best race of the series, with *Runaway* third, *Pilgrim* fourth and *Morning Cloud* fifth. *Pathfinder* had to start her engine after grounding heavily on a reef near Bradley's Head. She completed the course, after losing 10 minutes, for a provisional 11th, noting the circumstances on her declaration. But she was subsequently disqualified.

The line-honours battle was best of the series. *Kialoa II* outsailed *American Eagle* on the wind, eight miles to the windward mark, then hit the mark when set down on it by the current. While she re-rounded, *Eagle* gained the lead and held it on the two subsequent reaching legs and run in the harbour, to cross first by 18 seconds. *Ondine II* was again third home, another eight minutes behind.

Wai-Aniwa, for a mile running square to the finish in Sydney Harbour, set her drifter as a staysail alongside the spinnaker, which was pulled well around to the windward side. The British team said they had been prevented from using a similar rig at home. After discovering the only way to get a ruling on the sail's use in the Southern Cross Cup was to protest, Sammy Sampson of *Morning Cloud*

Brin Wilson's One Tonner 'Pathfinder' was 1971 Sydney–Hobart winner and helped New Zealand win the Southern Cross Cup

Slicing through the South Sea water, Jim Kilroy's 'Kialoa II' from the United States made the fastest passage down to Hobart in 1971

reluctantly lodged one. *Morning Cloud*'s protest alleged the rig infringed I.O.R. rule 860D, in that the staysail was set to fly 'kitewise' over the spinnaker. It alleged the staysail was set upside down, sheeted on the centreline at the bow with the luff outside the spinnaker. It was claimed the halyard was slacked off so the head was about six feet away from the forestay. The sail was sheeted to the end of the main boom.

A protest committee from the Yachting Association of N.S.W. deliberated for more than three hours in two sessions before dismissing the protest. It adjourned for the second session to allow further photographs to be produced in evidence.

The committee found as fact: that the sail was not set upside down. The spinnaker was sheeted outside the forestay and inside the headsail (normally the drifter) set as a spinnaker staysail. The tack of the headsail was down in the normal position. The headsail was sheeted legally to the end of the boom. The headsail was hoisted until the luff of the headsail was approximately three feet from the halyard sheave position. The sag of the luff of the headsail in relation to the forestay was about four feet. The committee found the facts did not indicate that the headsail was flown 'kitewise' and therefore did not contravene 860D.

The *Wai-Aniwa* staysail, invented by Chris Bouzaid, has since been widely copied internationally. It is known variously as a big boy, shooter, blooper, depending on which sailmaker one buys it from. And the rule-makers are still arguing about its legality.

Going into the Hobart race, Britain led with 200 points from New South Wales on 197 and New Zealand 196.

The New Zealanders were always well placed in the 630-miler, but an element of luck off the notoriously fickle Tasmanian coast enabled them to bury the British who, until then, on the radio position reports, looked set to win. The New Zealanders ran up on them before a fresh nor'wester, while the bigger British yachts were slowed in varying degrees by a calm off the Freycinet Peninsula. The Kiwi One Tonners then hammered home their good fortune with skilled and daring downwind sailing before strong winds, in the same tradition that won Chris Bouzaid New Zealand's first Sydney–Hobart Race in 1967.

A record fleet of 79 yachts got away to the slowest Sydney–Hobart start in memory in 1971. The eastern Australian States advanced their clocks one hour that year in a daylight-saving experiment, but the seabreeze nor'easter could not be advanced in the same manner. So when the gun went at 11 a.m. the fleet just drifted over the line on the dying wafts of the nor'westerly land breeze. After 10 minutes the first touches of the nor'easter came in and the yachts which, antici-

(Top) New Zealand sailmaker Chris Bouzaid, skippering 'Wai-Aniwa', stirred things up in Sydney in 1971 with his controversial 'big boy'. She set her drifter alongside the spinnaker, and the British lodged a protest. But the committee declared the sail legal

(Below) 'Runaway', one of the triumphant team of Kiwi One Tonners, was designed by her owner, John Lidgard

pating it, had hung towards the eastern shore, despite the tightly packed spectator fleet there, went to the lead.

All that day the fleet streamed south under spinnakers on an eight-knot nor'-easter and with some push from the southbound current, running strongly at up to one-and-a-half knots.

During the night the wind shifted to the south-east and freshened to 20 knots. *Buccaneer*, Tom Clark's 73 ft. plywood flier from Auckland, fractured the aluminium headboard on her mainsail. She was without a main for eight hours before the seas quietened sufficiently to send crewman Alister Lawrie aloft in a bosun's chair to retrieve the halyard. The Tasmanian One Tonner, *Maria*, pulled out with a broken cap shroud and the Sydney Swanson 36, *Mistress*, broke her forestay.

The shift put the fleet hard on the wind for most of the next day, with the port tack towards the coast, the favoured leg. A few gambled on the offshore leg, among them the Sydney 52-footer *Pacha* (Bob Crichton-Brown), winner of the 1970 race. But late in the day the wind shifted to the south-west, destroying *Pacha*'s hopes 110 miles off the coast, and those of the other offshore gamblers.

Kialoa II, working the rhumb line, gained a break on her big rivals with the shift. A lift on port tack encouraged her to go right into the coast, near Eden, until finally she had to tack to clear the shore. But after a few minutes on the dead losing starboard tack the sou'westerly shift picked her up and enabled her to lay right down the rhumb line, placing her to windward of the other fleet leaders.

The wind freshened and shifted farther to the west during the night. All day, on the third day of the race, the yachts reached hard across Bass Strait on a 20–25 knot west-south-west wind. Radioed positions, morning and evening, corrected by computer calculations, placed the British team one, two, three—in the morning it was *Morning Cloud* from *Cervantes IV* and *Prospect of Whitby*; in the evening, *Prospect of Whitby* from *Morning Cloud* and *Cervantes IV*. In the evening, *Wai-Aniwa* was eighth on corrected time, *Pathfinder* 10th and *Runaway* 12th.

That day *Kialoa II*, under full reaching gear, averaged 9·4 knots for five hours and hope began to grow that she would beat the race record. *American Eagle* was 22 miles directly astern of her with *Ondine II* another 10 miles astern, but 36 miles to the east, and 21 miles ahead of *Siska*. But on Tuesday night the leaders began to lose the wind. By early morning, they were struggling to find two or three knots, when the day before they had no trouble averaging nine. In seven hours, *American Eagle* covered 14 miles, *Ondine II* 20, *Siska* 28, *Ragamuffin* 29.

Prospect of Whitby's story is a typical one of those in the first 20 in the fleet caught in this calm stretching between Maria Island and Freycinet Peninsula, between 80 and 115 miles from the finish. From 5 a.m., off Freycinet, it took her five hours to cover 10 miles. 'At the same time,' her skipper Arthur Slater said, 'the New Zealanders were running down on a 25-knot wind under spinnakers. They did 40 miles in the same period.' *Prospect*'s team mates, *Morning Cloud* and *Cervantes IV*, also closed in on her—*Morning Cloud* from 16 miles behind to two miles and *Cervantes IV* from 23 miles to four miles.

The Sydney Cole 43 *Taurus* (Geoff Lee) showed up among the leaders at this stage. From Gabo Island at the head of Bass Strait, where she was eight miles offshore, she freed off and sailed low for speed, east of the rhumb line while others stood up to windward, anticipating a header. On Wednesday morning, from seaward, she closed rapidly on the slowly moving leaders, and by Tasman Island at the south-eastern tip of Tasmania she was alongside *Prospect of Whitby*.

As the wind came away again, fresh from the north-west at 25 knots, it gathered up the middle of the fleet first, bringing it up on the leaders, and gave everyone a fast spinnaker ride down the coast to Tasman Island. *Buccaneer*, hitting 14 knots and with two men on the wheel, ran up to *Ondine II*, caught and passed her rounding Tasman Island and held her off on a hard-on-the-wind duel in a 35-knot nor'wester up Storm Bay to the finish. *Kialoa II* was long gone. Jim Kilroy, trying to hang on to his spinnaker to the last possible moment rounding Tasman Island, had the decision made for him by a 50-knot clout out of Storm Bay which burst a hole in the top of it. She was first to finish, at 11.46 p.m. on Wednesday. Her elapsed time of 3 days, 12 hours, 46 minutes and 21 seconds was nine hours outside the record set by Huey Long with his first 57 ft. aluminium *Ondine* in 1962. *Buccaneer* was next, 2 hours and 41 minutes behind *Kialoa II* and 4 minutes, 58 seconds ahead of *Ondine II* across the finishing line in the Derwent. *American Eagle* finished 16 minutes, 59 seconds behind *Ondine II*.

Down the Tasmanian coast *Pathfinder* was building her corrected time win on a wild spinnaker run. 'For nine hours we had the most hair-raising ride any of us have ever experienced,' Brin Wilson said, 'going off the clock at 12 knots many times and broaching every five minutes. I think that's where we picked up our lead.'

But as the One Tonner rounded Tasman Island in the early hours of the following morning, a rain squall killed the wind. After drifting in nothing for a time, *Pathfinder* ghosted up Storm Bay and the Derwent River in light variables to the finish. She crossed at 11.02 a.m., followed by *Runaway* at noon and *Wai-Aniwa* at 12.15. After that came a gap. There was little wind until the south-east sea breeze came in at 2 p.m. This gave the New Zealanders the break they needed to stave off any challenges from lower-rating smaller yachts behind them.

Wai-Aniwa, the swing-keel Carter boat, came with a rush at the end, covering 220 miles in the 24 hours to Tasman Island, 128 of them in the last 12 hours. She had no control problems, skipper Bouzaid said. Her third made her top points scorer in the Southern Cross Cup series—a total of 133 points from *Runaway*'s 125, *Cervantes IV* with 120 and *Pathfinder* and *Morning Cloud* each scoring 118.

After *Wai-Aniwa*, four hours ticked by to the next finisher—the One Ton Cup winner, *Stormy Petrel*. She and the group which followed her, suffered in a calm off Tasman Island. It took the 38 ft. Tasmanian *Huon Lass*, which had featured in corrected time place calculations, nine hours to round the island. With treble points from this race the New Zealand team easily won the Southern Cross Cup with 376 points from Britain's 353 and New South Wales's 314.

Bob Miller makes it

The free-wheeling intuitive talent of Bob Miller upset the Sparkman and Stephens design domination of the Australian ocean-racing fleet in 1972. In the Admiral's Cup trials of that year, the Miller twin designs, *Ginkgo* and *Apollo II*, convincingly beat the latest S. and S. boats as well as a re-cut *Ragamuffin*.

Miller had really been waiting in the wings of offshore design since he collaborated with Ted Kaufman on *Mercedes III* in 1966. But the strictures of the new International Offshore Rule were against all his natural feeling and 'eye' for a boat.

Bob Miller has always inwardly known what makes yachts sail fast since the days of a not-too-happy childhood when he began making sailing models for himself because he could not afford the store-bought kind and there was no-one else around to make one for him. The models he fashioned from balsa wood, copied from an old Daniels book on model yachts, became the fastest around his hometown of Newcastle, an industrial city 100 miles north of Sydney.

Miller later designed and built a 20 ft. plywood sloop for himself, under the inspiration of Uffa Fox, that proved to be fast but kept falling apart because he just did not have the money for items such as frames to make it strong.

The young Bob Miller lived for boats but was bad at school—so bad that he could not achieve the educational qualifications needed to gain an apprenticeship with any of the Newcastle boatbuilders. He became an apprentice fitter and turner on the railways instead. But his sailing ability led him to be recruited by Ted Kaufman to crew on a Star class in Sydney and there he became an apprentice sailmaker to Peter Cole. Norman Wright persuaded Miller to join him and start a sail-making loft in association with the Wright family boatbuilding business in Brisbane.

Miller literally fell into his design career by accident: he plummeted from the mast of a 45-footer he was measuring for a new sail. He was in the hospital for three months while his smashed back mended. Norm Wright made him a drawing board to fit the hospital bed and kept him supplied with yachting magazines. From that bed, Miller designed *Taipan*, an 18 ft. skiff completely different in concept to the great sail-carrying five-man skiffs of that period. *Taipan* was extremely light, had a modest sail-plan, not much bigger than a Flying Dutchman's, and two men on trapezes—Norm Wright and Craig Whitworth.

He later joined Craig Whitworth as crew on a Flying Dutchman. Their successes through winning three Australian and an interdominion (Australia and New Zealand) championship encouraged them to move to Sydney and form a sail-making partnership, with Whitworth contributing business acumen and Miller sail-making talent. Bob's interest in design was renewed by his work on *Mercedes III* in 1966 and by his success with the trapeze-powered Contender with which he won the International Yacht Racing Union's trials to select a new single-handed dinghy in 1968.

When Miller and Whitworth in 1969 moved their sail loft from an old dance hall to a new 12,000 sq. ft. building, a design office was added for Miller. His first big-yacht commission, from Alan Bond for *Apollo*, came about the same time. The request for a 60 ft. yacht came out of the blue through Peter Nicol, at the time skippering an ageing metre yacht, *Panamuna*, for Alan Bond.

Miller's reaction was: 'Now a 60 ft. yacht is a pretty unusual thing, and I thought, "This is some screwball whose mouth is bigger than his pocket." I said: "Oh, yeah."

'But Peter came over to see me and proved to be a rational, intelligent sort of fellow. He told me they wanted a yacht to beat *Siska* without worrying about handicap.'

When they came to talk detail, it was established Bond wanted a 58-footer primarily for racing on the enclosed waters of the Swan River estuary in Perth, although capable of doing well in ocean racing. Rating did not matter. He wanted maximum performance for cost.

Both 'Ginkgo' (below, left) and 'Apollo the first' (below, right) were Bob Miller designs. Designed for Alan Bond, 'Apollo' was Miller's first big-yacht design commission and 'Ginkgo' helped establish him as one of the world's leading designers

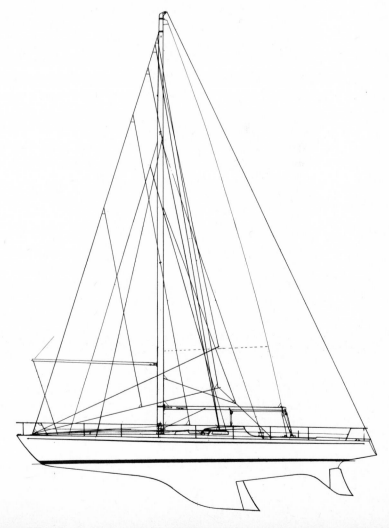

Miller concluded: 'The way to do that was to make the boat of reasonably light displacement, but a healthy type for going to sea, with a long waterline, not much overhang, easily driven, and for its size not a lot of sail. The same boat in Sydney could have had a bigger foretriangle and perhaps a bigger mainsail. But for Perth, where there is always lots of wind, the moderate sail area seemed ideal.'

The shape of the hull was dictated by reasons of economy as well as speed. As Miller put it, in his own original mode of expression: 'I gave her a long waterline to get speed without having to build a whole lot of boat hanging out in the air not doing anything except have the wind blow on it.'

This in turn dictated the shape of the bow section. The small overhang tended to make these sections very vertical in the topsides. Miller reasoned that when *Apollo* heeled, the wall-type topsides never reached the attitude where they were lying flat in the water as they do on boats with very long overhangs.

To dampen pitch, the sections between the front of the keel and the waterline are very U-shaped in *Apollo*. Big-transom stern and full sections aft act in opposition to these forward U-sections with both as far away as possible from the centre of pitch. She slams going to windward rather than pitches and while she can be uncomfortable to ride is always fast upwind in a moderate to fresh breeze.

Her principal dimensions are: length overall, 57 ft. 3½ in.; waterline, 48 ft. 3 in.; beam, 13 ft. 4 in.; draft, 7 ft. 11 in.; displacement, 33,000 lb.; ballast keel, 19,000 lb.; mainsail, 589 sq. ft.; no. 1 genoa, 933 sq. ft.

The keel and rudder are swept back and streamlined with the hollow trailing edges that have become something of a Miller trademark.

Apollo fully lived up to the expectations of Miller and Bond. She quickly proved herself 'fastest gun in the West' and encouraged Bond to take on the international big-time. He competed with her in the Newport–Bermuda Race, Cowes Week and Fastnet. As Miller expected, she went best in strong winds and tended to die because of her high wetted surface to sail area ratio, in light winds. And her high I.O.R. rating told against her. But in the 1973–74 season, under a new owner, Jack Rooklyn of Sydney, and with a very experienced crew, she notched up some impressive corrected time wins.

While Miller was happy with *Apollo* he was not happy with the way the newly introduced I.O.R. Rule was at that time encouraging yacht design. His feelings about the Rule in 1971 were these: 'Sometimes I look at pictures of yachts of the 1890s and wonder whether yacht design has advanced at anything like the pace of the materials in our boats. Because some of those old yachts make today's products look like boxes. It makes you wonder what designers like Watson and Herreshoff could have done given the sail-cloth, lightweight metal masts and rigging available to today's designers. They were on to small keels, with the rudder separate down the back; a practice that in modern times began to be really popular only five years ago.

'The modern offshore boats are designed to rules which distort their shape to make them really bitchy downwind, with enormous weather helm on a reach. This is because the International Offshore Rule evolves around measuring the length of the boat as a function of the proportion of the beam, encouraging beamier boats. But the bigger you make the beam, the crankier the boat will be downwind. These new I.O.R. boats go upwind not because they are fast, but because they have a lot of ballast. They have fine bows which throw a lot of water aboard. They are not the ideal cruising boat the rule makers think they are creating, but rotten boats to cruise because to windward the crew is saturated continuously, and downwind you can't steer them. They don't compare with light boats which are easy to steer downwind.'

Strong words those, and Miller was obviously thinking of *Apollo*, with her high performance but poor rating, as he expressed them. But early in 1972 Bob Miller did find a way to design a boat with the characteristics he liked within the confines of the I.O.R. With the help of Dennis Phillips, a draughtsman who joined him from the staff of Alan Payne, Miller found it was possible to design an I.O.R. boat that achieved a competitive rating without resorting to excessive beam. He looked instead towards making the hull deep, narrow and long.

The result was a 45-footer called *Ginkgo*, commissioned by Gary Bogard of Sydney. She and *Apollo II*, an aluminium sister ship built shortly afterward for Alan Bond, completely dominated the Australian offshore scene in the 1972–73 season, effectively ending the *Ragamuffin* era.

At launching, in mid 1972, Miller said he thought *Ginkgo* was the best boat he had designed to that time. He could not be certain—the design was 'intuitive', not tank tested. But the test tank of the Tasman Sea soon proved he was right. After competing in the 1973 Admiral's Cup to gain top scoring for the Australian team, *Ginkgo* was sold to Georgio Falck of Italy. She was still winning races in the Mediterranean in 1974.

Ginkgo's basic dimensions are: length overall, 45 ft. 6 in.; waterline, 41 ft.; beam, 12 ft. 12 in.; draft, 6 ft. 10 in.; displacement, 23,000 lb.; ballast, 12,800 lb.; mainsail, 400 sq. ft.; no. 1 genoa, 758 sq. ft.; rating, 36·3 ft.

Miller said of the boat: 'I tried to get a long waterline for the rating and the actual waterline of 42 ft. (if you include the transom-hung rudder) is very long. The displacement is very light for a 41-ft. waterline length boat.'

Compared to the Sparkman and Stephens boats she was competing against in Australia in 1972–73, *Ginkgo* was deep forward of the midship section, finer in the stern sections and slacker in the bilge. The fine, heavily-raked entry broadens quickly to deep, full U sections. Miller explains: 'The Rule dictates that. But it has got other benefits. It gives you a lot of room around the base of the mast (where all the halyards exit, below deck) and stops the boat pounding at sea. It is really the quietest boat I have ever been in in a seaway.'

The afterbody was flat with the waterline running out to a relatively fine transom where the topsides protruded beyond the transom in dinghy-style 'planing boards'. The rudder was swung on the transom from a small skeg. *Apollo II*'s rudder was tucked under the transom. With the rudder set a long way aft, and not too much bulk in the stern sections, these boats spun very easily through a tack.

Miller said of his general concept: 'I tried for a boat that will be at least equal to the others on the wind in shorter races and very fast downwind. After all, in most long ocean races you crack sheets wherever you can to gain distance, rather than point high towards the next wind change.' *Ginkgo* and *Apollo II* did prove fast on the wind as well. *Ginkgo* was able to beat the proven windward performer *Ragamuffin* in almost every race in 1972–73.

Ginkgo's hull was built by Halvorsen, Morson and Gowland, cold-moulded from two oregon laminates with one of lightweight Canadian cedar sandwiched between. It was heavily framed with Queensland maple laminates and had a laminated Queensland maple backbone. The skin was Dynel-epoxy sheathed. *Apollo II* was produced in aluminium by the same builder. She was built to Lloyds Register scantlings for Twelve Metres to give the builder practice for the 1974 America's Cup Challenger *Southern Cross*.

Ginkgo's deck layout and accommodation plan were quite unusual. Both were aimed at concentrating crew weight amidships and eliminating as many impediments as possible to the clean flow of air around the lower sectors of the sails.

Miller was influenced in designing deck and accommodation by his experiences sailing with Ted Turner aboard *American Eagle* in some of the 1971 Southern Cross Cup races. He placed a waist-deep cockpit just aft of the mast containing horizontal coffee-grinder type handles for the two Barlow 35 sheet winches. The helmsman had his own small cockpit right aft. Between the two cockpits on *Ginkgo* was a single hatch, protected by a tiny canvas dodger, leading to the main companionway below. Forward of the mast was a large hatch through which sails were handed. Otherwise, the clean, cambered shape of the deckline was unbroken.

Traditionalists looked with alarm at the lack of shelter on deck. Miller's reasoning was: 'Sailing on *American Eagle* showed me that the crew can stay on deck wringing wet and, provided they dress for it, it does not affect them. Once you have a little cabin to shelter behind, the crew tend to hide in the cabin and not do anything. On the *Eagle*, everyone on watch worked all the time. A fellow stood at the coffee grinder and trimmed the genoa or the spinnaker continuously.'

Below, there were no concessions to cruising comfort. *Ginkgo* provided only for communal living in a vast saloon in the centre of the boat. Two berths extended side by side directly under the cockpit and settee berths with pilot berths behind them were ranged on either side of the saloon. Abutting the bulkhead forward the saloon to port was the navigator's table and to one side of the mast was a compartment for the Perkins 4108 diesel auxiliary engine.

To pass forward into the fo'c's'le, to the side of the engine compartment, crewmen had to crawl on all-fours through a 'mouse-hole'. The fo'c's'le was given over to sail stowage. Directly beneath the sail hatch was the marine toilet, inside a box that doubled as a step.

Apollo II had a more conventional layout inside which meant some time after

*Gary Bogard's 'Ginkgo' meant the end of 'Ragamuffin's'
dominance of Australian racing*

launching that a small bubble coachhouse had to be added, to provide headroom over the galley and navigator's position which were located aft, just forward of the helmsman's cockpit.

The double-spreader masthead rig was very simple with fore-and-aft lower shrouds and no adjustment on the backstay. Miller reckons the only worthwhile adjustment on a backstay is to do it up as tightly as possible and forget about it: 'There is enough give in the rig to allow the mast to bend automatically to flatten the mainsail in fresh winds. An ocean racer has to have a flat main, anyway. You can take other measures to fill it up for light weather and for running.'

The mainsail was carried as close to the deck as the blocks would allow to achieve 'end-plate' effect—stopping the airflow escaping under the foot of the sail. The low mainboom also permitted precise adjustment of the mainsail's angle of attack for varying wind strengths. An elevated radial traveller track of the type used on Stars carried the mainboom vang. It meant the mainboom was effectively vanged at any angle immediately the mainsail was eased.

The sail plan was tall and narrow. Because the sail areas were all but on the point of being too small for light weather, *Ginkgo* and *Apollo II* called for careful and expert handling in the lower wind range. Both had excellent crews for that first season.

Miller sailed aboard *Ginkgo* himself, bringing along three close friends, Carl Ryves, Dick Sargeant and Pod O'Donnell. Sargeant and O'Donnell, besides being experienced offshore sailors, sailed together on *Gretel* in the 1962 America's Cup challenge and were with Bill Northam when he won his gold medal in the 5·5 Metre class at the 1964 Olympics. Ryves and Sargeant represented Australia in the Flying Dutchman class at the 1968 Olympics. Richard Hammond, veteran of two Admiral's Cups, was navigator; up-and-coming young designer Scott Kaufman added skill and enthusiasm; Alan Norman went aboard to cook, did that well and contributed more and more to the deck work as the summer went on.

Apollo II did not lack for talent, either. Jim Hardy, skipper of *Gretel II* and *Southern Cross* in the 1970 and 1974 America's Cups, joined Alan Bond as a watch captain. David Forbes and John Anderson, gold-medal-winning crew in the Star class at the 1972 Olympics, and John Bertrand, Olympic representative in the Finn class in 1972 and runner-up in the Finn world championship that year, also climbed aboard. Twenty-three-year-old Ron Packer of Perth navigated and other West Australians in the crew were John Phillips, John Longley and George Waring.

Never before had there been such a crossflow of talent from the Olympic classes into offshore racing, which in Australia had tended to be a separate compartment of the sport, jealously guarded by its specialist practitioners.

The *Ginkgo* crew was the more extraordinary group. Each man had so much

The Miller and Whitworth design team which produced 'Ginkgo'. From the left: John Bertrand, who also sailed on 'Apollo II', John King, Bob Miller and Dennis Phillips. They ultimately produced the Twelve Metre 'Southern Cross', too

sailing behind him, chain of command became mainly telepathic. Sometimes their whole approach appeared completely haphazard but it always got results. They were a compatible and understanding group. If something went wrong or a mistake were made, there were no recriminations, only a concentrated effort to improve from that position to the finish. There were no interminable post mortems around the bar; possibly because hardly any of them drank. But there was rapport, and there was humour.

Ginkgo began the 1972–73 season by winning the Montagu Island Race and was hardly ever out of a place after that. *Apollo II*, launched a little later, was just as fast but possibly fractionally behind *Ginkgo* in sailing skills. *Ragamuffin*, altered to keep her rating down under the provisions of the Mark III amendments to the I.O.R. rule, campaigned hard all season to keep up with them both.

The three comprised the Admiral's Cup team for 1973 with these individual placings in the trials: *Ginkgo*, first, second, first, first, first; *Apollo II*, third, first, second, third, second; *Ragamuffin*, second, fifth, third, second, third.

The Admiral's Cup trials concluded with the 1972 Sydney–Hobart. While *Ginkgo* won the Admiral's Cup division from *Apollo II* and *Ragamuffin*, first and second placings in the race went to Ted Turner's fire-engine red *American Eagle* and the vintage *Caprice of Huon*. Both were helped by an age allowance—each yacht more than three years old receives a reduction of 0·0030 from her time correction factor for each year of age allowance granted. (This system, introduced in Australia to encourage older boats to remain competitive, was roundly criticised by some new-boat owners following the 1972 Sydney–Hobart.)

But Turner and his crew sailed a fine race and *American Eagle* became the first yacht since John Illingworth's *Rani* to win on corrected time besides taking line honours.

The Australians headed for Cowes and the Admiral's Cup in 1973 confident in their new yachts and perhaps, after *Ginkgo* and *Apollo II* finished first and second in a fresh-wind Cowes–Dinard Race before the series, they were over confident. Their hopes were shattered by an effort, prepared in as determined a fashion as their own, by a new ocean-racing power, Germany.

Southern Cross Cup to Britain

With *Ginkgo* sold to Italy and *Apollo II* unavailable while Alan Bond began to prepare seriously for his America's Cup challenge, the Australian talent for the 1973 Southern Cross Cup was thinly spread. The New South Wales team, traditionally the strongest of the Australian states, comprised the new S. and S. 47-footer *Love and War* (Peter Kurts), a similar design to the German *Saudade* and *Prospect of Whitby* but carrying a taller rig and hence higher rating; Syd Fischer's 48 ft. veteran *Ragamuffin*; and the consistent S. and S. One Tonner *Pilgrim* (Graham Evans), a close second to *Wai-Aniwa* in the One Ton Cup of 1972.

Britain sent a strong team led by Arthur Slater. The three yachts were Arthur Slater's *Prospect of Whitby*, *Quailo III*, Donald Parr's Nicholson 55, and Alan Graham's and Dave Johnson's consistent Swan 44 *Superstar*.

The New Zealanders mounted a full-sized assault in Admiral's Cup rating boats in preparation for a challenge for the Admiral's Cup itself in 1975. All three yachts were new Sparkman and Stephens designs: Evan Julian's aluminium-hulled 45-footer, *Inca*; Brin Wilson's self-built 41-footer *Quicksilver* and Doug Johnstone's 42-footer *Barnacle Bill*. Much of the talent from the New Zealand One Tonners had percolated into these bigger yachts: Chris Bouzaid was aboard *Quicksilver*; Roy Dickson, who navigated for Bouzaid in his 1969 One Ton win, was with *Inca*; Mike Spanhake, Bouzaid's relief helmsman at the 1973 One Ton Cup in Sardinia, was helming on *Barnacle Bill*.

The New Zealand team spent a solid week training together off the Sydney coastline before the series and began each day with a 6.30 a.m. run around the park to shake off the cobwebs of Sydney's sweet night life.

A Hong Kong team was also put together around the new One Tonner *Ceil III*, newly built in Sydney to a Bob Miller design for Bill Turnbull. Two other Hong Kong yachtsmen chartered Australian yachts: Peter Jolly was fortunate to secure the still potent 57-footer *Apollo* from Jack Rooklyn, and John Park chartered the S. and S.34 *Aquila* from Ricky Laycock of Victoria.

The first race, over a 27-mile course, gave the New Zealanders a great start to the series. *Quicksilver* won by 23 seconds from *Ceil III* with *Inca* third, another 13 seconds behind; *Pilgrim* was fourth another 16 seconds behind, and *Barnacle Bill* fifth.

(Top) The clean simple deck layout of 'Love and War', a Sparkman and Stephens design built for Peter Kurts. She represented New South Wales in the 1973 Southern Cross Cup series and won the 1974 Sydney–Hobart

(Bottom) The 1973 Sydney–Hobart winner, 'Ceil III', in Constitution Dock, Hobart. She was designed by Bob Miller and features twin crew cockpits on either side of the mast

This race was the first in a Southern Cross series to be laid offshore over an Olympic-style course. Previously the short races had started and finished in Sydney Harbour because of the difficulty of laying marks in the 60 fathoms of water outside the Heads.

Prospect of Whitby failed to return for a recall signal at the start and was penalised two hours of her elapsed time. She would have won the race by a minute and five seconds had she not been penalised. Her crew protested against the decision, arguing that the starting procedure had not allowed the committee to accurately sight the line and that she was not over. Because of the difficulty of mooring the committee boat the race was started between two buoys forming the starting line, and the committee boat manoeuvred to sight down the line formed by them. *Prospect*'s crew claimed in the protest that the committee boat had drifted back from the line and that they could see daylight between it and the line. The protest was dismissed by a protest committee from the Yachting Association of N.S.W.'s rules panel.

The race was sailed in 7–15 knot nor'easter that provided a good test of sailing although there was definitely a right way to go on the first leg when the wind was light. Those yachts that held on on starboard in towards the coast longest were first to reach the freshening in the breeze and also picked a favourable lift for the port tack back to the layline. The New Zealanders inclined towards a middle course and were all well placed at the first mark, with *Inca* sailing a particularly good windward leg, moving fast and sailing very high.

The second race, which scores valuable double points, was sailed over a 180-mile course, down and up the New South Wales coast, around Flinders Islet to the south and Bird Island to the north, both about 45 miles from Sydney. From a down-wind start in a 15-knot southerly on Sydney Harbour, the yachts turned south at South Head for a beat into the moderate wind and sea.

The leaders all took a long starboard tack to pick up the best of the southbound current which was running at about 1·5 knots. A 20-degree shift then enticed most to tack on to port for a long slant down the coast. But those which stood further into the shift gained more from it and were able to lift to within five miles of Flinders Islet. These included *Apollo* which rounded 45 minutes ahead of *Quailo III*. Some yachts which tacked early just kept sailing out of the port tack lift and had to make up to 50 tacks in the quite different breeze inshore. *Pilgrim* was one to suffer dreadfully inshore.

Apollo's crew also gambled on her ability to 'lump' a number one genoa to gain power through the areas which had tended to stop her under the number two in the earlier stage of the beat. The sail and the boat held together and from this upwind advantage she took off on her best point of sailing, a reach, for Bird Island.

Under spinnaker before the 20 knot south-easterly, then starcut, and finally genoa as the wind veered east, *Apollo* averaged more than 10 knots over the 90 miles between the island, holding 12 knot speeds for long periods.

Then she reached back to Sydney Heads under genoa before running into the harbour under spinnaker to finish the course in 20 hours, 21 minutes and 15 seconds for an average of nearly nine knots, slashing 59 minutes, 39 seconds off the record for the 'two island' course. This record was one she held herself, established in 1970 when the boat was newly launched and owned by Alan Bond.

Apollo beat the New Zealander *Quicksilver* by the big margin of 39 minutes, 20 seconds on corrected time. *Inca* was third, another 8 minutes, 6 seconds behind and five minutes ahead of *Ceil III* in fourth place. Fifth-placed *Barnacle Bill* was 55 seconds ahead of *Quailo III*. The easterly faded after *Apollo* finished, ruling out the smaller yachts.

Race three, the second 27-miler, began in a 12–14 knot south-east breeze that collapsed to a calm by the end of the first round. *Apollo* scored her second win, having, as in the 180-miler, more use of a better breeze. She won by 5 minutes, 12 seconds on corrected time from *Love and War* with the West Australian 59-footer *Siska II* (second to finish) third on handicap. *Prospect of Whitby* was fourth.

Love and War, in her best race of the series, finished third across the line as well as second on handicap. She was the fastest yacht on the course in the light upwind haul to the second windward mark. The wind continued to fade so that the tail-enders, under floater spinnakers, were unable to make headway against the southbound current of nearly three knots. The last yacht to finish, *Aquila*, crossed at 1.24 a.m. the following day, more than 13 hours after the start.

With the Sydney–Hobart Race remaining, New Zealand led the series with 274 points. Britain had 217, Hong Kong 215, New South Wales 201, Victoria 164, the United States 138, Western Australia 132, South Australia 100, and Tasmania 41.

The 1973 Sydney–Hobart will be remembered mainly for the remarkable ferro-cement 72-footer *Helsal*, owned and skippered by Tony Fisher, carving 2 hours, 14 minutes and 7 seconds off the race record that had been unchallenged since 1962 when Huey Long's *Ondine* recorded 3 days, 3 hours, 46 minutes and 16 seconds.

An unusual weather pattern was ideal for breaking records. From the start, the leaders sailed in north-east, south-east and finally strong northerly breezes that kept them moving all the time without any real windward work. Most of the leading group had only to tack to clear Sydney Heads. They spent the rest of the race reaching and running. The first three finishers broke the record for the 630-mile race: *Helsal*, *Apollo* and *Siska II*.

The corrected time winner was *Ceil III*, but the British team took off the Southern Cross Cup, scoring heavily from a second, within the Southern Cross Cup fleet of 27, by *Prospect of Whitby*, fourth from *Superstar* and ninth from *Quailo III*. The final points in the Southern Cross Cup were: Britain 424, New Zealand 394, Hong Kong 373, New South Wales 366, Western Australia 273, Victoria 269, the United States 240, South Australia 196, Tasmania 59.

The New Zealand team suffered a tragic setback when a crewman on *Inca*, John Sarney, collapsed and died on the first day of the race. Sarney, a 20-year-old who joined as a replacement for a crewman who injured a knee in an earlier Southern Cross Cup race, collapsed in the evening when called out of his bunk for a sail change after a day's work in light-moderate conditions. A post-mortem showed he suffered from a rheumatic heart condition.

Inca's Mayday call brought the radio relay vessel *Mia Mia* alongside and a doctor from her pronounced Sarney dead. But, because of the heavy swell, transferring the body and skipper Evan Julian to *Mia Mia* was impossible. So *Inca* motored into Jervis Bay where Julian went ashore with the body and *Inca* resumed the race with an eight-man crew. Julian estimated the yacht lost seven and a quarter hours, plus a lot of weather gauge, and this compounded as the race went on because she fell into a less favourable wind pattern than the group she had been with, which included *Prospect of Whitby*. The whole incident must have had a depressing effect on the crew of *Inca* and on the New Zealand team. But it is to the credit of the Kiwis that they never claimed it as an excuse for being beaten. *Inca*, placed 23rd in the Southern Cross fleet of 27, made no claim for time redress to which she may have been entitled.

This was a race where, because of the easterly component in the breeze, it paid to be quite a long way east of the rhumb line for most of the course.

Ceil III's tactics were to haul off the coast to 20 miles east of Point Perpendicular and to keep climbing east of the rhumb line, fetching up 40 miles east of Freycinet Peninsula, mid-way down the east coast of Tasmania, before converging on the coast to round Tasman Island. The boat ran extremely well and was alongside the S. and S. 47-footer *Queequeg* for the first two days of the race.

Rounding Tasman, the relatively quiet ride in winds of 20 knots and less came to a sudden, violent end. The northerly wind built up to 30 and 40 knots. And the funnelling effect of the wind between the 900-ft. basalt columns of Cape Pillar and the 800-ft. high Tasman Island made the rounding a terrifying experience, with gusts variously estimated at between 50 and 80 knots raising an 8 ft. wall of spume and carrying many a spinnaker away.

Ceil III was knocked flat on her beam ends in a gybe-broach that looked so bad the skipper of *Callipyge* (Alain Streichenberger), running 400 yards away, lost sight of her completely and was contemplating a rescue operation. *Ceil III* was caught with three of the crew grouped around the base of the mast on deck, preparing to drop the spinnaker, and with the genoa hoisted ready for the fetch up Storm Bay to the finishing line. The boat was literally planing, at 12 to 14 knots, when it hit four steep waves in a row. The boat dug in and toppled over the bow, gybed and broached.

She lay on her side, held by both spinnaker and genoa, until the genoa sheet was knocked from its clam and the spinnaker halyard cut away. Then she came up, mast miraculously still intact, not a drop of water below and ready to race on.

'Only the eggs were broken,' said Bill Turnbull. 'She's a great boat.'

Ceil III's long-waterlined hull (33·5 ft.) and characteristically easily driven

Dave Allen's 'Improbable' from the United States. She was designed by Gary Mull to surf downwind—exactly what she is doing here during the 1973 Sydney–Hobart Race

Miller shape were made to order for the downhill conditions. But the boat was also extremely well prepared and sailed. Miller and Whitworth 'works team' members Craig Whitworth and Dick Sargeant, who manages the Miller and Whitworth sail loft, rigged and tuned the boat after its launching in Sydney from Doug Brooker's shed. They presented the boat to Bill Turnbull as a package and crewed on her along with other good Sydney sailors: John Wigan, who navigated, Doug Patterson and Scott Kaufman.

Ceil III beat *Prospect of Whitby* by 2 hours and 1 minute on corrected time. This was Arthur Slater's second second in the Hobart race, a replay of his performance with an earlier *Prospect* in 1969. He said downwind sailing was the boat's weakest point of sailing but a very determined effort on the part of the crew had kept *Prospect* right in the race.

Third was *Rampage*, another Miller design, of the same hull shape and dimensions as *Ceil III* but with a 4 ft. taller mast and 6 in. longer J measurement that pushed her rating from 27·5 ft. (One Ton) to 29·9 ft. A stock Cole 43 glass fibre production yacht, *Taurus* (Geoff Lee), was fourth and the U.S. 43-footer, *Improbable* (Dave Allen), fifth. Although this was a downhill race, the wind was not strong enough, except in the final few hours, to enable *Improbable* to climb out and surf to overcome her forbidding 38 ft. rating handicap.

Superstar was sixth, *Love and War* seventh and *Ragamuffin* eighth. *Quailo III* was ninth and *Mary Blair*, a 42-footer designed by Warwick Hood of Australia and launched in 1970 for Peter Riddle, returned her best performance so far with a 10th on corrected time.

Helsal's effort was a remarkable performance from a remarkable boat. Her owner, Dr. Tony Fisher of Sydney, set out to build a big, fast cruising yacht, that would get him quickly to the Barrier Reef. A structural engineer, Peter Ellen, convinced him that it was possible to build a hull in a refined method of ferro-cement construction weighing less than 10 lb. to the square foot. The method depended on a post-stressed framework of steel tubing containing tensioned high-tensile steel cables.

Joe Adams who designed the yacht calculated that using this method, with a designed displacement of 90,000 lb., the 'cruising boat' would be more than competitive as a line honours machine, considering that *Windward Passage* displaces 80,000 lb. and *Ondine II* 125,000 lb. Tony Fisher said he entered the Hobart race because Joe Adams convinced him that with a more favourable sail area to weight ratio than any of the other maxi-sized ocean racers, the crew would have only to step aboard and drive to take line honours and break records.

Unfortunately, it was not that simple. The original builder could not complete the yacht within his quote and it lay half completed for almost 12 months before building recommenced. Fisher employed two men who had been building ferro-cement yachts for themselves to complete the job—Mike Caponas and Tim O'Connell. With Fisher, they developed an even lighter form of ferro-construction than at first proposed, with a skin weight of 9 lb. per square foot.

The original ketch rig of the design was supplanted by a sloop rig on a mast

96 ft. high above deck and 103 ft. overall. Made by Alspar, it was the biggest mast ever extruded in Australia. Supporting this big mast and other difficulties with the equipment made the preparation for the race a race against time. Joe Adams pleaded with Fisher not to go. But he had made up his mind.

He imported three or four experienced American crewmen from *Blackfin* and *Windward Passage* to sort out the foredeck and, after a last minute rush, *Helsal* left for the starting line, freely tipped by many experts never destined to reach Hobart. She lacked a Starcut spinnaker and reaching headsails among other things. With a better selection of reaching sails aboard, she could have beaten the record by another two or three hours. As it was, she duelled all the way with *Apollo* and *Siska II*. Rounding Tasman Island, 40 miles from the finish, *Apollo* was only two miles behind and closing as *Helsal* had trouble with her spinnaker. The halyard jumped the sheave and jammed as the crew were trying to drop. Crewman Ian Moody went up the mast with a knife between his teeth and cut away the halyard.

Helsal then rocketed away up Storm Bay, doing 12 knots under cutter head-sails in the freshening northerly. Earlier, running before it outside Tasman Island, *Helsal* was doing 12–14 knots. No-one knows exactly how fast because she sailed the whole race without log or speedo. These instruments failed before the start.

While the leaders had an easy free-sheet ride all the way, the tail-enders and smaller yachts had to battle a progressively stronger northerly and finally faced a tough beat all the way up Storm Bay to the finish when the wind turned north-west. Wind estimates for the nor'wester varied between 40 and 80 knots but it was strong enough to blow the mizzen, mast and all, clean out of the 76 ft. ketch *Mia Mia*, accompanying the fleet as radio relay vessel.

Racing ahead

The glamour of international competition available through the Southern Cross Cup, Admiral's Cup and more recently the Ton Cups, plus, in many yachting centres, the sheer overcrowding of inshore waterways, is each year pushing more yacht owners and more skilled crewmen into ocean racing.

Despite a serious downturn in the Australian economy through 1974, the 1974–75 Australian offshore season is developing as a most interesting one with seven new yachts launched for the Admiral's Cup trials and two maximum I.O.R. rating boats launched to chase line honours and race records. But it was left to an older boat, Peter Kurt's *Love and War*, to win the 1974 Sydney–Hobart Race.

Two of the new boats are Bob Miller designed 54-footers, rating about 42 ft., built in aluminium for Syd Fischer and Alan Bond.

Fischer's boat, again named *Ragamuffin*, incorporates some of his own thinking. This boat and Bond's *Apollo III* are in the *Ginkgo* design theme with deep forward sections, relatively narrow beam and long, straight buttock lines. Fischer chose finer, rounded sections aft than those of *Apollo III* which has a chine in her stern sections to reduce waterline beam. The new *Ragamuffin* is 13 in. narrower in beam than *Apollo III*, slightly lower in the topsides and has a metre-yacht style flush-deck layout with a number of features devised by Fischer and his crew from their experience with the original *Ragamuffin*. She is furnished with only the barest comforts: 'She is a flat-out racing machine but one in which you will be able to sleep, eat and live reasonably well,' Fischer says.

Apollo III's deck layout is quite different, with a large cockpit surrounded by a raised coaming just aft of the mast. There is also a conventional cockpit right aft for the helmsman and afterguard.

A third new Miller-designed Admiral's Cup team contender was Geoff Lee's *Geronimo*, 48 ft. 6 in. overall and the first of a Miller and Whitworth line of production boats built in glass fibre by Olympic Yachts of Greece.

These yachts are to feature plush, space-age styled interiors to appeal to European tastes and are to be a good deal more comfortable below than *Ginkgo* and the new *Ragamuffin*.

For them, Miller devised gimballed glass fibre hammocks, about 6 ft. 9 in. long and 2 ft. wide, moulded to a roughly human shape. He picked up the idea from the Admiral's hammock aboard Nelson's flagship, H.M.S. *Victory* in Portsmouth, England.

Ray Kirby's new 47-footer *Patrice III* shaped well during the early races of the 1974–75 season in Sydney. She is a development of the *Saudade* theme by Sparkman and Stephens, built in aluminium. She carries a big sail area, with 160 per cent overlap genoas contributing to quite a high initial rating of 36·7 ft. that, it was hoped, could be whittled to less than 36 ft. as the season progressed.

Joe Adams, designer of the 73 ft. ferro-cement flier *Helsal*, the Sydney–Hobart Race record breaker in 1973, produced an unusual new Admiral's Cup candidate for Neville Gosson.

Like *Apollo III* and *Ragamuffin*, this boat, *Leda*, is built in aluminium which is becoming the favoured medium in Australia for one-off designs. While *Leda* is 53 ft. 6 in. overall, she has a 44 ft. waterline—a foot longer than *Ragamuffin*'s—and was expected to rate about 43·5 ft.

While the maximum beam, 15 ft. 7 in. is big, it fines down quickly to a 12 ft. waterline beam and the entire hull is well veed to make it go straight, especially downwind. *Leda* carries a seven-eighths rig instead of the conventional masthead, because Joe Adams believes the mainsail contributes valuable downwind power.

John Kahlbetzer of Sydney imported a new 53-footer from Palmer Johnson, of Sturgeon Bay, Wisconsin, U.S.A. Kahlbetzer, who campaigned his Van de Stadt-designed 42-footer *Bumblebee II* through the 1974 S.O.R.C., was so impressed by *Scaramouche*, winner of the series, that he ordered this updated, refined version from her designer, the young Argentinian, German Frers. *Bumblebee III*'s crew is headed by Australia's national sailing coach Mike Fletcher and she was second overall in the 1974 Sydney–Hobart Race.

Ted Kaufman won the first major race of the Sydney offshore season in 1974, the 350-mile Montagu Island Race, with *Mercedes IV*, a new Two Tonner he designed himself. She has a low-profile sleek green hull that looks fast and she points high under a lofty rig that would be ideal for British waters in August.

The 1974 Montagu was basically a downwind race before 25–30 knot reaching and running breezes, so *Mercedes IV* proved she could run fast as well. As with *Mercedes III*, Ted Kaufman got together with Cec Quilkey to devise a lightweight construction method that is vital to the design. They cold-moulded the hull with a one-inch thick core of end-grain balsa sandwiched between two double-lapped diagonal skins of King Billy Pine. Also sandwiched internally between the outer skins are full-length inch by inch stringers spaced 12 in. apart. The result is a 42 ft. hull with 35 ft. waterline displacing only 19,400 lb. And 11,800 lb. of this is in the lead keel and another 800 lb. in the diesel engine.

The two 'maxi' boats launched in Australia in 1974–75 are *Ballyhoo*, a 72-footer designed by Bob Miller for Jack Rooklyn, and Joska Grubic's 83 ft. Alan Buchanan designed ketch, 72 ft. on the waterline and rating about 68 ft.

Ballyhoo, 72 ft. 2 in. overall with a 65 ft. 3 in. waterline and 15 ft. beam, displaces 60,000 lb. and is in aluminium built by Halvorsen Gowland of Sydney. Seeking line honours, Rooklyn intends tackling the world's big offshore events with her. Grubic of Adelaide, well-known as a good competitor through his steel yachts *Adria* and *Anaconda*, intends his self-built glass fibre foam sandwich ketch specifically for the 1975 Financial Times Clipper Race from London to Sydney and back.

Interest is high in Australia in the level rating classes, particularly the Half Ton class which carries the most realistic price tags. The One Ton Cup class remains less popular, probably because of its proximity in cost and rating to the lower end of the Admiral's Cup scale. Level rating was encouraged in 1974 when the Cruising Yacht Club of Australia instituted a regatta for all the level rating classes and this is to become an annual event.

The appeal of close racing in the level-rating classes, and the narrowing of the Admiral's Cup rating limits to encourage what amounts to another class of boat racing at roughly the same speeds, is attracting top sailors from inshore one design classes such as the Solings and Dragons and from the dinghy classes. This follows a world-wide trend of small-boat sailors being drawn by the big boat challenge. To the basic ocean racing ingredients of adventure and camaraderie have been added the spice of boat-for-boat competition. More and more Australian yachtsmen are finding the mix irresistible.

PART THREE

Southern Ocean Racing Conference
and
Onion Patch

Goaded offshore

Real ocean racing in America got started with a contest that has, in some respects, never again been equalled. Late in the sailing season of 1866 a newspaper article was published in New York City that chided the members of the New York Yacht Club for bragging about their feats of seamanship in the placid waters of New York Harbour to Sandy Hook. The article suggested that New York's yachtsmen were really making much ado over nothing and that they should test their mettle in a real offshore contest. Indeed, since the formation of the New York Yacht Club in 1844, America's racing had been limited to the protected waters of the harbour, the Hudson River, Long Island Sound, with only occasional forays into the unprotected waters of Rhode Island Sound off Newport and the waters of the New Jersey coast.

After the article appeared ridiculing the N.Y.Y.C.'s race course, Pierre Lorillard and Franklin Osgood met one evening for dinner. Over what has been euphemistically called 'turtle soup', the two men decided that they would have a transatlantic race of their own in the dead of winter. The race would be between Lorillard's 105 ft. centreboard schooner *Vesta* and Osgood's 106 ft. keel schooner *Fleetwing*. Both men put up $30,000 apiece and the winner of the race, from Sandy Hook, New Jersey, to the Needles, Isle of Wight, would take all.

News of the race, and of the wager, spread quickly through waterfront streets of Manhattan and the next day 25-year-old James Gordon Bennett Jr. asked to be allowed in the race. Both *Vesta* and *Fleetwing* had polished off Bennett's *Henrietta*, a 107 ft. keel schooner, during the summer's racing, so it is little wonder that Lorillard and Osgood were pleased to see the pot sweetened with another $30,000.

Ironically, although Lorillard and Osgood had taken up the challenge to do some offshore racing, and in the icy North Atlantic at that, once the effects of the turtle soup had worn off it was disclosed that neither of these owners would be personally making the race. This was not particularly uncommon for Corinthian yachtsmen of the era as owners often watched their vessels race up the Hudson from the relatively comfortable surroundings of a patrolling steam yacht. This detachment from one's racing vessel seemed not to diminish the owner's feeling of participation. It is interesting to note that the yachtsmen who were most instrumental in establishing the sport in the United States would be called 'straphangers' or worse by the crews of contemporary ocean racers.

T. C. Wood's 'Water Witch' sailed in the inaugural, very rugged, Miami–Nassau Race in 1934. Twelve boats started: three finished, and one of them was 'Water Witch'. In 1936, under the ownership of C. A. Hansen, she won Class A in the 1936 Miami–Nassau Race

James Gordon Bennett was the only one of the three owners who set off on December 11th, 1866, on a cold, wet and miserable crossing. The 3,100-mile race finish was incredibly close, but *Henrietta* won, setting a transatlantic record of 13 days, 21 hours and 45 minutes for sailing ships that stood until 1905 when *Atlantic* sailed from New York to the Lizard in 12 days, 4 hours and 1 minute. That record still stands today.

By the early 1900s ocean racing was under way, although the start was a feeble one, and it was up to a few yachtsmen of stout spirit and an enthusiastic yachting press to force the issue. Thomas Fleming Day, the editor of 'Rudder' magazine during the late 1800s and early 1900s, was the most influential chronicler of the sport in those days and did much to allay his readers' fears of what lay beyond the horizon.

In 1930 the St. Petersburg, Florida, to Havana, Cuba, Race was started by George (Gidge) Gandy and was widely promoted in the Florida press as well as the national boating magazines. In 1934, Arthur H. Bosworth of the Miami Yacht Club and Sir Roland Symonette of the Nassau Yacht Club, seeing the success of the Havana venture, started a race of their own. It ended up being the Miami–Nassau Race and, like its Bermuda Race predecessor, had the full support of the island's Chamber of Commerce. (In fact, the business interests of island merchants figured strongly in the formation of many races off the Florida coast.) It was these two races, along with the Miami–Fort Lauderdale–Miami Race started in 1928, which formed the basis for the Southern Ocean Racing Conference which first took shape as the Southern Circuit in 1941.

While these East Coast races were being organized in the '20s and '30s, offshore races had sprung up earlier elsewhere in the country. The Los Angeles–Honolulu Race, a 2,250-mile event, was started in 1906, and in the midwest deep water racing had begun before the turn of the century—the Chicago to Mackinac Race began in 1898.

With the popular use of glass fibre in the 1960s, fleets became swollen with new participants and still more offshore races were instigated. Today, there are two or three long offshore races each season from every major yachting centre in the United States. Off Florida, in addition to the S.O.R.C., there are now races from Miami to Montego Bay, Jamaica; from Nassau to Kingston, Jamaica; from St. Petersburg to Isla Mujeres, Mexico; and from Fort Lauderdale to Charleston, South Carolina. Along the north-east coast of the country, in addition to the Bermuda Race and the Onion Patch Series, there is the Annapolis to Newport Race, the Marblehead to Halifax Race, and a race from Sandy Hook to the Chesapeake Bay. In the midwest the two Mackinac races now have the company of long-distance events across every one of the Great Lakes. In 1975, a race is planned from Port Huron to Chicago, a distance of over 600 miles, which will make it the longest freshwater race in the world.

On the American West Coast there is the Swiftsure Lightship Classic; the Victoria, British Columbia to Maui Race; the Los Angeles to Tahiti Race; the San Francisco to Los Angeles Race; plus races from Southern California to La Paz,

Cape San Lucas, Mazatlan, Puerto Vallarta and Acapulco—all in Mexico. Like the races into the Pacific, the ones to Mexico are also downhill slides. But the most popular Southern Californian race of all is the one from Newport Beach to Ensenada, Mexico—each year over 500 boats enter this overnight event, making it the biggest ocean race in the world.

From the sport's modest beginnings in 1866 it has grown in the last 100 years to a national fleet of nearly 14,000 boats across the country that range all the way from 20-footers to a number of 79-footers. Nearly 4,500 of this number are rated under the International Offshore rule. The number of boats rated under the I.O.R. nearly equals that of the rest of the world combined. The balance of America's racing cruising boats compete under a number of different handicap rules that vary from club to club. The largest fleets outside of those using the I.O.R. rule are the Pacific Handicap Racing Fleet, which numbers over 1,000 boats, and the Midget Ocean Racing Club (similar to Europe's Junior Offshore Group class) for boats up to 30 ft. overall, which now has about 2,000 boats.

During the last 100 years of American ocean racing obviously much has changed. Boats are no longer 105 ft. long, but rather 25 to 70 ft. Crews are no longer 90 per cent paid hands, and professionals now only man the largest of the yachts and serve more in the capacity of maintenance and delivery men. For the most part, owners sail their own yachts rather than watch from the sidelines. Most notably, ocean racing is no longer the province of the wealthy few. As for the boats themselves, instead of wood, they are now glass fibre and aluminium. Instead of their sails being of flax or duck, they are of Dacron or nylon. But for all the changes that have taken place over the last century, one thing has remained the same: men still want to challenge each other on the sea.

Southern circuit origins

Like so many ocean races in all parts of the world, the idea of the St. Petersburg to Havana Race was born in a bar. Its creator, Gidge Gandy, was sharing the good cheer of shipmates in a Cuban cantina when he devised what was to become the most glamorous and talked about ocean race on the American calendar.

The first St. Petersburg to Havana Race was held in the spring of 1930. Gidge and the St. Pete Yacht Club organised the start off the city's recreational pier and Rafael Posso organised the finish 284 miles later from Havana's famous Morro Castle. Eleven boats started and finished that race, the first long-distance ocean race from the Florida coast.

By today's standards, the Havana Race might not seem like a very challenging offshore event. But in 1930 it was the second longest regularly scheduled offshore race, superseded only by the Bermuda Race. The race took place in three bodies of water—Tampa Bay, the Gulf of Mexico and the Straits of Florida. Although the race usually could be counted on as an easy reach to Havana, it wasn't always so. Winter northers had a disconcerting habit of rolling down from the permafrost of Canada, across the frozen American plains, to smack the boats in the Havana Race with frigid, blustery winds.

In the first race the fleet dashed south with lifted sheets as a fresh northerly blew the odd combination of boats to Cuba. There were no restrictions placed on sails in that race, and canvas of all descriptions was in evidence. Spinnakers, balloon jibs, balloon staysails, fisherman staysails and club topsails were set. Gidge Gandy's *Cynosure* set a rafee and *Mallard* used a squaresail. More than one rig looked like a clothesline on Monday morning.

The pioneers of Florida ocean racing also discovered the surprising power of the Gulf Stream. Although everyone knew it was there, they found its set varied markedly depending on the weather conditions on the east coast of Florida and the Straits of Florida itself. Sometimes the effect of the current is negligible while in other years the Stream has been noted to course along at five knots. In the first Havana Race a few skippers miscalculated the strength of the Stream and were set to the east, forcing them to buck the current to get back to Havana.

The 44 ft. Marconi-rigged schooner *Haligonian*, owned by Houston Wall of Tampa, was the first boat to finish in 1930 in 44 hours and Garner H. Tullis' black schooner *Windjammer* from New Orleans' Southern Yacht Club had the lowest

The present-day courses for the Southern Ocean Racing Conference. In the old days there was a race from St. Petersburg to Havana

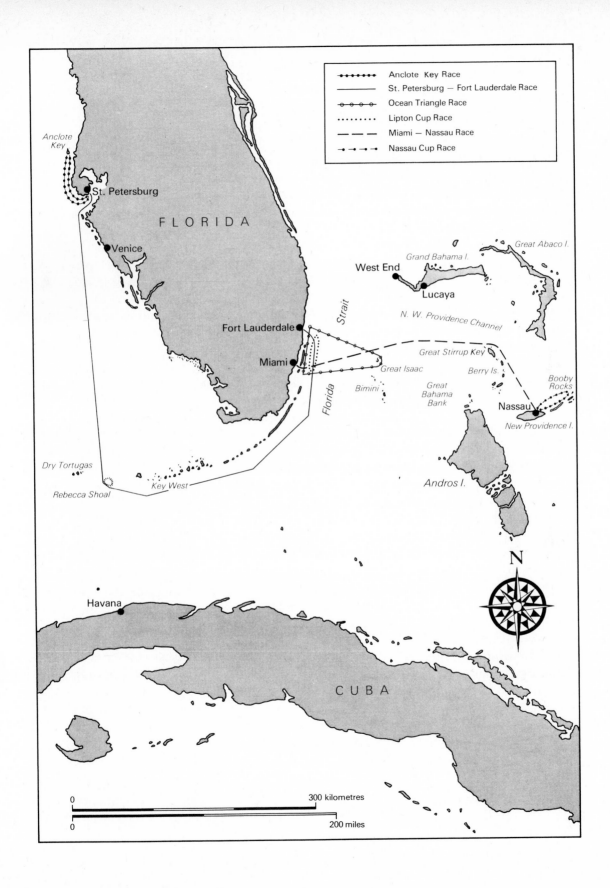

Anclote Key

St. Petersburg

FLORIDA

Venice

Fort Lauderdale

Miami

Strait

Florida

Dry Tortugas

Rebecca Shoal

Key West

West End

Grand Bahama I.

Great Abaco I.

Lucaya

N. W. Providence Channel

Great Stirrup Key

Great Isaac

Berry Is.

Booby Rocks

Bimini

Great Bahama Bank

Nassau

New Providence I.

Andros I.

N

Havana

CUBA

Anclote Key Race
St. Petersburg — Fort Lauderdale Race
Ocean Triangle Race
Lipton Cup Race
Miami — Nassau Race
Nassau Cup Race

0   300 kilometres

0   200 miles

corrected time in the fleet. In the harbour that winter were the ensigns of two nations and the burgees from eight different yacht clubs fluttering in the breeze. From the very beginning, the Havana race drew entries from many clubs, a tradition that was to grow over the years.

Reporting on the inaugural race, Gandy wrote: 'Yes, the social features of the race are a success! In fact, it seems to me that never have a group of sailormen become so well acquainted in so short a time.' One suspects that Gidge's omission of exactly with whom the sailormen became so well acquainted was not a lapse of grammar but rather the insertion of good taste, for in the 1930s Havana was the gayest and wildest city in that part of the world. Word quickly spread through yacht club bars far and wide of the beautiful and fun-loving women of Havana and of the gambling casinos and boisterous waterfront saloons that welcomed the warring yachtsmen, eager to replay the race over and over again until the wee hours of the morning. The Havana Race quickly became established as the most exotic race in the United States, not so much because of the course, but more by virtue of the good times to be had after the finish.

America's ocean racers didn't have long to wait for the northern gear-busters that would, over the years, spread the fame of southern racing as nature's test tank. In the second Havana Race, the eight-boat fleet beat out of Tampa Bay into the teeth of a dying south-easterly gale. Over 20 boats were expected for the event and possibly the smoky weather discouraged some of the faint-hearted.

Thrashing out the bay that afternoon was St. Pete Yacht Club Commodore Wall in his *Haligonian*; *Sunshine*, a 64 ft. schooner which was the scratch boat and had spent her early days fishing off New England's Grand Banks; and there was *Virginia*, a 54 ft. schooner which was built as a slaver during the Civil War. The smallest boat in the fleet was W. B. Allen's 30 ft. ketch *Gamecock*.

By the first night the wind had hauled to the north and the Gulf seas were in a rough and confused state that prepared the racers for what was to come. The second day out, the wind fell light and *Windjammer* and *Haligonian* (both class winners in the first Havana Race) gybed west of the Dry Tortugas, anticipating that the light air would hold for the rest of the race and that the Gulf Stream would carry them into Havana Harbour. The navigators on the two boats figured that the Stream would be running at its usual two knots. That race was to teach the sport's trailblazers something of the changeable personality of the Stream.

As the boats crossed the Stream on the second afternoon out of St. Pete, the navigators on nearly every boat were having second thoughts about their own abilities. Their sights placed them all much farther west than they reckoned they should have been because of the two-knot drift of the Stream. The cardinal rule when sailing in the Straits of Florida was taken as just that and nearly every navigator discarded his sights as inaccurate, and the fleet sailed on using dead

Since Olin Stephens designed 'Dorade' ocean racing has never looked back. Sailing her with his father and brother Rod in 1931, Olin won the Transatlantic Race and the Fastnet

reckoning. The lone exception was H. S. Denniston, skipper of *Sunshine*. He had faith in his sights and sailed right through the haze to Morro Castle, to be the first boat to finish and first in the fleet on corrected time.

Haligonian and *Windjammer* made their landfalls on the third night, 25 miles west of Havana, and had to use the time-honoured method of hoisting a man to the masthead to locate the loom of the city. In the meantime a fresh south-easter had sprung to life and their lot was a beat to the finish, the usual punishment for such an error in navigation.

Of course, it was the constant south-easterly that had been blowing at the start, and for days before, that had backed up the Stream until it flowed not at all—at least not on the surface. That year there was actually no set to the Stream.

On the third day, when most of the fleet had stumbled into Havana Harbour, a 50-knot norther swept in to lash the tardy. Race founder Gidge Gandy, who by now was called 'Admiral' by Florida yachtsmen, hove-to in the Stream to ride out the norther. Ashore, anxiety grew for Admiral Gandy and for *Virginia* which had also failed to arrive. The Coast Guard was dispatched on the fifth day. They discovered Gandy clawing his way off the lee shore of Cuba 40 miles east of Havana and *Virginia* snugly anchored in the security of the lee of one of the Florida Keys.

The little 30-footer *Gamecock* made a good account of herself by winning Class B and finishing third overall on corrected time and established the precedent in southern racing, to the consternation of many, that small boats could win races. There were some other firsts that year, too, most notably two women entered the race. As we have said, it didn't take long for word of the pleasures of Havana to get around.

Despite the great American depression, fleets continued to assemble each spring in St. Petersburg throughout the 1930s for the dash south. *Haligonian*, *Gamecock* and *Windjammer* turned up again and again for the next few years as class winners but it wasn't until 1937 that an overall corrected-time prize was awarded.

The second major race founded that would ultimately provide the framework for the Southern Ocean Racing Conference was the Miami–Nassau Race, begun in 1934. Twelve boats started the race and in the words of ocean racing's luminary Alf Loomis, who was there: 'At least half of them shouldn't have been allowed to start.' Although Loomis has sometimes been accused of overstatement, in this case he was giving a number of boats the benefit of the doubt. Nine boats quit.

The Miami–Nassau Race is exactly the same today as it was 40 years ago. The 176-mile race consists of three legs, the first from the sea buoy off Government Cut to Great Isaac Key, a small island that marks the western extremity of the Bahama Banks, the second leg is 65 miles to Stirrup Key, thence south-easterly for 55 miles to Nassau on New Providence Island.

The inaugural Miami–Nassau Race started off in a light easterly breeze that had many crew among the boats wishing for more wind. They got it a few hours later. Once the fleet had entered the Stream, low lying clouds came rushing westward to meet them, packed with 20-knot winds which set up a horrendous wave action. Nearly everyone racing was sick. As the breeze freshened, sails began ripping to shreds and more than one boat that had been over canvassed found that Mother Nature had quickly done the work of a reluctant crew.

Vadim Makaroff's 72 ft. *Vamarie* won the race in 32 hours, 38 minutes and 39 seconds. Philip Roosevelt was second in a boat he had chartered for the historic occasion—*Musketeer*, a 45 ft. ketch. She finished 17 hours behind the winner. The third boat was *Water Witch*, a 50 ft. schooner owned by T. C. Wood, which finished 18 hours after *Musketeer*. On the second day *Water Witch* blew out her jib and her main ripped along several seams. Though all on board were sick, the crew sewed sails all day while the vessel slogged along under a forestaysail and a jumbo. The crew of *Water Witch* fought to the finish and earned the respect of both the yachtsmen who finished and those that scattered for shelter around the course to places such as Great Isaac, Cat Key, and Bimini.

It was probably to the ultimate benefit of the sport that the Miami–Nassau Race started off with such a buster. It put yachtsmen on notice that they were racing in the ocean and gale-force winds can and do sweep through the land of sun and fun in the spring. There is no doubt that Loomis was right when he said that six boats shouldn't have started the race. One boat had an open cockpit, yet another had previously broken her back, and others couldn't go to windward. Even among the boats that finished, all suffered blown-out sails.

Olin Stephens, at the age of 65, still designs some of the world's most outstanding ocean racers, backed by a large staff at the New York based firm of Sparkman and Stephens

Lawrence Balliere's *Aweigh* won the 1935 Miami–Nassau Race and the proud *Water Witch*, under the ownership of C. A. Hansen, came back to win in '36. Then, in 1937, Robert W. Johnson began a winning streak with the Sparkman and Stephens designed *Stormy Weather*. She won the Nassau race five times in a row, in 1937, '38, '39, '40 and '41, the last two races under the ownership of William Labrot. The beautiful yawl went on to tie for overall honours in the first Southern Circuit in 1941 with Dudley Sharp's *Gulf Stream*. In 1948, 13 years after she began her ocean racing campaign, *Stormy Weather* won the Circuit in her own right under the ownership of Fred Temple.

Stormy Weather followed closely on the heels of the successful Olin Stephens design *Dorade* and replaced her as one of the classic ocean-racing designs of that era. Through the years *Stormy Weather* won her class in nearly every major event on the East Coast at one time or another, in addition to victories in the Southern Circuit. Stephens, ever mindful of designing racing boats to take advantage of the handicap rules, created in *Stormy Weather* a boat that rated well (41 ft. under the Cruising Club of America rule) and went fast.

Of the *Stormy* Olin said: 'She is really just exactly what I think the rule encourages. Her ends are short, beam ample, and displacement moderate. Personally, I should like her better with less beam, although she would be faster under the rule as she is. The beam and the displacement are both slightly under the figures set by the rule.' Her dimensions were 53 ft. 11 in. overall; 39 ft. 8 in. waterline; 12 ft. 6 in. beam; 7 ft. 11 in. draft; 1,300 sq. ft. measured sail area. She was built at the Nevins Yard on City Island. John G. Alden, who was probably still the leading naval architect at the time, said when he saw *Stormy Weather* in Nevins' yard that her hull was one of the most beautiful he had ever seen.

In 1937 *Stormy Weather* began what was to be nearly a lifelong career of chomping through southern ocean-racing fleets. Sailed by Rod Stephens Jr., brother of Olin, *Stormy Weather* won the '37 Miami–Nassau Race in just over 30 hours. It was a hard thrash to windward most of the way in moderate to fresh south-easterly winds for the best fleet of ocean racers ever seen south of Chesapeake Bay.

Of the 19 boats that started the race, two, *Stormy* and the 72 ft. Herreshoff-designed *Tioga*, would live on in the annals of yachting history. Later *Tioga*, under the ownership of Henry E. Noyes, would set an elapsed time record for the Nassau race of 19 hours, 36 minutes, 30 seconds. Years later she came under the ownership of Bob Johnson who renamed her *Ticonderoga*. In 1952 the mighty *Ti* set an elapsed time record in the Havana Race of 30 hours, 37 minutes, 28 seconds. But in 1937 the crew of *Tioga* had a few things to learn about ocean racing, coming abeam of the Stirrup Key light at night 12 miles to the north. Although such prudence might be laudable when cruising in the Bahamas it was no way to win a boat race. Rod Stephens rounded Stirrup close aboard an hour later and beat *Tioga* to the finish line by nearly an hour on elapsed time.

A little 30 ft. cutter named *Babe*, owned by Hugh M. Matheson, was second in the '37 Nassau Race and a month later went on to win Class B and the fleet prize in the Havana Race in a booming norther. The little *Babe* was sailed hard by her three-man crew and, when the wind piped up from the north-east, the crew set a large genoa as a spinnaker and boiled along at seven and a half knots, occasionally surfing to over 10. Small boats had become a fixture on America's southern ocean.

After winning his third Nassau Race, Johnson sold the *Stormy* to William Labrot, to make room for his new racer *Good News*, an S. and S. 64 ft. yawl which won the 1940 Havana Race. That must have been quite a ride because, as we have noted before, all sorts of wild ideas come to the heads of ocean racing men in the cosy confines of Cuban hostelries, particularly after a merry reach down to Havana on what was referred to by Florida's racers as the 'rumba' line.

While the 11 boats which had taken part in the race rode quietly at anchor, their crews were ashore and had turned the conversation to the serious business of handicap rules, always a favourite topic for discussion after an uneventful race.

The St. Pete and Miami Yacht Clubs rated the boats in the races under their domain in a somewhat arbitrary and unsophisticated manner. Basically, the clubs merely took the square root of an entering yacht's sail area and modified it slightly with propeller and rig allowances to arrive at a boat's rating. In the Havana Race, the scratch boat allowed the rest of the fleet 20 minutes for each foot of rating and that was that. Visitors from the north, who by 1940 made up nearly half of the small fleets, were used to racing under the Cruising Club of America rule on the Chesapeake Bay and in the Bermuda Race, and were anxious to see this rule extended to southern waters. A number of the northern yachtsmen contended that if the St. Pete and Miami clubs adopted the C.C.A. rule, more boats would be encouraged to go south for the winter to carry on old feuds started in the summer.

In 1941 the two presiding Florida clubs adopted the C.C.A. rule and for the first time formalised a loose, five-race 'winter circuit'. The races included the Lipton Cup, the Miami–Nassau Race, the Governor's Cup (held off Nassau), the St. Pete–Havana Race, and a race from Havana to Key West, Florida.

The first Circuit was a fierce tussle between Dudley Sharp's 70 ft. S. and S. designed yawl *Gulf Stream*, Labrot's *Stormy Weather* and Robert Johnson's *Good News*. *Gulf Stream* got off to a slow start, being placed sixth in the Miami–Nassau Race and third in both the Lipton Cup and the Governor's Cup, but then she won the Havana Race and the run back to Key West to tie for first overall in the series with *Stormy Weather*, which had won the Miami–Nassau Race. *Good News* finished one point behind the tied winners with 33 points.

It was this series that launched what was later to be called the Southern Ocean Racing Conference, a name that was not applied until the early 1950s ('Southern Circuit' is still used colloquially). The fleet for the first Circuit was small, with only six boats competing in the Havana Race. The Great Depression and the fact that a world war was being fought stunted the growth of the ocean-racing fleets in the early 1940s, and no long distance ocean racing was held during World War II. The Havana Race was re-instituted in 1946, and in 1947 the 'winter circuit' was held, and has been every year since.

Revolutions - in more ways than one

The new Circuit in 1947 was won by *Ciclon*, a Cuban boat owned by A. Gomez-Mena and M. Bustamante. *Stormy Weather* won in 1948, under the ownership of Fred Temple, and Palmer Langdon and Dick Bertram teamed up in '49 to win in *Tiny Teal*, taking the Havana Race in the process. In 1950 Walter Gubelmann's *Windigo* established a pattern that would only be broken once in the next 10 years—that whoever won the Havana Race won the Southern Circuit as well. The exception was in 1951 when James Crawford's *Lady Patty* won the Havana Race with Will Erwin's *Belle of the West* taking the Circuit. (In 1958 a race to Miami was substituted for the St. Pete–Havana Race due to revolutionary activity in Cuba at the time. However, *Ca Va* maintained the tradition by winning both the long race and the S.O.R.C. that year.)

When the Miami–Nassau Race was revived in 1947, King Neptune decided he'd give the 14-boat fleet a real slammer to windward to baptise the new ocean racers. Like the very first Nassau Race 13 years before, the event started out in moderate 15-knot breezes. Once the yachts were enticed out into the Stream by the balmy air, the gods turned up the wind valve as first a fresh, then a strong north-easterly wind lashed the fleet. With the Gulf Stream current running north at two and a half knots and the wind blowing south at 40 knots, the ocean was turned into a frothing grey maelstrom. Before the race was over one life and a number of spars were claimed by the deep.

The 72 ft. *Ticonderoga* quickly took the lead after the start at Miami's sea buoy as her New York crew drove the proud vessel into Stream at 11 knots. Gordon Raymond, her racing skipper, had just turned the wheel over to Corny Shields after about an hour of thrashing when the main mast crumbled. The spar broke off at the lower spreaders and, as it went over the side, it tore out most of the rigging and the mizzenmast. As the fleet neared Northwest Providence Channel, the wind built up to 45 knots and for the rest of the race blew between 45–50 knots true. Observers in Nassau reported that they had only ever seen conditions so bad in a hurricane.

With the crippling of the mighty *Ti*, Kenneth Stanford's 52 ft. yawl *Hostess II* became the scratch boat and Neptune took out his wrath upon her as well. After 30 hours of beating up the 65-mile leg from Isaac to Stirrup Key, *Hostess* gave up and turned on her engine. The 50 ft. schooner *Water Witch*, the graceful old lady that romped playfully to a Miami–Nassau victory in 1936, was also beaten into

The 72 ft. 'Ticonderoga', originally named 'Tioga', is a legend in the history of sailing. Designed by Herreshoff, she was a line honours champion

submission by the gale and retreated to the security of Miami. As the second day of the race wore on, one boat after another had the racing life pounded out of her by the wind and sea. *Estrellita*, the smallest boat in the fleet at 35 ft., took shelter in Bimini. The 38 ft. centreboard sloop *Bear Cub* was dismasted 20 miles west of Stirrup and ran across the treacherous Bahama Banks to Cat Key where she found the 50 ft. ketch *Malolo* disabled with rigging failures.

Late Thursday night with the gale howling at 50 knots and high seas breaking abeam, Angel Naya's 36 ft. Cuban cutter *Windy* was only 25 miles from Nassau— a few hours from the finish—when a huge sea washed across the boats, sweeping two crewmen overboard. The mainsheet parted and the boat's doghouse was swept away. Jose Kates grabbed a quarter-inch buoy line and hauled himself back aboard but the professional hand Francisco Garcia was apparently knocked unconscious and couldn't reach the life buoy thrown to him. He was never found. Before the race was over eight boats had dropped out.

Harvey Conover's winning 45 ft. S. and S. designed centreboard yawl *Revonoc II*, with veteran ocean racers Rod Stephens and Ed Raymond aboard, among others, proved that a centreboarder could go to windward in a gale.

Although it is generally accepted today that centreboarders can be the equal of keelboats to windward, it took many hard slogs to windward in the Southern Circuit to prove the point to many died-in-the-wool keelboat owners from the north. Historically, centreboards have been the point of design in particular that developed unevenly over the United States. Because of the shoal waters of Tampa Bay, the Florida coast and the Bahamas and even the Chesapeake Bay, yachtsmen in these areas tended to favour centreboarders. Yachtsmen from the traditional sailing areas in the north-east had no particular need for centreboarders so consequently keelboats were popular there. This is an important theme to remember for it was a problem throughout the development of the sport in the '50s and '60s to ensure that the handicapping rule fairly rated the two diverse types. The C.C.A. rule was able to deal with centreboarders and keelboats pretty much to everyone's satisfaction. However, when the S.O.R.C. adopted the I.O.R. Rule in the early 1970s, this old conflict came out into the open.

In 1952 Carleton (Mitch) Mitchell won the Miami–Nassau Race and launched what was to be the most spectacular ocean-racing career in the modern era of the sport. Mitchell's Phil Rhodes designed 57 ft. yawl *Caribbee* from Annapolis, Maryland, won the '52 Nassau Race, then went on to win the Havana Race and locked up the S.O.R.C. Aboard the flying centreboarder that winter were Ray Hunt, Dick Bertram, Walter Gubelmann, H. K. (Bunny) Rigg and many other veteran ocean racers. Mitchell duplicated the feat once again the following year, winning both the Nassau and Havana races and his second S.O.R.C. crown.

Fifty-two was quite a year for Mitchell. The Southern Circuit was now officially called the Southern Ocean Racing Conference and it included three distance races: the first event from Fort Lauderdale to Cat Key, Bahamas, as well as the Nassau and Havana races. *Caribbee* won all three both in class and fleet and swept the S.O.R.C. and its record 20-boat fleet by the widest points spread ever seen in Florida waters. The Havana Race was a fitting climax to a month of exciting racing.

That year a 40-knot north-easterly shoved the 29-boat fleet down to Havana across the finish line, smashing old records to smithereens. When yachtsmen arrived, they found themselves in the midst of a full-blown revolution as General Batista carried off a successful *coup d'état* that would leave him in power for the rest of the decade. Stories still circulate about the schooner *Ben Bow* finishing off Morro Castle not to a finishing gun, but to a machine-gun which reportedly added a new set of reef points to the yacht's mainsail. Although the story might not be true, there were certainly more fireworks in Havana than had been planned by the hospitable Cuban yacht clubs.

There were other fireworks that year though of a milder kind. The first of several rule-beating boats that would attack the Circuit over the years made her appearance.

A 39 ft. yawl called *Hoot Mon* was one of the strangest vessels ever seen on the Circuit and more than one mossbacked old yachtsman was heard to harumph that such contraptions should be banned from racing. Three dedicated Star-boat sailors figured that what was good in one-design racing might also be fast offshore and so built what amounted to a 40 ft. Star boat with a fin keel. Worth Brown who built her, Charles Ulmer who made her sails, and Lockwood Pirie, a former Star champion, all campaigned her hard. The strip-planked, edge-nailed yawl used an outboard motor for power and rated a low 22·6 ft.

Hoot Mon won the Lipton Cup in '52 first time out, then came up 12th in the Nassau Race to the relief of most of the fleet. But she won her class in the Havana Race and proved that, although she might not look seaworthy, she in fact could outlast some of her larger competitors. In 1953 she continued to play bridesmaid to Mitchell's *Caribbee*, and although she dominated her class, the Rhodes-designed yawl still proved superior on overall corrected time. However, *Hoot Mon* did manage to place second in overall S.O.R.C. standings, 40 points behind *Caribbee*.

The race to Cat Key was replaced in 1954 with one from Fort Lauderdale around Great Isaac to Miami, a race that is strikingly similar to the Ocean Triangle Race instituted in 1973 to replace the Miami–Lucaya Race, long a fixture on the Circuit. *Caribbee* picked up where she had left off the previous year by winning the new race, but just as it seemed Mitchell was untouchable, rule-beater *Hoot Mon* did what everyone had been afraid she could do all along—she skunked the fleet for an impressive run of firsts. Following up a fleet victory in the Lipton Cup she also took the Nassau Race in what was a spinnaker reach and run most of the way. She went on to win the Havana Race and took her first S.O.R.C. overall prize, becoming the first post-war design to win the Governor's Trophy.

Author, well known ocean racer, Carleton Mitchell came fighting back in 1955 with a new boat that was the latest product of the fertile mind of Olin Stephens. *Finisterre* was a 38 ft. centreboard yawl with graceful lines and she rated nearly as low as *Hoot Mon*.

Carleton Mitchell is one of the greatest ocean racing personalities of all time.

He was, and still is, an avid cruising man who wanted from one boat to be able to enjoy the best of both cruising and racing without compromising. In an article in 'Yachting' magazine in September 1954, Mitchell wrote:

> Every boat should be built around an idea. Years ago I decided that boats are nicer than houses, and little boats still nicer than big ones, mainly because they are more personal. As soon as you can't do things for yourself, but have to depend on others, a certain bond of closeness is lost; while there are advantages in size, such as comfort and the ability to make fast passages, gone is the casual freedom to move where and when and as you please. Which, after all, is one of the reasons for owning a boat.
>
> Yet I admit liking a certain amount of big-boat comfort, together with other assorted virtues. Not forgetting the maxim that you can't have everything in one hull, and that every boat must be a compromise, I must confess I wanted a boat that had everything: fast enough to be interesting around the buoys, yet rugged enough to face the possibility of a hurricane off the Azores; small enough to be easily taken for an afternoon sail by one person, yet comfortable enough to live aboard for weeks at a time even in areas remote from stores; draft shoal enough to poke into the byways of the Chesapeake or Bahamas or Baltic or the Mediterranean, yet possessing the ability to cross an ocean en route to the next gunkhole.

A flying centreboarder of the 1950s, Carleton Mitchell's 'Caribbee',
which won the S.O.R.C. twice

In the nine years after the war Mitchell had probably done as much cruising and racing as any man alive. He knew what he wanted and the result was a shoal centreboarder that was beamy for her time. The basic specifications for the boat were: 38 ft. 7½ in. overall; 27 ft. 6 in. waterline; 11 ft. 3 in. beam; 3 ft. 11 in. draft with board up; 7 ft. 7 in. board down; 18,640 lb. displacement; 740 sq. ft. of rated sail area. Although Mitchell stated that 'no attempt has been made to take advantage of the loophole in the Cruising Club rule which does not limit the weight of . . . tanks, bronze floors and diagonal strapping . . . or other metal items affecting the ballast-displacement ratio . . .' the C.C.A. rule was later changed to take into account these factors.

Below, the boat was open and efficient. Mitchell even went to the trouble of making a plywood mock-up of the interior to make sure everything was to his liking. *Finisterre* was even fitted out with an automatic pilot and a freezer to make cruising more comfortable. Also, Mitchell put wheel steering on the boat, practically unheard of on a racing boat under 40 ft. at that time. The boat was one of the first offshore racers in America fitted with a roller furling main. Although the

The yawl 'Hoot Mon' was an unconventional design, but she took advantage of the rating rule to win the S.O.R.C. in 1954 and 1955

system had been used in Europe for years, Stateside yachtsmen had been slow to adopt the system due to difficulties with early models.

Considering the fantastic racing record *Finisterre* was to have, her lines were remarkably conventional for Sparkman and Stephens. Later, Olin Stephens wrote of them: 'another controlling factor . . . is a conscious tendency to conservatism in sticking to a successful type and making only minor changes such as those I've described . . . It seems to me that existing conditions are very different from 20 years ago; now I think we have to consider a boat as an investment rather than an experiment, and while there is always something of the latter element involved, I have tried to keep that to a minimum.' If *Finisterre* had been commissioned a few years earlier there might have been some raised eyebrows by the traditionalist yachtsmen of America's north-east, but a number of successful Phil Rhodes and Olin Stephens centreboard designs that romped through fleets in the late 1940s and early '50s proved that such boats could win to weather. Mitchell got his cake and feasted on it for years.

The 1955 S.O.R.C. wound up being a ding-dong match between *Finisterre* and *Hoot Mon*. They both thrived on the large time allowances the rest of the fleet had to give them, yet in every other way the two boats were quite different. *Finisterre* had comfortable cruising accommodation while *Hoot Mon* had hardly any accommodation at all. *Hoot Mon* had slack bilges while *Finisterre* was far more conventional and seakindly. Significantly, both boats were among the very few racers that had been built after the war and both had expert crews aboard, including good dinghy sailors. Of *Finisterre*, the competition was wont to say that she had the best amateur crew aboard that money could buy.

Mitchell won the Bimini Race opener of the S.O.R.C., but *Hoot Mon* took the Lipton Cup. Then she won her second Miami–Nassau Race over a course that saw little windward work. *Finisterre* was second, 34 minutes behind on corrected time. *Hoot Mon* went on to win her second S.O.R.C. in '55.

The following year Carleton Mitchell accomplished what he set out to do in the first place—he swept the Havana Race and won the Florida Governor's Cup for highest-points scoring boat in the S.O.R.C. Mitchell was the first man to win three S.O.R.C.s. (Subsequently, he was the only man to win three Bermuda races, all in *Finisterre*.) But as Mitchell looked around at the audience at the trophy presentation, he must have realised that the S.O.R.C. would not be the easy pickings it had been in the past, for in the fleet that year had been Bill Snaith's *Figaro*, Luis Vidana's *Criollo*, Jack Brown's *Callooh* and John Price's *Comanche*— all boats that would figure prominently in future S.O.R.C. brawls.

In the winter of 1957 Carleton Mitchell and his beloved *Finisterre* were off sailing the Bahamas, having won the Nassau Race (Mitchell's third) and did not proceed to St. Pete for the Havana Race. It was a tough struggle just the same. For the first time in the 24-year history of the Havana Race, a Cuban won the event— Dr. Luis Vidana in his 67 ft. yawl *Criollo*—and the Circuit. Had *Finisterre* finished the Circuit that year she might well have wrapped up the top prize again.

In the Havana fleet that year was the little 32 ft. *Brisote*, owned by Spencer

Dr. Luis Vidana's 'Criollo' was the first Cuban yacht to win the Havana Race. The year was 1957 and she also won the Circuit

McCourtney, that was brand new for the race. She was so new, in fact, that her mizzenmast had only been stepped two hours before the start. Thus began the ocean racing career and the last-minute tradition of Charley Morgan. Morgan, who was at the time a struggling Tampa sailmaker, designed *Brisote* along with Charles Hunt who built the boat. This little fin-keel, hard-chine plywood boat was, in the words of Alf Loomis, 'as light as a politician's promise'. But she was up with the big boats going out of Tampa Bay and caused chills to ripple down the spines of more than one owner of a large goldplater. She finished second in Class C, losing to John Price's *Comanche* by 2 minutes 22 seconds.

In 1958 *Finisterre* won her fourth Miami–Nassau Race and Mitchell again declined the rest of the Circuit. By the time the record S.O.R.C. fleet made it around to St. Pete for the annual Havana Race, there were some serious fireworks in Cuba. The race course was changed, bent and elongated somewhat around Rebecca Shoal and up the keys to Miami, a 403-mile race that was destined to become the S.O.R.C.'s premier event. It all started because of another Cuban revolution.

The first race to Miami was a broad reach for 170 miles from the turning mark off Tampa Bay to Rebecca Shoal light; then with the wind out of the north it was first a beam reach, then a close reach and finally a dead beat for the final 40 miles to Miami—all of this for the larger boats. The wind slowly clocked through the race so by the time the small boats had the Florida Keys abeam it was a close reach. Class C finished under spinnakers which contributed mightily to their high fleet finishes. Jake Hershey's Stephens-designed *Ca Va* won the race and the whole S.O.R.C. as well. The key to her victory, in addition to the convenient wind shift, was that she, as well as second-place *Comanche* and third-place *Hoot Mon*, all in Class C, swung out for the Gulf Stream after rounding Rebecca. The two to three-knot boost from the Stream, plus the clocking wind, allowed these smart small boats to finish within a couple of hours of the big boats on elapsed time. *Brisote* hugged the Keys all the way up and could do no better than fourth in class as a result.

Ben Du Pont's *Rhubarb*, a Block Island 40, won the '59 Nassau Race but the most exciting event on that year's calendar was the Havana Race, the first time in 25 starts that the event was hard on the wind all the way to Morro Castle. Conditions were ideal for big boats and the first to finish was the 67 ft. cutter *Lobo de Mar* owned by members of the Havana Yacht Club. Unfortunately for the happy Cubans, *Lobo* had to give over nine hours to Jack Brown's *Callooh*. *Callooh*, which was steered much of the way by Emil (Bus) Mosbacher—who had come to national attention a few months before when he nearly won the America's Cup elimination trials in the old Twelve Metre *Vim*—took class and fleet honours with a corrected time of 1 day, 21 hours, 37 minutes, and 47 seconds for the 284-mile race. There were 32 boats in the race that year, including a number of former winners—*Caribbee*, *Hoot Mon*, *Criollo*, *Ciclon* and *Ca Va*. Also in the fleet were two of the first popular glass fibre production boats built in the United States—the Bounty IIs. George Pearson's *Celia II* and M. H. Hogan's *Glass Skipper* were Bountys and *Celia II* finished second in Class B to *Callooh*.

The Bounty IIs marked a real watershed in American ocean racing. This boat dates the beginning of the glass fibre era in ocean racing and the sport has never been the same since. The boats were built by the Coleman Boat and Plastics Co. of San Francisco, California, and were designed by Phil Rhodes. Designer William Garden collaborated on the glass construction and tooling. Specifications of the Bounty II are 40 ft. 10 in. overall; 28 ft. water line; 10 ft. 3 in. beam; 5 ft. 10 in. draft; with 717 sq. ft. of rated sail area. The lines of the boats were conventional for the day, with the forefoot slightly cut away and a large keel-hung rudder. The counter was long and sloping, and the boat had the low and graceful lines that typified all new C.C.A. rule boats of the day. The layout below was remarkably advanced with all weight concentrated in the middle of the boat and over the keel. The main saloon had a large dropleaf table mounted on the centreline with four berths in the main cabin along with a large galley and chart table. Forward was a good-sized toilet room and a large forward cabin. The engine was mounted under the sole in the main cabin and the ends of the boat were empty.

Carleton Mitchell's 'Finisterre', the only boat ever to have won the Bermuda Race three times, was responsible for a number of changes in the C.C.A. rule. When she was built in 1955 it was unusual for a yacht under 40 ft. to have a wheel rather than a tiller

The sixties breakthrough

If '59 was a watershed for ocean racing in the United States, 1960 marked a new beginning for the S.O.R.C. By that year Fidel Castro was firmly in control of Cuba. The casinos were closed down and the luxury hotels taken over. Yachts and yachtsmen were nothing more than decadent reminders of crass capitalism as far as the new regime was concerned and although the Cuban yacht clubs had not formally closed down, the S.O.R.C. fathers decided to stop the classic race to Havana. In its place they substituted an event from Miami to St. Petersburg, just the reverse of the '58 course. This was done largely because the Havana Race and the short Havana–Varadero races had always been the last events on the S.O.R.C. calendar and it seemed a waste of time and effort to ferry the fleet to St. Pete only to have it return to Miami. The Lipton Cup, Miami–Nassau Race and Nassau Cup were still the first three events of the season.

Much of the enthusiasm for the Circuit dissipated in 1960 because of the demise of the Havana Race and only 12 boats started the long Miami to St. Pete race after James Rider's *Tigress* had won the Nassau Race. A brisk, cold northerly prevailed at the start as the tiny fleet ran down the Florida coast, being sure to stay as close to the shoals and keys as possible without running aground. Because the fleet had to stay between the Gulf Stream (which flows north) and the line of government buoys marking the shoals, there was little room for tactics until after Rebecca Shoal was cleared at the end of the Florida Keys. Pure reaching and running boat speed was the decisive factor and after the boats turned north they got the thrash to windward that would separate the straphangers from the racing yachtsmen. Luckily for the race, the breeze, which unfortunately for the participants was icy cold right off the great American plains, held from the north until the last boat had rounded Egmont buoy for the final sprint to the finish off St. Pete's famous municipal pier. Thor H. Ramsing's 46 ft. sloop *Solution* won the race—the first and last ever held from Miami to St. Pete.

Bar-room talk being what it is—just that, bar-room talk—no-one paid much attention when 31-year-old sailmaker Charley Morgan kept saying he could design a boat that could win the S.O.R.C. But when Florida Flying Dutchman sailor Jack Powell heard Morgan's boast, he put his money where Morgan's mouth was. Powell, an American yachtsman widely known for his impish sense of humour, no doubt started savouring his new boat right from the moment he dropped the commission in Morgan's lap. The result was *Paper Tiger*, Powell's first ocean racer and a radical new glass fibre construction design which not only established that glass boats could hang together and win ocean races, but also launched Morgan on a career that was to make him a millionaire.

Jack Powell's 40 ft. yawl 'Paper Tiger' ushered in the era of glass fibre ocean racers in the United States, and also launched the career of her designer, Charley Morgan

Paper Tiger was built over a male mould with a steel pipe running from stem to stern, embedded in the glass. Steel tubes were then welded on to the pipe along the backbone and run up to the chainplates and bulkheads. Morgan had studied the C.C.A. rule carefully and placed the yacht's tanks and engine as low as possible. Her lines were not as radical as her construction, yet the fullness of her beam was carried well aft to increase the boat's sail-carrying capacity and to keep her stern from dragging. The yawl's measurements were: 40 ft. overall; 27 ft. 9 in. waterline; 11 ft. 7 in. beam; 4 ft. 4 in. draft; 20,800 lb. displacement; with 765 sq. ft. of rated sail area. The boat was finished two weeks before the S.O.R.C., much like Morgan's earlier *Brisote*. She hit the Miami–Nassau Race starting line with Powell, Morgan, Ted Tolson and George Pearson aboard along with some other Florida hotshots, after coming in second in the St. Pete to Fort Lauderdale Race.

The '61 Nassau Race was a fresh beat to windward all the way to Stirrup Key and should have been a big-boat race. The 73 ft. *Ticonderoga*, Huey Long's 57 ft. *Ondine* and a number of other large goldplaters figured they'd be in the money when they began the 50-mile slide down to the Bahamas' capital. But before all the Class A boats had finished and well before any Class B boats were even near the finish line, Class C *Paper Tiger* came surging across the finish line to save her time on the fleet. Given all of the condescending talk around the Miami docks about the lack of virtue of this new plastic soap dish, the victory was particularly sweet for owner Powell who revelled in the humour of it all. There had been six non-finishers in the Nassau Race and his glass speedster had proved herself more than up to the task at hand.

Paper Tiger won the S.O.R.C. that year, the first year of the modern Circuit. Both Morgan and Powell now had a good dose of ocean racing in their blood and would figure prominently in S.O.R.C. racing for the rest of the decade. But there were some other names in the **Circuit** that year that would become fixtures in American ocean racing. Huey **Long**'s *Ondine* was one of the first aluminium ocean racers on the American scene and she won Class A in the St. Pete–Fort Lauderdale Race and was second in her class in the Nassau Race. There was also a man by the name of Ted Hood, a sailmaker from Marblehead, who sailed his Class C *Robin* to a second in class, and a third in fleet, in the Nassau Race.

Powell, Morgan and navigator Ted Tolson again won the Southern Circuit in '62 in *Paper Tiger*, proving that their first victory was not a fluke. Ted Hood was second overall in his 45 ft. steel yawl *Robin* after trailing *Tiger* around most of the Circuit and winning the Nassau Cup. Dick Carter proved in '62 he would be a force to reckon with in the future by finishing third in the Nassau Race and Nassau Cup, and coming second in the Lipton Cup in his Tripp-designed *Medalist*. Also, Vince Lazzara, who had figured prominently in the success of the Bounty class and who would later be instrumental in a number of glass fibre boat companies including Columbia and Gulfstar, did well in his Class A *Avante*. A record 41 boats took part in the Nassau Race.

Joe Byars' 38 ft. yawl *Doubloon* won the '63 S.O.R.C., but to this day is remembered more for her two 360-degree somersaults off Cape Hatteras during a delivery. It was a dramatic capsize in which the young helmsman, Gene Hinkle, had been thrown overboard during the gale and climbed back aboard 20 minutes later. She won both the Nassau and Lauderdale races and swept the Circuit. New York boatbuilder, designer and dockside character Robert E. Derecktor figured prominently in '63 with his yawl *Grey Goose* for a sixth in the S.O.R.C. Florida ocean racer Homer Denius bought *Paper Tiger* and she proved still to be a good design, taking a third in the Circuit.

It was during the early and mid-1960s that many of the men who were later to dominate the modern Circuit were just getting their feet wet in ocean racing. It was a period of a changing of the guard. The old timers, men who had raced hard in America's southern waters in the late '40s and '50s, were now being replaced by a new breed. The yachts, too, were changing. The old wood designs were not able to win year after year as they had done in the '50s. Design competition intensified and each year a significant part of the fleet was made up of new boats, whereas in the '40s and '50s the fleet was always of old boats with maybe only one or two new ones.

It was also a time when the type of crewmen who raced was in a period of transition. Throughout the history of the S.O.R.C., most boats were owned and crewed by middle-aged, or older, men who could afford to participate in the costly sport. Crew members were usually friends of the owner and of his generation. But in the early and mid-1960s things began to change. Glass fibre boats, being less costly to construct, opened up ocean racing to the less wealthy and so it is not surprising that younger men began showing up in Florida each winter. Also, as competition became keener with the influx of dinghy racers, crew skill and agility became more important and younger men began finding their way on to the yachts. In the 1950s a crew member in his late teens or early twenties would be a rarity, but in the '60s it was becoming commonplace.

There is nothing that points up the changing of the guard more dramatically than the 1964 S.O.R.C. victory of *Conquistador*—a production Cal-40 glass fibre sloop designed by Bill Lapworth. *Conquistador* won the Circuit by a scant $1\frac{1}{2}$ points over *Sabre*, a new Morgan-designed prototype for the Columbia 40. Not only did these two young designers dominate the Circuit with their modern glass creations, the Cal-40 proved to be a design breakthrough.

Fuller Callaway's Cal-40 took the East Coast yachting fraternity by surprise. The tradition-bound yachtsmen of the Chesapeake Bay and the north-east had hardly become accustomed to the idea that boats could be made of glass fibre when they had yet another bitter pill to swallow—a light-displacement (for those days), flat dead-rise, glass sloop with a rudder *separate from the keel* had won the S.O.R.C. Not only had the boat been fast off the wind, she could hold her own to windward and was easy to steer.

Bill Lapworth had performed major surgery on the bottom of the conventional ocean-racing hull and boats have never been the same since. The forefoot was completely chopped away and the hull of the boat drew only about one and a half feet before the keel was added. The cord length of the keel itself was far shorter than most boats of the time, thereby eliminating many square feet of wetted surface and drag. Aft, the bottom rose gently from the keel into very flat buttocks, thence into a low counter. The spade rudder was mounted just forward of the end of the waterline aft. Measurements of the Cal-40 were: 39 ft. 6 in. overall; 30 ft. 6 in. waterline; 11 ft. beam; 5 ft. 6 in. draft; 15,500 lb. displacement; 6,000 lb. ballast; with 699 sq. ft. of rated sail area.

By this time the S.O.R.C. had settled down into a five-race series that is nearly identical to its present six-race format. Throughout the '60s the S.O.R.C. opened with a 105-mile race from St. Pete to Venice, Florida, via the Boca Grande buoy. The concept of the race was to be a shakedown cruise for the yachts before sending them around Florida's Key West version of Cape Horn, where fresh northers and a choppy Gulf Stream can combine to shake apart all but the strong. Most years the weatherman has granted the S.O.R.C. fathers their wish as a number of the Venice races have been gearbusters.

After the 403-mile Lauderdale Race, the 28-mile Lipton Cup—from Miami to Lauderdale and back to Miami—was held a few days prior to the race to Nassau. The finale of the Circuit was the 31-mile Nassau Cup Race from Nassau to Booby Rocks and back. Unlike most major ocean-racing series in the world, the S.O.R.C. has always had fixed courses for every race. In theory, then, it is possible for the whole Circuit to be sailed without even one windward leg. In practice, however, most S.O.R.C.s have had their share of beating.

Bill Snaith, one of America's greatest and most colourful ocean racing men, won the '65 S.O.R.C. in his 50 ft. yawl *Figaro IV*, which had been designed and built by Bob Derecktor. Snaith had won the St. Petersburg–Fort Lauderdale Race, and, with consistently high scores in the rest of the events, he took overall honours. Back in the ruck that year was a 25-year-old one-design sailor who had entered the Circuit as a lark. He could hardly find his way around the course in his Class B *Scylla*, but somehow he managed to take a second prize in the Lipton Cup and that was all the silverware necessary to spark the imagination of the young man who would turn the S.O.R.C. upside-down—Ted Turner.

The '66 Circuit started off with a howl—and not from the wind gods. It was from the contestants and one of them, Turner, immediately earned the reputation as a person who couldn't hold his tongue. Usually he couldn't hold it because it was moving too fast to catch. It seems that the turning mark of the Venice Race had been changed by the Coast Guard between the time the race circular had been printed and the race itself. A buoy with a long and short flashing light had been changed for one with a six-second light although it was located in the same place as the first. A number of racers had a hard time finding it, including Turner, and he, along with veteran Jack Price and a couple of other owners, protested to the race committee for prejudicing their chances by not notifying the fleet of the change. In fact, the previous five issues of 'Notice to Mariners', published by the Coast Guard, mentioned the change but no-one piped up with the news at the skippers' meeting. The race was thrown out.

Turner went on to win the Lauderdale Race in his Cal-40 *Vamp X*. The year before he had navigated simply by following the fleet, but this year he had a real navigator aboard as well as Buddy Friedrichs, a New Orleans Dragon champion whom he had met the month before. Together they pulled off one of the biggest coups in S.O.R.C. history. Ted went on to win the Lipton Cup and was placed well up in the rest of the races to take the shortened four-race Circuit. *Geechee*, a Columbia 40 owned by John Baker, won the Miami–Nassau Race that year in a booming north-easter that allowed the 72 ft. *Escapade* to better *Tioga*'s 26-year-old elapsed-time record with a time of 19 hours, 33 minutes and 37 seconds.

George Moffett won the '67 S.O.R.C. in his 48 ft. Alan Gurney-designed sloop *Guinevere* by half a point over Bill Snaith's *Figaro*. The final score after the five-race Circuit was 943·25 to 942·75. It was a tough loss for Snaith, who had just recovered from a long, serious illness. The boat that seemed to all to be the sure winner that year was Perry Connolly's *Red Jacket*, a 40 ft. fin keel stripped-out racer from the Canadian design team of George Cuthbertson and George Cassian. Connolly represented the Royal Canadian Yacht Club of Toronto and came close indeed to being the first Canadian to ever win the Circuit. After wins in the Venice Race and the Lipton Cup and a second place in the Lauderdale Race, *Red Jacket* was the points leader. Then a 23rd in a light and fluky Nassau Race put her out of the running.

It was a great shock to the traditionalists when 'Conquistador' won the S.O.R.C. in 1964—glass fibre and of revolutionary design, too. But the Bill Lapworth designed Cal 40s soon became firmly established on the American racing circuits

Perry Connelly's 'Red Jacket', a 40 ft. fin keel stripped-out racer from Canada, launched the reputation of the Canadian design firm of George Cuthbertson and George Cassian

The '67 Lauderdale Race was one of the gearbusters that Florida yachtsmen dread. Despite the fact that the race was started on February 11th instead of the middle of January, when previous races had been held, a typical cold norther came blowing down on the 47 boats in the race. As the intrepid fleet rounded Rebecca Shoal the wind began building and, just after the first boats finished, the wind was howling a steady 40 knots, with gusts even higher as squall after squall ripped over the racers.

The north-easterly blowing across a three-knot Gulf Stream quickly built up steep, short seas that pounded the boats, causing them to shudder from masthead to keel bolt. Things got so bad that at one point Bob Derecktor aboard *Vamoose* (a contraction of Turner's *Vamp* and Derecktor's *Goose*) ordered co-owner Ted Turner to strike the main and put up the storm trysail. A short argument ensued. However, aboard other boats there was no argument about shortening down and most carried mere handkerchiefs for sails. Those that didn't found their Dacron finery in ribbons. One observer described the race as Florida's Fastnet as yachts began to get into trouble. Jim Doane's Cal-48 *Flame* went aground near Fowley Rock and was pounded unmercifully until she got off on the next high tide. Wally Frank's Cal-40 *Old Salt* was dismasted, as was Ted Hood's *Robin*. As the storm made up into gale proportions, breaking seas swept life rafts from the decks of *Stampead* and *Red Jacket*.

Red Jacket was another important design that surfaced in the S.O.R.C. and set trends that outlived, by years, her competitive racing days (although with a good crew she is still able to place well even today under the I.O.R.). With a total displacement of just over 17,000 lb., she certainly wasn't the lightest 40-footer ever built but her secret was that her balsa-core hull and minimum interior joinery work allowed as much weight as possible to be put into the keel. She was scant on headroom, her head and hanging lockers were not enclosed and even her cabin sole was a series of strip planks to save weight. It was little wonder that *Red Jacket* came back in 1968 to take the Lauderdale Race and the Lipton Cup, and a seventh in the Nassau Race gave her a well-deserved S.O.R.C. victory.

There was another success story in 1968. Young Lee Creekmore, a 23-year-old boatbuilder from Miami, won a light and fluky Nassau Race in a 30-footer that he both designed and built over a span of four years. A 90-mile race from Miami to West End, Grand Bahama, was added that year to round out the Southern Ocean Racing Conference to six races. Sixty boats participated in the Nassau Race as the influence of the lower-priced glass boats was making itself felt—the fleet had doubled in just eight years from the time of the first victory of glass fibre design.

By 1969 ocean racing had worked itself up to a fever pitch in the United States as hundreds of new sportsmen entered the fray, mostly in the new glass boats being turned out by a score of boat companies across the United States. The winner that year was Jack Powell's 46 ft. aluminium yawl *Salty Tiger*, which was designed and built by Bob Derecktor. Although *Salty Tiger* had not won a single event on the S.O.R.C. calendar, she was placed well in all of them for a 54-point lead over

'Salty Tiger', an aluminium 46-footer, won the 1969 S.O.R.C. with
fine, consistent performances in all the races. Designed by Bob
Derecktor, she was owned by Jack Powell and Wally Frank

Melee, Don Ayres' Cal-40. This was an impressive showing for Derecktor's new
design, which Powell owned in partnership with Wally Frank, but the series
also showed the staying power of the Cal-40 which by that time had been going
strong on the Circuit for five years.

There were many other good new boats that year and with six races and four
classes almost all of them had a chance to shine. The winner of the Nassau Race
was *Lively Lady*, a 30 ft. design from the drawing board of young Gary Mull, a
relatively unheard of designer at that time. Most impressive of all was Bob Johnson's new *Windward Passage*, a beautiful, white 73 ft. ketch designed by Alan
Gurney. Just as *Paper Tiger* had launched the career of Charley Morgan, so did
Passage and *Lively Lady* launch the design fortunes of Gurney and Mull. *Passage*
was the speed sensation of the Circuit, winning both the Venice Race and the
Nassau Cup. Most impressive of all, she knocked 3 hours, 39 minutes off the
Miami–Nassau elapsed-time record, averaging 11 knots in the process.

The series marked a turning point in American ocean racing. First, there was a quantum jump in the number of entries. In the Miami–Nassau Race, the most popular event on the calendar, 100 boats participated. Even in the St. Pete to Fort Lauderdale Race, which had by now garnered the reputation of a brutal gearbuster, there were 75 boats, 21 up on the year before. With the appearance of so many new designs, the competition was feverish. The reputation of the S.O.R.C. had now spread far and wide and the Lauderdale Race had gained the reputation of being America's foremost ocean race, surpassing even the classic Bermuda Race. It was a breezy series and one that will be remembered for a lifetime by those who participated in it.

It began as a dead beat out of Tampa Bay with Ted Turner quickly taking the lead in Class A with his newly purchased converted Twelve Metre *American Eagle*— 'The Bird' as she was affectionately known for many years. *Eagle* had been built by a syndicate composed mostly of Du Ponts for the 1964 America's Cup defence. After being defeated in the American trials by *Constellation*, she was sold to a Canadian who converted her to an ocean racer but with little success. Turner bought her in November, just before the Circuit, for $70,000, then ferried her south with a small crew just in time for the S.O.R.C.

As soon as the Class A boats were able to ease sheets after getting out of Tampa Bay, the mighty *Windward Passage* smoked by the fleet down to Rebecca Shoal.

Halfway down to Rebecca, north-westerly squalls accompanied by a classic cold front moved in to sting the fleet. Almost immediately, the sea began collecting its toll. *West Wind II*, an Islander 37, was dismasted, *Lively Lady* lost her rudder, *Turnbull IV* pulled a chainplate and had to retire, and rigging failures on two other boats forced them to seek shelter. Even among the finishers there were the disabled, with *Indigo* and *Bikini* losing part or all of their centreboards.

As the fleet rounded Rebecca, every captain was faced with the decision either to sweep around the Keys on a rhumb line course, skirting the government buoys, or to head out to sea to pick up the Gulf Stream boost. Interestingly, *Eagle*, *Passage* and a number of other Class A boats, chose to take the most direct course and in doing so broke the elapsed time record for the race. Bob Johnson's *Windward Passage* was the first to finish, bettering the record he had set in 1962 in his old *Ticonderoga* by four and a half hours. As the fleet started north-east the wind clocked to the north, then to the north-east, and it was a hard beat in 30-knots of wind all the way up the Florida coast in rough, steep seas. Probably the most outstanding performance of all in that race was turned in by *The Hawk*, a 37 ft. wooden boat designed to the R.O.R.C. rule, a fact that allows her to still be competitive today. *The Hawk* reached to pick up the Stream immediately after rounding Rebecca and by so doing finished third overall and first in class.

It was a bumpy ride up to Miami that year with boats falling off 10 ft. waves. Steve Kastnet on the Cal-48 *Yankee Girl* broke his leg after the boat fell off a particularly high wave. Aboard Pat Haggerty's *Bay Bea*, a gooseneck on the main boom failed and struck one of the crew on the head, tearing a long gash in his scalp. Both crew members insisted that their boats continue in the race, despite their injuries. Turner won the bash in *Eagle* and looked as if he might be on the road to his second S.O.R.C. victory. *Eagle* took second in the new race from Miami to Lucaya, Grand Bahama (another Chamber of Commerce promotion) and seemed to have the Circuit won.

The Miami–Nassau Race that year started in a light south-easterly, but another cold front was on the way. As *American Eagle* approached the Bahama Banks, she found herself only a few yards from Northeast Rock and immediately gybed. A block on the windward running backstay broke and a few seconds later *Eagle*'s mast was over the side and Turner was robbed of the title. Jack Powell benefited from Turner's misfortune and became the first man to win three S.O.R.C. titles under the modern format.

When the norther hit that year, carrying winds of 40 knots gusting to 50, a number of boats were dismasted and sails blew out all over the fleet. The leg from Stirrup Key to the finish line off Hog Island (later called Paradise Island after some hotel developers took ownership). The 55-mile run became a surfing contest as nearly the whole fleet romped south at hull speed or better. There were many speed duels throughout the fleet but one of the most interesting was between Charley Morgan's new 33 ft. *Outrageous* and the ultimate winner *Lively Lady*. *Lively Lady* prudently set her no. 2 genoa for the gusty run as Morgan under a storm chute, quickly closed. Finally Morgan's spinnaker halyard chafed through and *Lively Lady*'s victory was assured. In the meantime the Cal-40 *Melee* had broached under spinnaker, like many other boats in the fleet, and had lost her

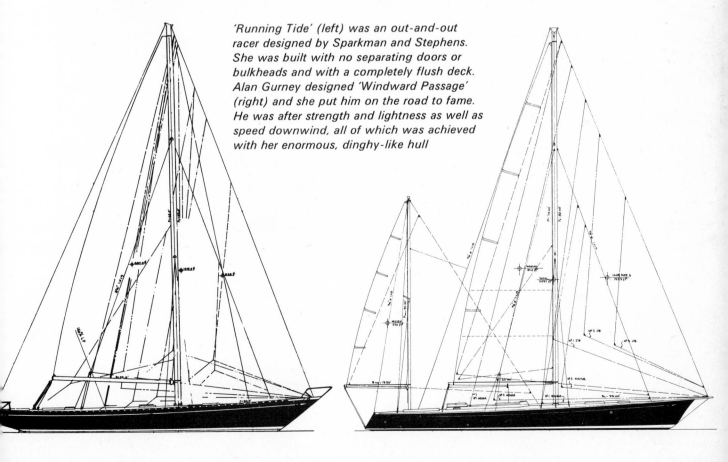

'Running Tide' (left) was an out-and-out racer designed by Sparkman and Stephens. She was built with no separating doors or bulkheads and with a completely flush deck. Alan Gurney designed 'Windward Passage' (right) and she put him on the road to fame. He was after strength and lightness as well as speed downwind, all of which was achieved with her enormous, dinghy-like hull

helmsman overboard. Because it was daylight the man was found and hauled aboard, but if the incident had occurred at night he would have been impossible to find.

The year 1970 marked the last time the S.O.R.C. was sailed under the C.C.A. rule, a fact that Florida yachtsmen especially, and others from all over the U.S., have been mourning ever since.

The 1970 Circuit was a duel between the leviathans *Windward Passage* and *American Eagle*, a rematch to play out the feud started the year before. This time Turner kept the mast in his rig to win, *Passage* was second overall and the '70 series was the swansong for those two great American ocean racers. As the International Offshore Rating rule was instituted the following year, these and many other great old designs would no longer stand much of a chance against the new designs coming up. Again, participation in the Conference took a great leap forward as a total of 137 different boats sailed at some time or another in the series.

John Potter's 57 ft. S. and S. design *Equation* won the Lauderdale Race by hugging the Keys much of the way. She led on S.O.R.C. points going into the Nassau Race, when she broke her headstay. There were some other great American boats battling in Class A that year which showed promise. Jim Kilroy's 73 ft. *Kialoa II* took some class prizes and was third overall in fleet; Huey Long's new 73 ft. Bill Tripp-designed *Ondine* took a third in Class A in the Lauderdale Race, George Coumantaros' 73 ft. *Baccara* didn't win any class prizes but she was undoubtedly the most luxurious racer in the fleet. Halsey Herreshoff dominated Class B with a boat of his own design called *Cosette*.

The effect of the I.O.R. on fleet standings was not immediately felt in the Circuit, nor would it be for a couple of years. Jakob Isbrandtsen's 61 ft. S. and S. designed sloop, *Running Tide* won in 1971. The pale green hull was long, narrow, deep, and designed during the waning days of the C.C.A. rule. In many respects she resembled a Twelve Metre, which is not surprising as she was designed about the same time the Sparkman and Stephens staff were working on their 1970 America's Cup defence hopeful, *Valiant*. *Tide* ended up being a far better ocean racer than *Valiant* was a Twelve Metre. Built in Holland, *Tide* was finished off Stateside and her graceful lines and flush, efficient deck make her one of the most beautiful modern ocean racers to sail anywhere in the world. Unlike many of the pre-I.O.R. designs, *Tide* has survived well and is still able to take both class and fleet prizes on occasion.

Most of the racing in 1971 was to windward, a factor that greatly helped *Tide*, but below the surface the I.O.R. boats were beginning to rumble. Second in overall fleet standing, just 3·75 points behind *Tide*, was David Steere's *Yankee Girl*, a new aluminium hull from S. and S. built by Palmer Johnson in Wisconsin and one of the first Stephens boats built to the I.O.R. rule. With nearly a 50 per cent ballast/displacement ratio she had the ability to carry a tremendous amount of

As a Twelve Metre, 'American Eagle' was beaten by 'Constellation' in the 1964 America's Cup trials. Under the ownership of Ted Turner she won the 1970 S.O.R.C.

sail area up to 28 knots of apparent wind. Lynn Williams' 60 ft. Mull designed C.C.A. *Dora* was third overall, but her competitive racing days were over almost as soon as they began. Turner managed a fifth overall in *American Eagle* by virtue of the great amount of windward work in the Circuit, but Turner loathed being beaten by men he felt were not his peers and he put the old warhorse up for sale. He sold her to Bermudian Warren Brown who re-christened her *War Baby* and repainted her baby blue.

Had there been an award for the most outstanding achievement in the '71 Circuit, it would have gone to the little 30 ft. *Smuggler*, a Peter Norlin designed Half Tonner and the first of her type to appear on the American side of the Atlantic. *Smuggler* was campaigned by young Bengt Jornstedt and four Swedish friends who had saved their money and taken up a collection to make it to the S.O.R.C. campaign. They lived aboard the boat and hammered their little I.O.R. design around the Circuit—through cold fronts and high seas that had even the Class A crews wishing they were at home before a cosy fire—in such valiant style that they won the respect of everyone in the fleet. *Smuggler* also swept Class E, winning nearly every race.

American yachtsmen breathed a sigh of relief after a boat called *Condor* won the 1972 S.O.R.C. Seven fellows, unknown beyond their own yacht club, quietly ambled down to the Southern Ocean Racing Conference and cleaned up, one of the few times in the history of the series that such rank newcomers to the grand-prix circuit had ever pulled off such a feat. Not only did they wipe up some of the most sophisticated racing machines ever to hit an American starting line, they did it in a four-year-old C. and C. designed Redline 41, a C.C.A. boat. The 'old' boat was in need of a paint job and its one go-fast feature was a sign in the cockpit that read, 'The windward rail is where it's at'.

With that homily, a broken speedometer, a borrowed Loran direction-finder that didn't work, a couple of new sails and even more old ones, and a helmsman's seat scrounged from a lawn tractor, Hill Blackett and his band of Chicago sailors calmly hammered the likes of Ted Turner, Pat Haggerty, Jim Baldwin, Wally Stenhouse and a 120-boat fleet of glory-hungry racers.

According to a poster taped to *Condor*'s forward bulkhead, 'Hill Blackett is America's No. 1 skinflint.' If that was true it may have explained why *Condor* won the light-air Circuit. Virtually every expense was spared in preparing the boat for the S.O.R.C. Most important, when it was recommended that Blackett buy a new 170 per cent genoa, if not a smaller one, he steadfastly refused. Winds during the whole spring were light and *Condor*'s 180 per cent genoa—the greatest overlap in the fleet—paid off in performance.

Other factors contributing to the Cinderella story were the boat's crew—a

The 1972 S.O.R.C. winner 'Condor' (top) thrived in a light-air series with a 180 per cent headsail when the rest of the fleet were using 150 per cent rigs. Hill Blackett (centre, with pipe) and his young crew proved an old boat can be a winner if she's well sailed and of good design and has some luck

cadre of youth and experience that had sailed together on *Condor* since she was new and who understood how to get every bit of speed out of her. Most important, *Condor* was in the right place at the right time, most notably in the Miami–Nassau Race when she went far north of the rest of the fleet (thus breaking a cardinal rule of how to win that race), picked up a favourable wind shift and flew home to win class and to take sixth overall. That was the only race in which *Condor* won her class, but consistently high finishes allowed her to stave off the determined assault of Wally Stenhouse in his new 49 ft. *Aura*. Stenhouse finished second in the Circuit and thereby joined the ranks of Jack Price, George Dewer and many other veteran S.O.R.C. ocean racers who have campaigned for years, only to be nosed out of first, time and again, by a few points. *Condor*'s victory was a shot in the arm for the sport as it seemed to indicate that even low-pressure local yacht club sailors might have a chance in the big time, given a few breaks.

Ted Turner and Perry Bass teamed up that year and chartered *Running Tide* and were leading on overall points in the Circuit until midway when they began to slip into the tank. Light air, old, tired sails and a few tactical errors had conspired against Turner, who had won the World Ocean Racing Championship a few weeks earlier. Competition in Class A turned into a shooting match between Jesse Philips' 56 ft. S. and S. designed *Charisma*, a sistership to *Yankee Girl*, and the C. and C. designed custom one-off 53 ft. *Bonaventure V*, owned by Bernie Herman of Toronto. Even though *Charisma* won the Nassau Race, *Bonnie* was able to take Class A honours for the most consistent performance. New that year was Jack Potter's 68 ft. Britton Chance designed *Equation*. This boat was a breakthrough design for larger boats, having a very shoal canoe underbody with a swing keel that completely tucked up into the boat's belly off the wind. Even though she smashed *Windward Passage*'s elapsed-time record for the Lauderdale Race by 45 minutes, she could get no better than third on corrected time. *Celerity II*, a brand new Cal-33 with a double-head rig, shot around Florida in an off-the-wind slide which took her to the Lauderdale Race silverware.

19, 20, 21 *The victorious American Admiral's Cup team of 1969. Dick Carter's brand new 'Red Rooster' (above right) won the Fastnet Race overall. There's plenty of activity aboard the blue-hulled 'Palawan' (above), owned by Thomas J. Watson Jr. And Dick Nye was back again with 'Carina' (right)*

22 *'Windward Passage', the speed sensation of the '69 Circuit. She broke the Miami–Nassau record that year by over $3\frac{1}{2}$ hours. At the helm, Peter Bowker*

23 *Home safe and sound after her triumph in the 1972 Bermuda Race, Ron Amey's 'Noryema VIII'*

New forces at work

A number of forces converged on the '73 Circuit to make it one of the most tumultuous contests in S.O.R.C. history. First of all, the I.O.R. rule had finally caught up with the Circuit. Thousands of I.O.R. boats had been produced and they were rapidly pushing the C.C.A. boats off the race course. A few of the better old designs, such as Wally Stenhouse's *Aura* and *Running Tide* owned by Albert Van Metre, could still win, but for the most part they were buried or put out to pasture in the form of cruising boats.

The second force that for the first time made itself known was the advanced development of the One Ton Class. Second and third generation I.O.R. One Ton designs were now hitting the starting line and their development had far outstripped anything done in the open-class racing boats. Designers had finely tuned the lines of these little speedsters so that they packed a wallop of power that was unmatched by the large lumbering goldplaters. It was not until the spring of '73 that the American racing fraternity began to realise how fast this class was developing in relation to other boats.

Thirdly, there was the glaring loophole in the rule that was exposed by M.I.T. ocean engineering professor Dr. Jerry Milgram when he built his infamous cat-ketch *Cascade*. Even though she was about the size of a One Tonner, she could carry far more sail off the wind than anything near her 37 ft. and she terrorised East Coast yachtsmen. Surprisingly, she could even hold her own on the wind and when her chance came to ease sheets she was off in a flash. Worse, her rating of 21 ft. was a bitter pill to swallow. All of these forces and more were brought to bear in the '73 Circuit and the very best ocean racers in America were assembled there with 112 boats making the Lauderdale Race. They were the nucleus of the Circuit and the largest congregation racing might ever see in Florida's waters, and that year's fleet included yachts which have shaped America's current ocean racing fortunes and thinking.

In Class A in '73 was Jesse Philips' 56 ft. *Charisma*, a first-generation S. and S. I.O.R. design that had turned out to be a classic ocean racer in the tradition of *Stormy Weather*, *Finisterre* and *Dorade*. She was heavy and strong, a powerful boat that excelled in fresh, windward work in moderate seas. Invariably when she was behind her crew prayed for 25 knot winds on the nose and 4 ft. seas. But when she was well sailed she was also fast in light air and could tack downwind with any boat in the fleet. But the factor that had brought *Charisma* alive in the racing seasons of '72 and '73 was her new and very young crew.

In 1973, America's Cup skipper William Ficker was signed on as *Charisma*'s sailing master. He brought to the boat the intense concentration of a Star world champion and an America's Cup helmsman. With Ficker aboard, the boat was run much the same as his Twelve Metre *Intrepid*. When he was at the helm he concentrated on only one thing—boat speed. On the wind, his eyes would rarely leave the telltale woollies on the luff of the massive genoa. When they did, it was to check boat speed in an effort to wrench an extra 1/10th of a knot out of the boat.

While Ficker steered, watch captain Andy MacGowan would feed him tactical information, watch for wind shifts and keep track of *Charisma*'s relative position to her competition. North sailmaker John Marshall would call genoa and main-sheet trim and constantly adjust the sails to get the shapes he felt were optimum. Below deck, *Charisma* had two navigators—one for each watch—who spent their entire time checking the boat's position, progress over the bottom and monitoring the radio for weather information. Forward, a veteran crew of racing men never cleated a sheet and constantly played the sails, day and night. When Ficker was not at the helm, he expected the same concentration and devotion to boat speed that he displayed.

Charisma won Class A overall that year, coming first in her class in the Lauder-dale and Nassau Races as well as the Lipton Cup. The reason for her victory was simply the concentration and hard work of her crew. But even that could not overcome the irresistible force from Class E—the One Tonners were on the march and *Charisma* had to content herself with being the first non-Class E boat in overall S.O.R.C. standings.

Pushing *Charisma* that year was the brand-new *Salty Goose*, a 54 ft. aluminium sloop designed and built by Bob Derecktor who owned her in partnership with Wally Frank. *Goose* was a consortium of Derecktor ideas fashioned together to provide a real match for *Charisma*. Below the waterline *Goose* had slack bilges that led back to a skeg-hung rudder just below her transom which was pulled back to nearly make her a double-ender. She had a swing keel that could be pulled up about halfway into her underbody. Eventually, this versatility was discarded and her keel was pinned in place. Below deck, *Goose* was as stripped-out as any One Tonner ever built, with the forward third of the boat containing nothing more than a head bolted to the bottom and a few pieces of tubing to hold sail bags.

But with the exception of *Goose*'s lack of accommodation and swing keel, both she and *Charisma* were basically conservative boats in concept. Challenging that philosophy was Norman Raben's 50 ft. Gary Mull designed *La Forza del Destino*. She was a light displacement boat (28,000 lb.) with an 'I' of 68 ft. This gave her one of the highest sail-area-to-displacement ratios in Class A. Raben wanted a boat that would move in the light zephyrs usually found on Long Island Sound in the

(Top) Bob Derecktor and Wally Frank owned 'Salty Goose', a 54-footer designed by Derecktor, built in aluminium with few concessions for comfort below

(Below, left) Bill Ficker, 1970 America's Cup defending helmsman and 1974 Congressional Cup champion, is seen here steering 'Charisma' to first place overall in class A in the 1973 S.O.R.C.

(Below, right) The 37 ft. Milgram designed 'Cascade' nearly won the 1973 S.O.R.C. with her radical cat-ketch rig which made her very fast downwind

summer, and that is what he got. In a mere breath of air *La Forza* moved and, like a Twelve Metre, she created her own apparent wind. Raben, who is one of the most game competitors on the American racing scene these days, has a den full of Long Island race trophies to prove the worth of his concept. In '73 *La Forza* held on doggedly during the Circuit but seemed unable consistently to break through the class leaders, yet she was able to take third in Class A in both the Venice and Lauderdale races.

Although no one seemed to realise it at the time, *La Forza*'s tall stick would have an influence on American ocean racing that would not be fully felt until 1974. The rig was designed for light air but the high stick was also an advantageous rating/sail area trade off. German Frers proved the point in '73 and '74 when the boat he designed for Chuck Kirsch, the 55 ft. *Scaramouche*, cleaned up on the Great Lakes and almost won the '74 S.O.R.C. Pat Haggerty went up on his stick and that, along with other modifications, made his C.C.A. boat *Bay Bea* competitive again. Later in the spring of '74 Lynn Williams paid $30,000 to have the mast of his 61 ft. *Dora* increased six feet and Steere did the same with *Yankee Girl*. By the summer of '74 everyone was acutely aware of the rating advantage to be gained by going up on the mast, and it had all started with *La Forza*.

Another goldplater that was active and moderately successful in the Circuit during the early '70s was Jim Baldwin's C. and C. 61 ft. *Sorcery*. This boat is noteworthy for a number of reasons. First, when she was built she was the largest production glass fibre boat in existence. After her would come *Robon*, which was first to finish in a rough 1972 Bermuda Race, and *Sassy*. All three boats had their share of racing success, but not so much as one might have expected.

One of the problems was that *Sorcery* was designed just prior to the introduction of the I.O.R. rule and so was never able to compete under the handicapping formula to which she was designed. The man who had originally placed the order with C. and C. wanted a boat that would be competitive with Twelve Metre yachts, so it is not surprising that in many respects she resembled a Twelve. With a 26 ft. J and a 75 ft. mast, her sailplan of 1,712 sq. ft. is roughly similar to that of a Twelve and her 50 ft. waterline and 8 ft. 3 in. draft also approximated the America's Cup boats. Yet she was beamier (15 ft. 1 in.) and a bit lighter than many Twelves at 48,155 lb. displacement with 22,122 lb. of ballast. Her fin keel and cantilevered spade rudder were characteristic C. and C. shapes, and her flush deck was equipped with two large Barient coffee grinders, making her truly one of the first large flat-out glass ocean racers.

Just as some of the large Class A ocean racers were sorting things out, the One Tonners were getting into their stride in the United States. Although there was nothing new about One Ton racing in Europe, the concept of level racing was slow to gain acceptance in the United States. In 1971 and '72 there was only one real regatta for One Tonners—the N.A.Y.R.U. championships—and in both years (and every year since for that matter) the fleets only numbered a handful. A Swan 37, *Bullet*, won the United States championship in '71, with the new Stephens designed aluminium *Lightnin'* winning in '72. *Lightnin'* was a fire-engine-red, full race sloop that had been built by Minneford's on City Island on speculation to acquaint its yard personnel with the methods of aluminium construction. Although the boat reportedly cost Minneford's over $100,000 to build, she was eventually sold to Ted Turner for around $60,000 in late '72.

By that time the first wave of One Ton interest had swept over the really keen American yachtsmen and a number were jumping into One Tonners. Ted Hood had designed and built the first of many One Ton *Robins*, and a number of America's stock-boat companies were tooling up with their own entries, apparently unaware of the short competitive racing life of designs in the class.

Ranger Yachts of Costa Mesa, California, was the first American company to pump a stock One Tonner out the door. With an all-star crew of one-design sailors aboard, including sailmaker Click Schreck, O. J. Young and John Dane III, a Ranger 37 owned by Jack Valley and called *Muñequita* won the '73 S.O.R.C. Designed by Gary Mull, the most eye-catching feature of the boat was its sleek blister deck with portlights mounted flush in the deck.

That year Classes E and D were full of most of the fastest small boats in the country. The fleet was divided in such a manner that half of the One Tonners were in D and the other half in Class E. *Muñequita*, for example, rated just over 27·5 and was therefore in Class D. This was probably a wise move on the part of Schreck and company because Class D is traditionally the weakest of the five S.O.R.C. classes. Even before the Circuit, Schreck guaranteed Jack Valley that they would win overall title for their class. He should have displayed a bit more optimism.

In Class D, along with *Muñequita*, were *Elixer* and *Orpheus*, both Swan 37s. *Elixer* had done well in the Circuit the year before and David Veitor's *Orpheus* had been the scourge of small boats in the north-east. Three other Ranger One Tonners were in D, Bob Mosbacher's *Semloh*, and *Ramrod*, owned by the Flitman/Graves partnership and Dyer's *Dirego*. A Chance designed stock One Tonner *Fou de Vous*, and a Yankee Yachts' One Tonner *Family Affair*, sailed by S.O.R.C. veteran Dr. Herb Virgin, were also in the D fleet, and for the first time these four stock designs went toe-to-toe—hundreds of thousands of dollars' worth of tooling and promotion were riding on the outcome.

There was another One Tonner in the D class that deserves special mention. That was an aluminium Van de Stadt design built in Europe called *Pied Piper*. She is noteworthy because, far from being a stripped-out racing machine, she had teak decks as well as a beautiful, and heavy, teak interior. Although she didn't shake up the fleet, she did manage a class second and third during the six races, a testament to the fact that boats can still be beautiful and do well.

Ted Turner's 38 ft. *Lightnin'*, which was the prototype for the Yankee Yachts' production One Tonner, was the boat to beat from the outset. Trying to do just that was Ted Hood in *Robin*, Jerry Milgram in his radical *Cascade*, Murphy and Nye sailmaker Bob Barton in a Peter Norlin-designed 37-footer called *No Go V*, and Martin Field's *The Magic Twanger*, a Swan 37 with microballoons added to her beam, sailed by one-design hotshot Tim Stearn. Stearn received recognition a year later around the world when he introduced his double-grooved headstay device called the Twin Stay. This rotating stay would allow a second headsail to be hoisted before the first was taken down, eliminating the necessity for a boat to be bareheaded during a headsail change.

Class B that year was made up of about 25 boats that measured from 42 ft. to 50 ft. overall, a relatively narrow range of boats that offered good racing possibilities. Heading up the B fleet were three near sisterships all closely related to the classic S. and S. *Bay Bea* that first came out of the Palmer Johnson yard in 1968. The three aluminium sisters were Wally Stenhouse's *Aura*, Chuck Kirsch's *Scaramouche*, and Commodore Kilpatrick's *Bandit*. *Aura* had been winning races or finishing well up in the events all over the world while *Scaramouche* had done well on the Great Lakes, and *Bandit* had swept the board at Chesapeake Bay under the ownership of Al Van Metre.

Only the absence of Haggerty's *Bay Bea* kept the '73 Circuit from being a sail-off between these four classic boats. They had dogged each other around the Circuit the year before in a dazzling display of tactics and sailing that none aboard would ever forget. *Aura* had won Class B the year before, thus topping her sisters, and had nearly won the Circuit, save for the good luck of *Condor*. A rematch was certainly in order.

Going up against the dynamic trio from S. and S. were three 43 ft. sisterships designed and built by the Canadian firm of Cutherbertson and Cassian. All three, Russ Hoyt's *Destination*, Buzzy Schofield's *Arieto* and Mel Holstein's *Alethea*, had banged heads with the S. and S. sisters the year before and in '73 they were even better prepared, even more finely tuned, for the Class B clash. Like the S. and S. 49s, these three semi-custom 43s had been designed just before the I.O.R. rule came out, so in this respect they were all racing with the same handicap. On the other hand, all six were ripe for picking by a new I.O.R. designed flyer. and there were a number of them in the same class.

Six Nautor-built, S. and S. designed 48s (called Palmer Johnson 48s in the States because they were marketed through the P.J. network, but referred to as Swan 48s in the rest of the world) had found their way to the '73 S.O.R.C. and their owners had high expectations. After all, they were designed to the I.O.R. rule by Olin Stephens and company and the British *Noryema*, a Swan 48, had won the Bermuda Race the year before. These six I.O.R. boats were accompanied by three new 44 ft. Brit Chance designed ketches, two of which were built by DeDoode in Germany and one, *Jemel*, by New Orleans Marine with the newly patented undirectional glass material called C-flex. *Jemel* was the lightest and, with Buddy Friedrichs at the helm, the best sailed of the three.

Class C was an interesting combination of Canada's Cup boats, I.O.R. designs, dated I.O.R. designs and a few old C.C.A. boats. The summer before, Llwyd Ecclestone's Hood-designed *Dynamite* had won the Canada's Cup, thus returning the old trophy to the United States. The cup is sailed for in Two Ton level-rating boats (32 ft. I.O.R.) and practically all of the participants except *Dynamite* showed up at the Circuit to settle old scores.

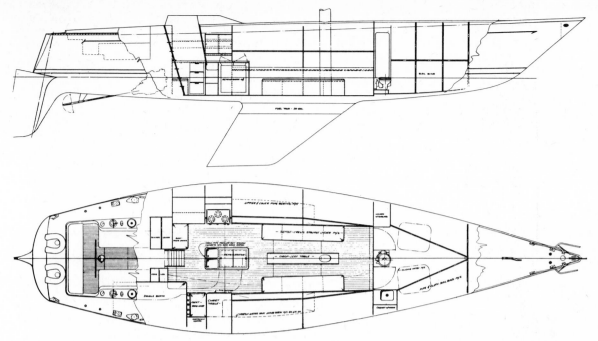

'La Forza del Destino' has a high sail area to displacement ratio—she displaces 28,000 lb. with an 'I' of 68 ft.—and set a fashion others copied

Canadian construction contractor Gerry Moog had purchased the defeated defender *Mirage*, a racy-looking 40-footer that was as bare as a hound's tooth below decks. Also in the fray was Maury DeClercq's 43 ft. *Spirit of Michigan* and Frank Piku's 42 ft. Dick Carter designed *Aggressive*. Both *Aggressive* and *Spirit of Michigan* were in the elimination series among the contending challengers, in part because they were designed for heavy air. The elimination series had been held in light air and, ironically, the Canada's Cup match itself—usually held in gusty late season breezes—also proved to be a light-air series, thus putting *Mirage* at a disadvantage. The '73 S.O.R.C. would be the showdown for heavy-air Canada's Cuppers.

Also in the batch of Class C boats were two brand-new Swan 44s, Sam Lightner's *Scarlett* and Mark Ewing's *Harpoon*. These two S. and S. designed production boats had a similar deck layout to the Swan 48s.

Class A that year was made up of 22 of the most glittering goldplaters to have ever hit the Circuit and, since the class was divided the following year, that aggregation of sailing power might never again be assembled in one class. Rounding out the '73 fleet were such boats as *Windward Passage* (73 ft.), *Blackfin* (73 ft.), *Kialoa II* (73 ft.), *Baccara* (73 ft.), *Equation* (68 ft.), *Sorcery* (61 ft.) and sistership *Sassy*, *La Forza* (54 ft.), *Congere* (54 ft.), *Running Tide* (61 ft.), *Charisma* (56 ft.), *Yankee Girl* (56 ft.) and many others. New among this high-strung fleet were Frank Zurn's 61 ft. McCurdy and Rhodes designed *Kahili II* and Lynn Williams' 61 ft. S. and S. cutter *Dora IV*. The new *Dora* had a tremendous sail-carrying capacity, had come in second in her class in her maiden Bermuda Race the year before, and looked to all the world like a major Class A threat. *Kahili II* was fresh from double wins in the Great Lakes, taking the Chicago–Mackinac and Port Huron–Mackinac races. A nightmare of winches and complicated sheet leads on deck, below *Kahili* had some of the most sumptuous living accommodation seen on any of the modern ocean racers.

The Circuit's opening 105-mile Venice Race started off in a 20-knot southerly but by the time Class D made its way to the line a cold front had hit the fleet. The icy norther had stabbed through the bay, sending temperatures plunging and gave the fleet a wild ride south and a tough beat 30 miles north to the finish line in 35-knot winds. It was a tough gearbuster that caused *Running Tide*'s headstay to break, *Charisma*'s headsail luff-feeding device to break off (and thus keep her crew from hoisting a headsail for 20 minutes) and *Sorcery*'s spinnaker halyard to jam at the turning mark, forcing her to sail two miles to leeward. *Yankee Girl* blew out four spinnakers during the hairy ride south as gear and sails exploded all over the fleet. One crewman suffered a broken arm and an owner holding on to a wayward spinnaker sheet had his hand yanked into a block, crushing one of his fingers.

As seems so often to happen in the S.O.R.C., Mother Nature couldn't wait to wallop the weekend sailors. The sea was so rough at the finish line off the Venice breakwater that the Venice Yacht Club race committee first lost its anchor, then its heart, and abandoned the line after the first 10 boats had crossed, leaving the rest of the fleet to take their own times. This is never a particularly good way of obtaining accurate times and when the fleet discovered that the race committee hadn't even bothered to walk out to the end of the jetty to clock the boats only a few hundred yards offshore, bitter complaints were issued up.

Because of the Venice Yacht Club's lack of contrition over its finish-line foul-up, the S.O.R.C. fathers later in the year eliminated the Venice Race and for '74 substituted in its place a race from St. Pete up to Tarpon Springs and back, now called the Anclote Key Race. This race serves the same purpose as the Venice event—a good shakedown for the fleet with a good chance of some wet thrashing to windward.

Sassy won the race, and Class A, followed in both class and fleet standing by *Equation* and *La Forza del Destino*. Many aficionados were impressed by the strong performance of *La Forza* in the fresh conditions, but of course the downwind slide was just her meat. Nevertheless, she had proved in the beat to the finish that she was a better all-round boat than many had imagined. Olympic gold medal winner Buddy Friedrichs steered *Jemel* to a first in Class B, with *Aura* second and

(Top) 'Muñequita', one of the Mull designed Ranger 37s, won the 1973 S.O.R.C. Sailed by a cadre of New Orleans one-design champions she created a reputation that resulted in over a hundred being built

(Below, left) Ted Turner was one of the first people to bring the techniques of small boat sailing to the S.O.R.C. He won it outright in 1966 and 1970

(Below, right) M.I.T. professor of ocean engineering Dr. Jerry Milgram maintained throughout the 'Cascade' episode that the Offshore Rating Council acted too quickly in first giving 'Cascade' an arbitrary 10 per cent penalty and in later changing the rule to affect only his boat

ORIGINAL BEAM

BEAM AFTER ADDITION OF BLISTERS

BLISTERS, IF WELL DESIGNED, DO NOT AFFECT SPEED BUT DO REDUCE RATING!

Arieto third. These three diverse designs, evidently the best from their respective classes, would battle throughout the rest of the Circuit for the Class B overall prize.

In Class C, the heavy-weather Canada's Cuppers got just what they had wanted the summer before. *Aggressive* won the division with *C-Mirage* (ex-*Mirage*) second and Englishman David May's new S. and S. aluminium *Winsome*, an Admiral's Cup hopeful, third. The third Canada's Cupper, *Spirit*, stumbled in last in class and at the tail end of the fleet, reeling from gear failures and a crew injury.

Muñequita began her winning ways by taking the Class D prize, followed closely by two Swan 37s, John Graham's *Elixer* and David Veitor's *Orpheus*. Schreck and crew were lucky that race as a sistership had a bulkhead split completely through just below the starboard chainplate, and nearly lost her mast. Turner's *Lightnin'* thrived in the rough water and won E with Elliot Siegel's *No Go V* up to the task for second and Hood's *Robin* third.

The 403-mile St. Petersburg to Fort Lauderdale Race held a few days later was a perfect example of what this classic race can be like. The fleet beat out of Tampa Bay in a moderate southerly. The wind clocked around to the west, then to the north, and at nightfall it lightened.

Aboard Class A *Charisma*, which had been sailing along about eighth in her class, boat-for-boat, all the crew stayed on deck for most of the night, gybing the vessel constantly, always looking for the fastest sailing angle. Within a few hours *Charisma* led the entire S.O.R.C. fleet—an incredible example of downwind tacking.

As the fleet rounded Rebecca Shoal, every boat had to decide how to play the Stream. The wind was still out of the north, making it a reach around the tip of Florida—first a broad reach, then wind abeam, and finally a close reach heading up the east coast of Florida.

Finding the Gulf Stream is not as easy as it may sound. It is not a yellow brick road. It is in the Straits of Florida however and the sharp observer can usually find it. Nautical charts show the axis of the Stream about 50 miles south of Key West; then, according to the charts, the axis moves closer to the coast as it swings northward around the east coast of Florida until it reaches a point about 20 miles off the coast near Alligator Reef. However, the northern edge of the Stream and a good two-to-three-knot push is far closer to shore. For years S.O.R.C. navigators have generally considered the edge to run along the 100-fathom line. This topographical line is about 13 miles off Key West and stays about 10–12 miles offshore until the top of the Keys where it swings dramatically close to shore, being only two miles out off Miami. Quite often the northern edge of the Stream does run roughly along this line, but quite often it does not and that makes locating the Stream a giant guessing game.

After rounding Rebecca a skipper is faced with a dilemma: should he hope the Stream can be found at the 100-fathom line and go for it, or should he take the shorter rhumb-line course around the Keys? Further, what happens if the Stream is not at the 100-fathom line? Does he then go even farther out until he finds it or settle for the distance he has already given away to those who stayed inside? Boats have been known to go as far as 50 miles south searching for the Stream and, having found it, were unlucky enough to have the wind shift to the north-east, making it a beat to the finish line. The pitfalls of the Stream are obvious and far more boats have been hampered in their quest than have been helped.

Another interesting aspect of the Stream is what its two-to-three-knot boost means to a boat's overall speed. Obviously a three-knot boost to a 30-footer that might average six knots under the right conditions means a 50 per cent increase. However, a 50-footer averaging about nine knots in the same conditions receives only a 33 per cent increase. The really big boats that might do 12 knots receive only a 25 per cent speed bonus. Fantastic increases in relative speed over the bottom can be had, then, but the relative benefit decreases as the boat gets larger. Yet, if it is potentially dangerous for the large boats to venture out in search of the Stream, it can spell disaster for the small boats if it is 30 or 40 miles south and only a knot or less in set, as is often the case.

The last five years or so, the keen (and wealthy) S.O.R.C. competitors have been taking the guesswork out of finding the Stream by flying small airplanes over the Straits of Florida a couple of days before the race. There are a number of tricks to locating the Stream, such as watching for tankers. Tankers going east can be expected to be in the Stream (if their navigators are at all conscientious about their duties) and ships going west should be north of the Stream. Occasionally one will see tankers headed in opposite directions with the edge of the Stream right down the middle.

If the wind is blowing against the grain of the Stream white caps will be kicked up, and when this happens there is literally a 'white brick road' to follow. Without this indicator, scouting parties look for a line of Sargasso weed that usually piles up along the northern edge of the Stream. Other indicators are a chain of knotty clouds directly over the Stream and increased wind turbulence. Possibly the best time of all to discover this undulating river is in the late afternoon looking west. The setting sun backlights the sea, highlighting its different textures, and it is then that the location of the Stream is most easily discerned.

Ironically, when Jesse Philips, owner of *Charisma*, flew his navigators and tacticians over the Stream in 1973 the very knowledge that they gained could well have been the factor which kept them from winning the race. The *Charisma* crew charted the Stream about 20 miles south of the Keys and two days later, when they arrived there by sail, they knew right where to go. In the meantime, Wally Stenhouse in *Aura* steered around Florida's answer to Cape Horn on roughly the 80-to-100-fathom lines and won the race by virtue of good speed and sailing less distance, for she had picked up the Stream off Alligator Reef as it swung in. The speed that *Charisma* picked up by going out to it was offset by the reduced mileage of *Aura*'s course. *Charisma* was second.

When Class A, B and C boats were south of Florida the wind was booming in from the south at 28 to 30 knots, making it a fast reach around the 'Horn'. As night fell the wind piped up to 35 knots, making it a wild spinnaker ride down the breaking seas of the Gulf Stream and across the finishing line off Fort Lauderdale.

As the bigger boats were finishing, the crews looked overhead to see a low layer of clouds scuttling north, but a few thousand feet above the light of the moon illuminated higher clouds tearing south-east—a norther was on the way!

An hour later it hit, turning the last 50-mile leg up the coast into a wet beat for the small boats. Within an hour the temperature plunged 25 degrees and the winds freshened to 40 knots, now and again gusting to 50. While the big-boat crews were enjoying a tot of rum in the snug bars ashore, the bulk of the fleet found itself rail down in icy winds. The 40-knot norther hit the Stream, turning it into a maelstrom of turbulence which sent wave after wave of green water washing over the decks. The last of the Class E boats didn't finish until the following night after 24 hours of thrashing through wet and miserable conditions. After the race, many of the Class E crews vowed that they would never again go racing offshore!

But if *Charisma*'s second place was ironic, given all of the trouble she had gone to to find the Stream, more ironic was the near miss of Jerry Milgram's *Cascade*. With an arbitrary 10 per cent penalty handed out to her by the Offshore Rating Council, she now rated 22·8 instead of a bit over 20. Nevertheless, she flew around the course and continued to do well after coming on the wind. When she crossed the finishing line she appeared to be the overall winner, but a few hours later she was protested against for going inside the government buoy off Miami. Upon checking with his navigator, Milgram discovered that they had indeed gone inside the mark. Milgram admitted the error and *Cascade* was penalised three hours, which pushed him down the placing list and out of the running.

The winds piped up to 40 knots again as a northerly stabbed the fleet on its way across the Stream to Lucaya, the last time that race was part of the S.O.R.C. There were a number of gear failures throughout the fleet, and many skippers, particularly those in the larger classes, thought the race was tougher than the Lauderdale Race had been. Wind conditions were made to order for *Cascade* and she reached across to win by over an hour. That victory was followed up by another in the Lipton Cup, the 28-mile dash from Miami to Lauderdale and back. In the Miami–Nassau Race conditions again favoured easy reaching in moderate winds and *Cascade* shot to victory again. Only a poor showing in the final Nassau Cup, which had a long, hard windward leg in fresh winds, plus her Lauderdale Race mistake, kept the radical *Cascade* from winning the Circuit. The Bob Derecktor-designed *Salty Goose* won the Nassau Cup and that victory was instrumental in her being picked for the American Admiral's Cup team a month later.

Ted Hood's Circuit

The 1974 S.O.R.C. had two important changes to the six-race Circuit. First, the race to Venice was eliminated and in its place was an event from St. Pete, out to Tampa Bay to Tarpon Springs, then back to the channel leading into the bay. The second change was the institution of what was called the 'Ocean Triangle Race', an event from Miami across the Stream, leaving Great Isaac Island to port, back across the Stream to Fort Lauderdale, then down to Miami. This 132-mile giant triangle replaced the Lucaya Race which was usually a reach.

One Tonners came into their own in 1974 and so completely dominated the Circuit that only one race was taken by something other than a One Tonner. This time, no fewer than six of the world's fastest custom One Tonners were entered and the stock raters didn't have a chance. Nor did the rest of the fleet.

Martin Field's brand new Doug Peterson designed One Tonner *The Magic Twanger* from King of Prussia, Pa., won the hard-fought Anclote Key Race after sistership *Country Woman*, owned and sailed by Murphy and Nye sailmaker Bob Barton, was penalised time for not having the two obligatory orange smoke flares aboard. The time assessment dropped *Country Woman* down to third, behind George Tooby's *America Jane II*, a 39 ft. S. and S. custom One Tonner.

Both *Twanger* and *Country Woman* were built from the same lines as the famous *Ganbare*, which nearly won the 1973 World One Ton Cup in Porto Cervo, Sardinia. Both boats were also made of genuine tree wood by Carl Eichenlaub in San Diego, California. Eichenlaub had also built *Ganbare* and quickly gained a reputation for being able to knock out reasonable facsimiles of boats in about 60 days.

In the time-honoured tradition of the S.O.R.C., both Peterson boats were still being hammered together as the first race began. In fact, minor construction continued on *Twanger* all during the race. But it was the year of the Tonners and in spite of a dead beat back down the coast to the finish line near the Skyway Bridge, the One Tonners were able to dominate the top positions. The only boat that broke their hold, because of Barton's penalty, was Kirsch's new Frers designed *Scaramouche*, which finished third in the fleet. Norm Raben's *La Forza* won Class A despite being over the line early and losing 14 minutes on a restart. In fact, starting late might have even helped Raben as he was able to then pick the right side of the course. His boat likes nothing more than light-air beating, the conditions of the day.

In Class D, Dick Carter showed what a production boat could do by winning the class in *Rabbit*, a 39-footer of his own design.

The St. Petersburg to Fort Lauderdale Race started out under clear skies and balmy south-easterly winds that made it one of the most enjoyable ocean races of the year, although the south-easterly did not allow the fleet to lay the big turning mark at Rebecca Shoal. All through the fleet fierce covering manoeuvres took place as the top boats tried to cover their major competitors in each class. In Class E, for example, Ted Turner, sailing *Lightnin'*, and Ted Hood in his new *Robin Too II*, tacked and covered each other for nearly 30 miles as if they were in an America's Cup match race. Finally Turner tacked to port and Hood decided to hold on starboard to sail his own race.

It seems that the boats which decided to bite the bullet and tack back to the rhumb line (nearly 90 degrees to the course) early in the leg, were the boats that generally fared well. For example, *Scaramouche*, *Yankee Girl* and *Charisma* sailed in sight of each other well down the coast. Finally *Scaramouche* and *Yankee Girl* decided to make the seemingly unprofitable, but conservative, starboard tack to the original rhumb line while *Charisma* headed west for the Dry Tortugas. She eventually found them and bounced over part of them. But as *Scaramouche* neared Rebecca she got a lift right from heaven and swept past the shoal on a favourable tide.

Approaching the door at Rebecca with a favourable current was just as important in 1974 as had been in the very first race to Havana 40 years before. Dick Carter was one of a number of old hands who knew what he was about and purposely timed his arrival at Rebecca with the ebbing tide. Hood's *Robin* arrived soon after and received the same lift and favourable current that had helped others. This was one of the keys to the race.

As Class E and D boats neared Fowley Rock, south of Miami, a dry front swept in from the Florida mainland, and again the small boats found themselves with a tough beat to the finish. However, unlike the year before, the plunging temperatures and gale-force winds did not accompany the front. But the norther did not turn into a trump card for the large boats as it often does in the Lauderdale Race. Hood had made all the right decisions, including going out about 18 miles off the southern coast of Florida, and he finished 12th on elapsed time and only nine hours after the 55 ft. *Scaramouche*. Hood won the race, the *Mouche* was second and Dick Carter's *Rabbit* was third. Llwyd Ecclestone's *Dynamite* won Class C while *Running Tide* won Class A—all these boats ended up in the top 10 in the fleet, a strong testament to the sailing skill aboard these fine yachts and to the I.O.R. rating system.

The new Ocean Triangle Race turned into a showdown of sorts between *Charisma* and *Scaramouche*. Had the S.O.R.C. been a big-boat circuit the year before, *Charisma* would have won it. A win in the Miami–Nassau Race, a second in the Bermuda Race and with fleet and class wins world-wide, the big blue beast, registered out of Dayton, Ohio, had terrorised fleets all over the world. Even

'Robin Too II' in which Ted Hood sailed to victory in the 1974 S.O.R.C.

(Inset) Sailmaker, designer and champion helmsman Ted Hood

though *Scaramouche* had won the two Mackinac races the year before and despite the fact that *Wa Wa Too*, also designed by Frers, had displayed good speed in the Solent the previous year, few people knew about her until the Anclote Key Race. That was when the *Charisma* crew first learned that big blue couldn't hold the little *Scaramouche* in light air. With about the same overall dimensions, more sail area and over a foot less of rating, Kirsch's grey ghoster was unbeatable in light zephyrs.

After the start of the Ocean Triangle both *Charisma* and *Scaramouche* stayed close together while the new Chance designed *Gannet*, a sistership of Sir Max Aitken's *Perseverance*, tagged along a few yards to leeward. The three boats, with some of the best men in American ocean racing sailing them, worked their boats hard for every fraction of a knot boat speed the entire 55 miles across the Stream to the island on the Bahama Banks. As they neared the island, *Scaramouche* was finally able to break free on the close reach, gaining over a half-mile lead on *Charisma*, which in turn had managed to slip away from *Gannet* after hours of close hull-to-hull racing.

The A and B boats rounded at sundown and it was an eerie feeling as the depth-sounder went from off soundings to just a couple of fathoms in a distance of a few hundred yards. The boats sailed up on to the bank, swung around the island and, with the breeze freshening, started their return trip across the Stream. In the night *Charisma*, with all hands on deck for the duration of the 132-mile race, set a Starcut, the famous blue-and-white Banks 'chute which she had first used two years before in winning the Venice Race, and slipped by the troublesome *Scaramouche*. The latter was late in getting up her Hood flanker and the time lost there allowed *Charisma* to ease a half-mile into the lead.

Approaching the Lauderdale sea buoy, it soon became obvious that *Charisma* had overstood. The set of the Stream fooled many navigators that night and it became commonplace to see boats running down to the mark under spinnaker. Nevertheless, *Charisma* managed to stay in front of *Mouche* in the gruelling beat dead to windward down the Florida gold coast to Miami. The wind freshened to 28 knots over the deck as *Charisma* repeatedly tacked to cover *Scaramouche* in the narrow band of water from the beach out to the Stream. As the crews on these two mighty racers sweated it out over coffee grinders, the gay lights of 15 miles of solid high-rise hotels glittered in the background. But during that long 15-mile beat—which comes as close as any racing in the United States to the short tacking conditions usually found in the Solent—*Charisma* was unable to break away and save her time. *Scaramouche* won the race with *Charisma* second. The *Mouche* was firmly in control of the overall S.O.R.C. point standings and had knocked off America's best ocean racer in the process.

As Chuck Kirsch entered the Nassau Race, he had the S.O.R.C. in the palm of

The spinnaker being handed on Dick Carter's 'Rabbit'

(Inset) Dick Carter, a favourite designer around European shores and one of the few visionaries in the sport

his hand. All he had to do was keep his sleek, grey sloop out of trouble and finish well up in the fleet for the rest of the Circuit. But unfortunately a norther was brewing that would turn the Nassau event into a small-boat race. Kirsch and his crack crew of Great Lake sailors would have to wait until the Bermuda Race later that year before they would receive the laurels they richly deserved. The cold, 30 knot winds made for a rough and wild reach across the Stream and a beam reach on to Stirrup Cay. What happened that night was nearly tragic and marks one of the most fascinating episodes in recent S.O.R.C. history.

The north-easterly and a strong current setting on to the banks caused many racers in the fleet to sail farther on to the shelf than they had thought. This, together with the fact that boats have been closely skirting the chain of rock piles that mark the northern Bahama Banks the last few years (some even going inside, which is against the racing rules), caused a number of boats to hit the coral. One boat, *Wimoweh*, an Ericson 46 owned by a syndicate of sailors from New Orleans headed by Temple Brown, racing along at eight knots, hit a rock, bounced off and then came down firmly on another. Within minutes it was obvious that the boat was taking in water faster than the crew could pump it out. The hull had been gashed along the starboard side and the hole could not be reached because it was behind a hanging locker. Unable to stem the flow, the crew radioed a Mayday signal and released their distress flares. Since there were a number of boats in the area many saw the flares but, sadly, only a few boats responded.

But three boats did answer the Mayday call and one, Mike Fisher's *Osprey*, ventured into the shoal water to rescue the crew before the boat sank.

In one of the most novel race committee decisions ever, *Osprey* was awarded 1 hour, 23 minutes off her elapsed time for the time spent on the rescue, *plus* another 37 minutes for the burden of the added crew weight, some 2,000 pounds.

Although no one quibbled about the 1 hour, 23 minutes, the 37 minutes extra that race committee chairman Robert Symonette insisted upon was generally considered to be 'bonus time' by the S.O.R.C. folks. Symonette was understandably upset because many more boats had seen the flares or had heard the Mayday, yet failed to offer assistance. (Many boat owners later reported that since they knew by listening to the radio that one boat had gone to the rescue and two others were standing by outside the rocks, there was no need for more boats to pile into the confusion.) Fisher's seamanship and that of his watch captain John Rumsey was of the highest order and the 'bonus time' made *Osprey* the winner of the race. This knocked the rightful winner, George Tooby's *America Jane II*, into second place. (Later that year, at the One Ton Cup in Britain, the ultimate winner, *Gumboots*, went to the assistance of a burning cruising yacht. She took aboard the hapless crew and did not finish the high-points scoring race, but was given a well deserved position.)

Because *Scaramouche* tanked the Nassau Race, *Robin Too II*'s fifth overall was enough to push her into the lead on overall point standings. For 15 years Ted Hood had been sailing and winning races in the S.O.R.C., but overall victory had eluded him. Now all he had to do was turn in a credible finish in the final 30-mile

Norm Rabin's 50 ft. 'La Forza del Destino' was designed for the light airs and smooth waters that predominate on Long Island Sound during the summer

Nassau Cup Race, from Paradise Island out to Booby Rocks and back, and he would be the new king of the S.O.R.C. Close behind him in points was a cluster of hot One Ton boats crewed by some of the best small-boat men in the country. Ted Turner's *Lightnin'*, George Tooby's *America Jane II* and Bob Barton's *Country Woman* were all within three points of each other.

The first leg of the race was a beat to windward and halfway up the leg Hood was in a good position. Then, unexpectedly, Hood's Kevlar mainsail began tearing from the leech toward the luff. A spinnaker sheet had chafed through the leech of the main in the Nassau Race and a hasty patch sewed on by Hood had not held. Victory was being torn from his grasp. Quickly, his crew, which included Hawaii hotshot Cy Gillette, reefed the main above the tear. The wind thoughtfully freshened and Hood's chances didn't seem to be appreciably harmed.

Incredibly, as *Robin* neared the windward mark, the toggle holding the headstay broke and his genoa sagged off to leeward. It was as if fate had not counted on Hood winning this or any S.O.R.C. Gillette took over the helm as Hood himself rushed to the bow to make repairs. Luckily the luff wire held as the boat bore off. A spare toggle was fitted and *Robin* was off once again and flying with renewed determination. In spite of his gear failures, Hood still managed a fifth in class and fleet, good enough to win the '74 Circuit by over 40 points.

Hood's S.O.R.C. success proved to be only the first of what was bound to be the most spectacular of his 35 years of racing. The following September he successfully defended the America's Cup in the Twelve Metre *Courageous*—the dream of every American racing man, including Ted Hood.

The Bermuda Race

Although it is not the oldest ocean race in the United States, the Bermuda Race is certainly by all accounts America's classic blue-water event, and provides the treble-points scorer for the Onion Patch team series. Started in 1906 by Thomas Fleming Day, the editor of 'Rudder', America's foremost boating magazine at the time, the event was designed to encourage the use of small boats at sea. For decades, Day had been the leading exponent in the States for taking seaworthy small yachts to sea. Eventually, he took his own 25-footer across the Atlantic to prove the point. Throughout the late 1800s and early 1900s, Thomas Fleming Day worked tirelessly to promote the sport of offshore racing (and cruising) and it is due to his efforts that the yachtsmen of America began to get their feet wet beyond the Gulf Stream.

Only three owners were intrepid enough to enter the first Bermuda Race, held from Gravesend Bay in Brooklyn, New York, to St. David's Head, Bermuda. Frank Maier won the race in his 38 ft. yawl *Tamerlane*. News of the race spread throughout Long Island South and up America's north-east cruising grounds to Maine that summer and word got around that the little boats didn't fall off the ends of the earth and no sea monsters had been sighted. In 1907, 12 boats entered and Harry A. Morss's Clinton Crane designed 85 ft. *Dervish* won easily. Participation fell off the next three years with only five boats entered in '08 and '09 and only two boats making the event in 1910. One of the two boats was Harold S. Vanderbilt's 76 ft. Herreshoff schooner, *Vagrant*, which won the event, the last of the original Bermuda races.

The event lay dormant during the years of the first world war and it was not until 1923 that the next race was held. This time the editor of 'Yachting' magazine, Herbert L. Stone, was the instigator and 22 boats showed up at the starting line in the mouth of the Thames River off New London, Connecticut. It was a wild and wet ride that year with wind on the nose for practically the entire 660-mile race. Surprisingly a schooner, *Malabar IV*, designed and sailed by John Alden, won the race. It was after this Bermuda classic that Judge S. B. Coffin was quoted as saying: 'The next time I come to Bermuda it will be in a submarine. Then I can be under water all the time instead of half under all the time.'

Robert N. Bavier Sr. made some yachting history that year by having the only Bermuda-rigged yacht in the fleet. In fact, his New York 40 was nearly prevented from entering because many of the old cruising salts of the day figured the rig was unsafe, as gaff-mainsails were still the order of the day. Bavier not only proved that he could make it to Bermuda, but was the first boat there, being narrowly beaten by *Malabar* on corrected time. It is interesting to note that the

R. W. Ferris's schooner 'Malay' won the Bermuda Race in 1930

revival of the Bermuda Race was two years before the first Fastnet Race, held in 1925.

Bavier returned to win the following year in a 59 ft. Herreshoff designed yawl called *Memory*. Alden won the 1926 Bermuda Race in his 54 ft. schooner *Malabar VII*. In '32 Alden would win yet a third time in his famous *Malabar X*, a 58 ft. schooner that still sails in American and Caribbean waters, often in the charter trade. From 1926 onwards the race was staggered and thereafter it was always to be held on even years, with only one lapse during the war.

The 1926 race is, perhaps, notable for two reasons. First, the first entry from Britain was in the race—*Jolie Brise*, a bluff-bow cutter which, having won the first Fastnet Race, had sailed all the way to New London just for the race. Secondly, the use of radio aboard racing vessels 'came into its own'. *Malabar VII*, *Dragoon*, *Cygnet* and *Jolie Brise*, among others, had radios. Their main use was to get an accurate time check with which to reset the yachts' chronometers if need be. One owner reported that he would have missed Bermuda by eight miles had it not been for the correct time being received by radio. Thus the marine electronics industry was born.

Twenty boats entered the Bermuda Race in '28, but most were still gaff-rigged. The winner, however, was not—R. Grinnell's 59 ft. Herreshoff *Rugosa II*. The race was sailed in fresh breezes down to the Gulf Stream where the boats encountered a few squalls. Then it went light for the duration.

In 1930 a lovely schooner called *Yankee Girl II*, owned by Dr. G. W. Warren, was first to finish in one of the most closely contested Bermuda Races of the early years. Within four-and-a-half hours after *Yankee Girl* had finished, 16 boats had passed by St. David's Head. The young and virtually unknown designer Olin J. Stephens sailed his yawl *Dorade* to second place in Class B, his first success in ocean racing. R. W. Ferris's 45 ft. Roué designed schooner, *Malay*, won the event.

The '32 race was started off Montauk Point, which put Bermuda a few miles closer than previous races from New London. The fleet was down from the record 42 boats in 1930 to 27. Although the Depression had not bottomed out, the Bermuda Race fleet had. In succeeding years the fleets would grow in size with 43 yachts starting in 1936—the greatest number in any Bermuda Race from 1906 till 1950.

The race was a tough slam to Bermuda with three days of blustery winds and heavy seas. But the wind was from the south-west and it turned into a record passage for the event. With little to do except shorten down and occasionally shake out a reef, it might sound like an easy ride. But when the wind pipes up the Bermuda Race is never easy. Green water was taken aboard all the boats and by St. David's Head the fleet was exhausted from the thrash. Alden's *Malabar X* schooner won the race, a victory that was saddened by news of the loss of a life when the 78-footer *Adriana* burned and sank.

Ten of the crew were rescued by *Jolie Brise*, which had her rail and stanchions smashed during the operation. This is the same boat which had come out from Britain in 1926. This time she had returned under the command of Bobby Somerset, Commodore of the Royal Ocean Racing Club.

R. J. Schaefer Jr. won the '34 Bermuda Race in his 56 ft. Stephens designed *Edlu*, with Robert N. Bavier Sr. serving as skipper. With an ideal sailing breeze of 20 to 30 knots for most of the race, the fleet slid south with eased sheets in the south-westerly. *Vamarie* set an elapsed-time record of 3 days, 3 hours, 37 minutes, 32 seconds for the course.

Because of the strong tides and light air that often exist in Long Island Sound, the start of the '36 Bermuda Race was moved to Brenton Light off Newport, Rhode Island. Newport was ideally suited to handle and provision the fleet and the waters off her shore usually have wind. A record nine foreign entries raced to Bermuda that year, with boats coming from Sweden, Holland and six from Germany. There were 43 official starters plus another boat that insisted on sailing over the course in spite of being turned down by the Cruising Club of America as being potentially dangerous.

A tropical storm descended on the fleet as it sailed into the Gulf Stream, with winds being registered up to 45 knots. This was one of the roughest Bermuda Races that had been experienced since 1923 and it would be another couple of decades until a fleet would have to endure it again. Eight boats dropped out of the race and a ninth was disqualified because her engine was used to manoeuvre the boat after the topmast had been lost. *Mandoo II* was disabled when a fitting on her headstay broke. *Winsome* dropped out when her mast partners split. *Salee* retired because nearly her complete sail inventory had blown out. *Zala* dropped out because her radio didn't work. R. P. Baruch won the race in his 53 ft. S. and S. cutter *Kirawan*.

Henry C. Taylor's beautiful 72 ft. S. and S. yawl *Baruna*, with Rod Stephens on board, won the '38 Bermuda Race, which was a frustrating, light drifter. But to prove that her victory was no fluke, Taylor won with *Baruna* again in '48, a contest filled with fresh breezes and stiff competition. *Baruna* was the first boat in history to win two Bermuda races.

The intervening race, in 1946, was a light-air affair won by A. H. Fuller's 57 ft. S. and S. sloop *Gesture*. The great race had been called off in 1940 due to war and American yachtsmen had to content themselves to race elsewhere. Although most of the distance races closed down around the United States, freshwater yachtsmen kept racing throughout the war as the two long races to Mackinac rumbled on without a murmur.

The prevailing wind for the Bermuda Race is usually from the south-west. Traditional race strategy in these conditions is to work to the west during the early half of the race to a spot some 30 to 60 miles west of the rhumb line, then to ease the sheets and fly home to the silverware. This makes it one, long starboard tack to Bermuda and hard on the wind much of the way.

The notorious Gulf Stream. (Left) Its approximate track across the Newport–Bermuda course. (Right) A typical meander, similar to the 1974 loop, and the course which that year gave most advantage over it

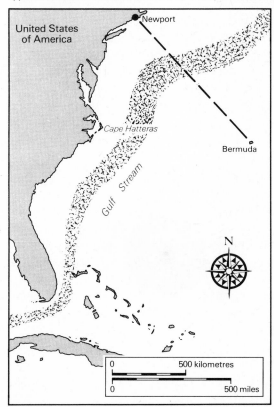
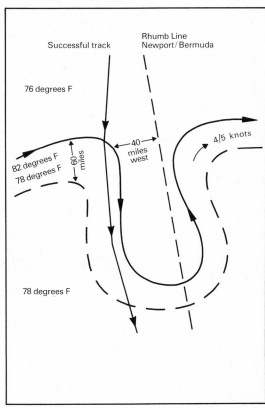

The old timers didn't have the benefit of Coast Guard infra-red photos charting the meanders of the Gulf Stream or satellite photos that use both visual and infrared reconnaissance. Consequently, until 1952 (Woods Hole Oceanographic Institute began charting the Stream in 1950) fleets were often confused by the Stream. They knew the temperature of the Stream and about where it was to be found, but what they didn't know for certain was which way it would be flowing.

Because of almost daily observations instigated since the employment of weather satellites, we now know that there is often a large loop in the Gulf Stream near the Newport–Bermuda rhumb line. The loop moves from east to west or sometimes flattens out giving the Stream a north-easterly flow. Because the loop in the Stream moves a matter of a few hundred miles, it is possible for boats taking the rhumb line in two successive years to get a two-knot boost from the Stream one year and lose two knots over the bottom the next because they are sailing right up the Stream. In fact, this exact change occurred between the '72 and '74 Bermuda races. In '72, the Stream was flowing in a south-easterly direction east of the rhumb line. Boats such as the British winner *Noryema VIII* and runner-up *Charisma* went east after they started and picked up the boost. (They also ended up being on the right side of the course because of it.) In 1974, the Stream formed a surprising double loop. This time, to get into favourable current, boats had to go west of the rhumb line. Boats that took a course east of the rhumb line, as had been used in '72, found themselves paddling up Stream.

As it turns out, the term traditionally used by yachtsmen of 'crossing the Stream' is a bit misleading. No doubt some years the Stream is, indeed, crossed. Those are the years when the Gulf Stream is flowing as one might naturally think it would, north-easterly or easterly. A track down the rhumb line might take one through the Stream for 30 to 50 miles, and all the while being pushed to the east. Just as likely, however, one might find oneself not crossing the Stream at all but sailing right down (or up) the centre of the mighty river. In this case a boat might sail for 100 miles down or up the Stream, depending into which loop one happened into. Obviously the effect of the Stream doubles if one boat is sailing in the favourable meander and another boat is sailing up river. Unfortunately, few, if any, yachtsmen were aware of this phenomenon before the early '50s.

William Moore won the 1950 Bermuda Race as the sport got off to a fresh start. New yachts were being built and raced and the changes were coming fast as the pace of yacht design became even more competitive than it had been before the war. Moore's 57 ft. S. and S. yawl *Argyll* beat John Nicholas Brown's famous *Bolero* by an hour on corrected time. Both *Bolero* and *Argyll* sailed a fine race, but for the former to have won she would have needed to average 8·5 knots for the distance. That was nearly an impossibility and this fact of American ocean-racing life points up the difficulty of big boats winning races.

Dick Nye won his first Bermuda Race in 1952 (and his second in 1970) in one of a number of boats called *Carina* that he has owned over the years. His 46 ft. yawl thrived in the light airs that reduced the race nearly to a drifting match. These conditions put the big boats on the shelf with each passing hour, with first

24 Jessie Philips' 'Charisma' was one of the first American yachts built for
I.O.R. and dominated American offshore racing circuits in 1972 and 1973

25 (Previous page) The eye-catching red hull of Ted Turner's One Tonner,
'Lightnin'.' She was runner-up in the S.O.R.C. in 1973 and 1974 and
up-rated to take part in the 1973 Admiral's Cup series

26 The Frers designed 'Scaramouche' was the only yacht to break the
domination of the One Tonners at the 1974 S.O.R.C.

John Nicholas Brown's famous yawl 'Bolero' which took part in the
Bermuda races in the 1950s

Class A, then Class B, and so on slipping into the tank. There were 10 foreign
entries that year, six from Britain.

By '54 the Bermuda Race was riding a crest of popularity that was to keep it
as America's foremost ocean race for the rest of the decade. Among the 77-boat
fleet assembled that year were some of the greatest names in the sport, yachts that
will be remembered by enthusiasts into the next century. *Bolero* was there and
won Class A, and along with her in that class were *Cotton Blossom IV*, *Good News*,
Escapade, *Fortuna*, *Barlovento*, *Niña* and *Ticonderoga*. In Class B were *Stormy Weather*,
Gesture, *Ondine*, *Merry Maiden* and *Caribbee*. It was truly a great fleet.

Again, the weather killed off the big boats the first two days of the race as the
flotilla glided through light air and glassy-smooth water all the way down to and
through the Stream. At night, stars twinkled brightly overhead and enough men
became addicted to the pleasures of ocean racing to keep the sport going for 50
years—just in search of another crossing like that one. The breeze didn't pipe up
until there was only 375 miles to go and with handicaps based on 675 miles the
smallest boats were in good standing. Dan Strohmeier won the race in his 39 ft.
Concordia Inc. design yawl *Malay*. But there was more to Strohmeier's victory than
size and rating. He also hit the south-easterly flow of the Stream just right—and
a good deal farther to the west than many of the hotshots.

This was the year almost everyone was putting great stock in the Woods Hole Oceanographic Institute's prediction of the location and flow of the Stream, and Strohmeier was no exception. A number of boats that year reported discovering temperatures of 82 degrees F. on the northern edge of the Stream.

After a number of years of generally calm weather, Bermuda Race veterans were hankering for a real blow for the Onion Patch, the nickname for Bermuda Island which was once famous for its robust and tasty onions. They got their blow in 1956, a race that has gone down in the books as one of the greatest blue water events ever held.

The wind was from the classic south-western quadrant making the course to St. David's Head a close reach—just the right condition for a record breaker. *Bolero*, under the ownership of Sven Salen, set a new elapsed time record of 2 days, 22 hours, 11 minutes, 37 seconds, which broke *Highland Light*'s old record, established in 1932, by nearly an hour and a half. This record stood until 1974, when *Ondine* reached south in much the same weather pattern in 2 days, 21 hours, 42 minutes and 14 seconds.

With 20 to 30 knot winds and squalls blasting much higher, and with an overcast sky for nearly the entire race, good navigation was at a premium. Carleton Mitchell in his 38 ft. 8 in. *Finisterre* knew that the shortest distance between two points on a screaming reach is the rhumb line, stayed on it the entire show to finish 20 hours after *Bolero* and win both Class D and fleet. Bill Snaith came within a hair's breadth of winning in his *Figaro* (as would be his fate so many times throughout his illustrious sailing career), finishing second, 14 minutes behind on corrected time. Incredibly, DeCoursey Fales' *Niña*, a schooner built in 1928 under a different handicap rule, won Class A while *Bolero* had to settle for second in class. *Bolero*'s headstay toggle had snapped and she finished the race under full main and staysail.

Disaster struck the Class C cutter *Edla*, owned by Henry Wise Jr. when she hit Northeast Breaker off Bermuda. At two o'clock in the morning her hull slammed into two coral pinnacles which ripped open her bottom on either side of her keel and she filled immediately. Wise rushed below and handed out lifejackets and the crew clung to the backstay. For eight hours the eight hapless men hung on desperately while wave after wave pounded down upon them from the breakers cresting at the shoal. For a couple the temptation was great to try to swim the seven miles to shore. However, good judgement prevailed and all held on until daylight. The chief lookout at St. Georges spotted them as he ranged his glass along the distant reef and within minutes two liferafts were dropped by a Coast Guard plane. (Wise, like so many men who have been beaten by the elements going to Bermuda, has raced numerous times since, no doubt with a score to settle.)

But if 1956 was one of the greatest Bermuda Races ever, the '58 race was one of the most unusual. Light south-westerlies had been predicted for the 1 p.m. start. It ended up blowing from the north-west—almost unheard of at a Bermuda Race start—at 30–35 knots. So much for the weathermen around Newport!

Those watching that start from the spectator fleet might well have thought that since the trip to Bermuda is nearly always on the wind, the contestants didn't quite know how to use their spinnakers. In the strong gusts boats were rolling from side to side, with first their starboard spreaders in the water, then their port spreaders. A crewman on one of the boats was yanked nearly up to the lower spreaders as the halyard he was holding got away from him. There were spinnaker hour-glasses, blown out chutes and broaches all over the starting line, but somehow all but one boat got away (and she had a frozen steering gear), sailing 174 degrees magnetic to the little island beyond the Stream.

The 111 boats in the fleet covered three-quarters of the distance to Bermuda under spinnaker—nothing even remotely like that had ever before occurred. With only a hundred miles to go, the leaders fell into a frustrating calm and the small boats came marching up.

Again, Carleton Mitchell and his crew of sharpshooters sailed the shortest route to Bermuda, driving *Finisterre* to her maximum potential day and night. Action at the finishing line was chaotic as boats sailed in from everywhere, with 62 boats finishing within 4 hours and 20 minutes of each other—after 635 miles! Thirty-four boats crossed in one hour alone. If that sounds incredible, consider that the winning *Finisterre* finished just 3 hours and 10 minutes after the very first boat, *Good News*, on elapsed time!

Obviously, there was quite a bit of luck involved in a 38 ft. 8 in. boat winning two Bermuda Races in a row (the first boat ever to do so, *Baruna* having left a gap of some 10 years between her victories). But much of Class D had the same air as *Finisterre*, so why not another boat this time? In addition to picking her way around the holes and parking lots, there were a few other virtues that *Finisterre* had working for her. First, she had been designed by Stephens to the C.C.A. rule. Secondly, Mitchell had assembled an energetic and able crew of young men who were of Olympic medal calibre. At least four were national or international dinghy champions. All were seasoned offshore veterans. Mitchell's '58 Bermuda Race crew list included Corwith Cramer Jr., Durward Knowles, Dick Bertram, Charles Larkin II, Bobby Symonette, Bunny Rigg and professional Mel Gutman. It was a star studded cast.

Virtually the same crew shipped aboard with 'Mitch' in the 1960 Bermuda Race, an event that has gone down in yachting history as one of the roughest. Those who grumbled that *Finisterre*'s back-to-back victories were a fluke had to swallow hard after the '60 race because Mitchell and clan did it again. Moreover, the little centreboarder won in tough conditions. When 'Mitch' discovered at one point in the race that he couldn't foot and point with the boats around him, he drove off his grey yawl and went for speed. There was nothing lucky about her '60 victory. It was a combination of rating, boat speed and an over-abundance of

(Overleaf) The 58 ft. schooner 'Niña' was designed for the 1928 season. That year she did well in the Transatlantic Race and won the Fastnet for owner Paul Hammond. In 1962, under the ownership of De Coursey Fales, she won the Bermuda Race

skill and experience that popped up through the companionway every four hours.

Hitting the meander of the Gulf Stream spot-on was the first duty at hand as it started its 60-mile south-easterly flow about 47 miles west of the rhumb line. At a point about six miles from the rhumb (but far to the south) it hooked north-east again. *Finisterre* entered the Stream 42 miles west of the rhumb line and then was lifted 33 miles south and 23 miles east by its mighty flow.

On the second night out one boat noticed a cooling of the water temperature while at the same time running lights began appearing aft over the horizon. The boat altered course a little to the southward and a couple of hours later the lights had disappeared. Such is the power of the Stream.

The wind was light and variable the first four days of the race, making it one of the slower Bermuda passages on record. Then the glass rapidly fell and what started out as a light south-easter rustled up to 40 knots within an hour. Heavy, cold rain shot through the black night air as 135 helmsmen squinted into the battering, stinging salt spray. The wind quickly built up to 50 knots and ranged between 45 and 65 all night with occasional gusts to 80. As the eye of the tropical depression passed over the fleet, stars could be seen overhead and the wind abated, but only for a time and soon crests were being again blown off the 15 ft. seas in streaming grey beards. The howl of the gale continued throughout the night and at dawn the 1,000-plus intrepid racers could see for the first time the immensity of the seas boiling up around them. By mid-morning wind gauges had dropped back to 35 knots. The worse of the storm had passed and the first boats finished off St. David's Head a few hours later, but many boats were damaged by the blow. A headstay fitting on *Windrose* let go during the gale, forcing her crew to run halyards forward to keep the mast in. But soon they, too, parted and the vessel was lucky to finish only 12 hours after her E.T.A. Another Class A boat, Henry Morgan's elegant *Djinn*, was knocked flat in the water and five men were swept overboard—all to be saved by their safety lines. Later, her mainsail blew out. *Souvenir* lost her headstay, *Stormy Weather* had her boomkin torn out, *Highland Light* and *Cotton Blossom IV* had their rudders ripped off and *Windquest* and *Donchery* lost their spars.

Considering the size of the fleet, the gear failures that occurred were not terribly numerous. However, a tragedy nearly took place aboard the yacht *Scylla*, owned by sailmaker Charley Ulmer. Crewmember Jack Westin had just been relieved to go off watch and had unhooked his safety line when the boat lurched in the gale. Westin fell overboard into the midnight sea in conditions that normally would have precluded him from ever being found. But if there was ever a case to prove that God watches over children, drunks and yachtsmen, this was it. Ulmer had shipped aboard one of the new-fangled Guest strob lights (before they were required for offshore racers) which was attached to the stern pulpit. The strob light and the horseshoe life preserver were immediately tossed over the side into the frothing Atlantic, but there was probably no-one aboard who seriously thought that Westin would ever be found. The sails were quickly dropped and the engine, after a new battery was put on the line, was cranked up.

After recovering from his initial shock, Westin pulled off his heavy foul weather gear. While on the top of a crest he could faintly see a flicker of light in the distance—then it disappeared. It was the strob and Westin made for it. After 30 minutes *Scylla* arrived back at the strob light and, to the disbelief of everyone involved, the boat and Westin met. Strobs have been compulsory equipment ever since.

The Bermuda Race fleet was treated to fair, moderate winds from the southwest in 1962, just what the doctor ordered for Fales' ageing *Niña*. This grand old schooner, built in 1927, won the 1928 Transatlantic and Fastnet Races and cut a dashing figure throughout yachting history during the mid 1900s. With her 2,700 sq. ft. golliwobbler there was simply no holding her with sheets eased, and she capped her marvellous career by winning the 1962 Bermuda Race.

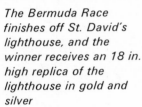

The Bermuda Race finishes off St. David's lighthouse, and the winner receives an 18 in. high replica of the lighthouse in gold and silver

An invitation overseas

Noting the success of the Admiral's Cup in Britain, Bermudian and American yachtsmen decided to start a similar four-race team contest, hoping to entice more foreign competition to their shores. It was called the Onion Patch Series because the Onion Patch, Bermuda, is the finish for the final race, much the same as the Admiral's Cup concludes with the Fastnet. The little island comes alive every two years at the end of the Bermuda Race, and the locals there wanted to add more incentive to bring overseas yachtsmen their way and also to give their own yachts more reason for slogging northwards to Newport, only to slog the 600-odd miles back again. The Royal Bermuda Yacht Club presented the Onion Patch Trophy in 1962 and the first event was held in '64.

The series these days begins with the 175-mile Astor Trophy Race from Oyster Bay, New York, to Newport, Rhode Island. This is an old event on the Long Island Sound racing programme and serves the secondary purpose of being a feeder race to Newport. The two middle races of the series are 25-mile Olympic courses held off Newport in Rhode Island Sound.

With the Astor Trophy Race beginning on a weekend and the Bermuda Race held on Friday, the two day races fill out a busy week of sailing and socialising. But even though there are nearly 200 boats in Newport that week, it's a far cry from the Admiral's Cup and Cowes Week. It seems that it is simply too expensive and too difficult for foreign yachting communities to field competitive three-boat teams so there have never been more than six international teams engaged in the Onion Patch.

In 1964 there was Bermuda, the U.S. and Argentina. The States won this inaugural series, an event that passed almost unnoticed in the host country, much less around the world. But the '64 Bermuda Race had a record 143 starters.

The fleet thrived on moderate south-westerlies for 500 miles down the track until the wind gave out. It was a classic situation of the big boats stuck in the Atlantic tar as the small classes came rushing up with the dying breeze, turning a 635-mile race into a short overnighter. Milton Ernstof's 37 ft. yawl *Burgoo*, the lowest rating boat in the fleet, won, the smallest boat ever to win a Bermuda Race.

The entry list took another leap forward in '66, to 167 boats, with entrants from eight different countries, and news of the Onion Patch had spread. Teams came from Germany, Great Britain, Argentina and Bermuda to challenge the United States. From Germany there was Alfred Krupp's elegant *Germania VI* and N. Lorck-Schierning's *Jan Pott*. *Duchess of Devonshire* and *Whistler of Paget* were up from Bermuda while German Frers brought his *Fjord V* from Argentina with *Fortuna* and *Nike* completing the Latin American team.

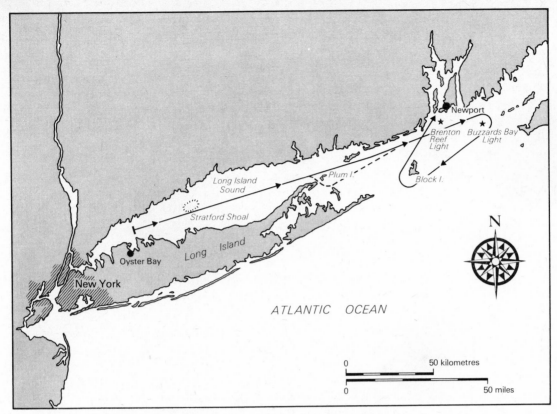

The Astor Trophy Race course in the Onion Patch series

The British won the series that year with Dennis Miller's *Firebrand* and Ron Amey's *Noryema IV* tying for second place in individual standings. The third British boat was R.O.R.C. Commodore Mike Vernon's *Assegai*, overall sixth out of the 15 boats competing.

Heading the defending American team was Bob McCullough's 47 ft. *Inverness*, from the Stephens board, which scored first overall on points. Backing up McCullough was *Illusion*, sailed by the Mosbacher/Monte-Sano team and E. Newbold Smith's *Reindeer*. That the American team wasn't up to the foreign challenge is demonstrated by the Bermuda Race. While Vince Learson won the race in his Cal-40 *Thunderbird*, Curt Steinwig's *Nike* was second, *Noryema* was fifth (and second in Class D) and *Fortuna* won Class A.

The race that year began in a calm and ended with a gale. In fact, most of the fleet had finished before the gale swept over the course, but enough yachts were caught in it to end up with 11 non-finishers, the largest number up to that time. What wind there was came from its traditional location.

The 73 ft. *Big Toy*, the largest glass fibre boat at the time, slipped her lower spreader and put in to Norfolk, Virginia. The 72 ft. *Royono* started leaking and a

Coast Guard pump had to be dropped aboard. The wood 44 ft. yawl *Alert* also began to open up and was taken in tow by the escort destroyer *USS Norris*, which also picked up Howard Read's dismasted *Seeadler*. As if two boats were not enough, *Norris* took on a third yacht, a 29-footer disabled in a Single-handed Transatlantic Race going on at the same time. A couple of boats also dropped out because their sails had been blown out. Although the gale was short and did not hit the entire fleet, it was reported by Bermuda Race veterans to be far worse than the 1960 storm. Certainly it took a greater toll.

Because of the grumbles that always accompany this or any long race, to the effect that one or another class didn't get a fair shake because of the fickle weather patterns that can switch the fleet positions from the one class to another, the C.C.A. decided in 1966 to institute a performance factor. Basically, class finishes were fed into an I.B.M. computer to establish a speed curve. Each boat's performance was related to its rating and the average speed of the rest of the boats in that rating band. The object was to discover which boat had sailed closest to its theoretical maximum capability—thus producing the winner. Ironically, the eventual winner of the race, Vince Learson, was president of I.B.M. The result was also calculated, for intellectual curiosity, using the conventional N.A.Y.R.U. Time Allowance tables and under that system *Thunderbird* would have won by an even greater margin.

For the '68 race, and all following Bermuda Races, the C.C.A. abandoned the computer and returned to the N.A.Y.R.U. tables. Sailmaker Ted Hood won the race in what he guessed was about his eighth *Robin*. Like most of the rest of his boats, she was a Hood design, a 51 ft. steel yawl built by Maas in Holland in two months. The winds were kinder than in 1966, being generally moderate and from the south-west. For the most part, *Robin* followed the time-honoured tactic of staying close to the rhumb line. She was also driven hard by Hood and his all-star crew.

The Onion Patch Trophy returned to American hands when five foreign teams took part. The first race was a 25-miler in Long Island Sound, when 14 boats representing Bermuda, Canada, Germany, Great Britain and the United States came to the line. In winds which at times brought the race almost to a halt, the German *Germania* won, followed by a two, three, four for America's *Thunderbird*, *Inverness* and *Robin*. Fifth was Britain's *Noryema VI* (formerly Dick Carter's *Rabbit*) and sixth, *Whistler of Paget* for Bermuda.

The second race was 112 miles from Oyster Bay to Newport. It was won by Canada's *Spirit*, with *Germania* second, *Robin* third, *Noryema VI* fourth, *Inverness* fifth, *Privateer* (Bermuda) sixth, *Thunderbird* seventh, *Truant VI* (Canada) eighth, *Firebrand* ninth and *Prospect of Whitby* (Britain) 10th. On points the United States had a healthy lead with 132 points to Britain's 104, Germany's $94\frac{1}{4}$, Bermuda's 83 and Canada's $65\frac{1}{2}$.

A popular Bermuda Race and Onion Patch competitor: 'The Duchess of Devonshire', owned by Sir Bayard Dill of Bermuda

A slight bias at the windward end of the starting line for the third race, in Rhode Island Sound, resulted in a general mêlée there and several yachts being over at the gun. A protest was lodged when the recall procedure was not correctly adhered to and the race was declared void. So there was no change in points standing before the Bermuda Race. *Robin*'s overall win kept America well ahead but Britain put up a good performance with two seconds in class for *Firebrand* (Class D) and *Prospect of Whitby* (Class E), so the final points position was U.S.A. 297, Britain 252, Germany 218½, Bermuda 179, Canada 177½.

In 1970 the American team won again, fielding three of the hottest custom ocean racers in the country: Dick Nye's 48 ft. sloop *Carina* (the Bermuda Race winner), Jack Potter's Stephens designed *Equation* and Pat Haggerty's classic 49 ft. *Bay Bea*, another S. and S. design. This American power was too much for the British team, Arthur Slater's latest *Prospect of Whitby*, a new Swan 43 *Firebrand* and the Lloyds' Yacht Club boat *Lutine*, and they could do no better than second in a four-way series. The Argentinians were third and the Bermudians fourth.

It should be pointed out that until 1970 the British and European entries were suffering under a grave handicap and it was a credit to the British that they were able to win in '66. The European boats were, of course, designed to the R.O.R.C. rule while the American and Latin American boats were designed to the C.C.A. rule which was the system employed for the series.

Dick Nye came back to win his second Bermuda Race in 1970 in his new aluminium sloop *Carina*, designed by McCurdy and Rhodes. The course had been slightly altered, with the addition of a turning mark in the form of the Argus Bank Texas Tower south-west of Bermuda, making the rhumb line 679 miles long. But as many competitors had difficulty finding the tower its use was discarded in later races.

The fleet generally suffered through a low pressure system which dusted off the yachts with vicious blasts of cold air and bullet-like rain. Squalls peppered the fleet with nasty 60-knot winds that mowed down a lot of masts. In all, seven boats were dismasted during the second night and third morning of the race in what for a while threatened to be wholesale destruction of the fleet.

But the 1970 race only put crews on notice as to what the Atlantic could dish out if it got serious. In the '72 race, the sea gods really got down to business. In what was probably the roughest, toughest Bermuda Race of all times, 13 boats were unable to finish out of a record 178 starters, as a gale lashed the big boats for over 24 hours and hammered the small boats for nearly three days. To the crews on the 40-footers it must have seemed like an eternity. Yet the winner was only 48 ft.—Ron Amey's *Noryema VIII*, a glass fibre production Swan 48, the first non-

'Windward Passage', carrying a tiny storm trysail, shows what conditions were like for the 1972 Bermuda Race. She lost her port lower shroud and her mainsail pulled out of the mast track, so great was the punishment she encountered

(Inset) Wind, rain and spray can all take their toll of the helmsman's eyes. Luckily there were goggles on board the British yacht 'Noryema VIII'

American boat ever to win the race. Despite this victory, Britain still could not win back the Onion Patch Trophy.

Six teams, the most ever, raced in the series: U.S.A., Argentina, Brazil, Britain, Bermuda and Australia. The first race was the feeder from New York to Newport for the Astor Trophy.

Sir Max Aitken's *Crusade* went ahead for Britain out of the Onion Patch yachts and led them westwards past Block Island and Buzzard Tower and back for the dog leg around Block Island. But this was a dead beat to windward in a fresh 20 knots and she was unable to lay the course and headed southwards. Astern of her, *Charisma* and *Yankee Girl* found a different wind and could lay the course. The Brazilian *Saga* did best of all—second overall and top Onion Patch boat—but the U.S. team still took a points lead with a second, third and 15th.

Erling S. Lorentzen's 57 ft. *Saga* was to prove the star of the series and won the first inshore race off Newport with a superb windward performance. But the Americans seemed unbeatable, with *Yankee Girl* second, *Charisma* fourth and *Aura* (Wally Stenhouse) eighth. L. Kocourek's *Matrero* took fifth place for Argentina, Richard Thirlby's *Maverick* a sixth for Britain, but neither had strong support from their team mates. Jim Baldwin's *Sorcery*, representing Australia, sailed well but Alan Bond's *Apollo* and the third member of their big boat team, the 71 ft. ketch *Benedic* (G. J. Dusseldorp) let her down.

At the end of the third race, the British team was feeling a little happier with a first for *Noryema VIII*—a good omen for the big one—third for *Maverick* and 12th for *Crusade*. Argentina, with a fourth for Frers's *Fjord* and sixth for *Matrero*, were also in a strong challenging position but it was difficult to break the stronghold of the home team. The points position was: the United States 149, Argentina 131, Britain 114, Bermuda 103, Brazil 100 and Australia 87.

Halfway through the Bermuda Race the gale hit. The sea built up to 20 ft. with foamy crests being chopped off and shot to leeward at 50 miles an hour. On the wind, the yachts rose with the crests then fell into the canyons on the other side. Few boats gave any more concessions to the gale beyond reefed mainsails and storm jibs and the fearless racers pressed forward at top speed, shooting off the tops of the swells at six to nine knots, then smashing down on the other side. Wood, glass and aluminium boats alike took a horrible pounding as their crews relentlessly drove them into the snarling teeth of the 45 knot gale for hours on end, driving their bows into the waves, hell-bent for Bermuda. With yachts falling off 10 to 20 ft. cliffs for hour after hour, failures were bound to occur.

After eight hours of unmerciful slamming that often left sleeping crew members suspended in air as the boat dropped out from under them, *Windward Passage*'s

(Top) Sparkman and Stephens 1974 style: 'Siren Song' a 58 ft. cutter owned by Joseph S. Wright, impressed many with her performance on her first major outing in the Bermuda Race

(Below) One of the newest maxi-boats in the United States is Huey Long's 79 ft. ketch 'Ondine' which set a new elapsed time record in the 1974 Bermuda Race. She cost over half a million dollars and her smart accommodation includes a sauna

port lower shroud fell to the deck, threatening to bring down the mast. The head-sail was dropped and staysail set. Then her main pulled out of the mast track at the headboard and the storm trysail was set. Vin Learson's *Nepenthe* fell off three waves in succession and her mast came down. The 45 ft. *Duchess of Devonshire* lost a spreader and was dismasted 150 miles from Bermuda, as was *Skylark*. *La Forza del Destino* lost her steering quadrant north of Bermuda and was disabled. *Rage* lost her headstay and the glass fibre *Nike* fractured her bottom and began taking in water.

Crusade carried away her port intermediate shroud and, unable to sail on port tack, had to heave-to for seven hours. Even though she eventually finished un-aided, her poor position killed any chance Britain had of winning the Onion Patch Trophy. *Noryema*, in the middle of this maelstrom, suffered nothing but the loss of a speedo transducer which was torn off when she fell down a wave. *Maverick*, too, of cold-moulded plywood, suffered no structural damage.

Owner Amey wasn't on board *Noryema* because of business commitments in England, but veteran yachtsman Ted Hicks brought the Swan 48 home a winner by going east to pick up a favourable meander of the Gulf Stream. Then he ended up being on the right side of the rhumb line as the gale hit.

Hicks's spot-on navigation also played an important role in *Noryema*'s victory as many boats approaching Bermuda were not sure of their exact position. For ex-ample, Dick Nye hove-to aboard *Carina* during the night for fear of hitting the shoals north of the island. *Equation*, for safety reasons, turned on her illegal Omega to confirm her position. With R.D.F. bearings unreliable and practically no visibility in the gale while approaching Bermuda at night, yachts and the lives of many crewmen were in danger. It is a tribute to the good seamanship of the skippers that almost to a man they followed a prudent course in keeping their vessels off Bermuda's vicious coral bricks that dark night.

Line honours went to the C. and C. designed 61 ft. sloop *Robon*, on her maiden voyage, although she was far from being maximum rater. She was followed by more A class yachts, and only five B class had finished when *Noryema*, from C Class, crossed the finishing line at her second attempt—bad visibility from rain squalls had kept her away the first time. The Onion Patch overall team rankings were U.S.A., Britain, Argentina, Bermuda, Australia, Brazil.

The 1974 event was gentle compared with the '72 bash but nevertheless the 167 boats were buffeted by rough, confused seas in the Gulf Stream and 20–30 knot south-westerlies that had the fleet reefed down for almost the entire distance. Huey Long's 79 ft. new Britton Chance designed *Ondine* took advantage of the close-reaching conditions to smash the old elapsed time record by two hours— 2 days, 19 hours, 52 minutes and 22 seconds for the 635-mile race. She beat another new maxi-rating boat, Eric Ridder's 79 ft. Stephens-designed *Tempest*, by nearly two hours.

But the battle for overall victory was between Chuck Kirsch's year-old German Frers designed 55 ft. *Scaramouche* and Jesse Philips's 56 ft. Stephens designed *Charisma*. Both boats went west to pick up the Stream and stayed west of the rhumb line by 50 miles before cracking sheets in the south-westerly for Bermuda. It was a tough hull-to-hull battle all the way with *Scaramouche* beating *Charisma* to the line to win fleet and class by nearly half an hour. *Charisma* was second in fleet for the second Bermuda Race in a row.

Lynn Williams's 61 ft. S. and S. designed *Dora IV* won the goldplater class with Frank Zurn's *Kahili II*, a McCurdy and Rhodes 61-footer, just minutes behind. In Class B the feuding was as close as any seen in the Bermuda Race for years with the new 58 ft. Stephens yacht *Siren Song*, owned by Joe Wright, finishing only a few minutes behind *Charisma*.

C. A. Corna's 49 ft. *Recluta III*, a Frers design, won Class C and was third in fleet. Jim Mattingly sailed the PJ (Swan) 44 *Diane* to first in Class D while Don Tate's *Cayenne* won Class E. The Ericson 37 *Hot Canary* (Stan Rubenzahl), won Class F with Ted Hood second in *Robin*, one of his new One Tonners.

Only three foreign teams entered the '74 Onion Patch—Great Britain, Bermuda and Canada. To nearly everyone's surprise the British team dominated the series. Going into the Bermuda Race all they needed were moderately good placings in the final and the trophy would have gone to Britain for the second time. Unfortunately for the British team, they put in a poor showing in the heavily weighted Bermuda Race. One boat, Chris Dunning's beautiful *Marionette*, which had sailed a near-perfect series to that point, is reported to have not gone for the boost of the Gulf Stream, but instead took the rhumb line. This broke a cardinal rule of the race and it was little wonder that *Marionette* finished 143rd overall. But Ron Amey's year-old 52 ft. S. and S. *Noryema* did little better with a 119th and Powell and Martin's 50 ft. S. and S. *Oyster* was 137th. It is hard to know why this powerful team fell into such disaster and it is certainly a shame since the American team was being propped up by one outstanding race winner, *Scaramouche*. Overall, the British team was consistently better until they hit the Stream.

German Frers originally worked for Sparkman and Stephens. Now his designs in his own right are winning on both sides of the Atlantic. This is his drawing of 'Recluta III', owned by Argentinian Carlos Corna

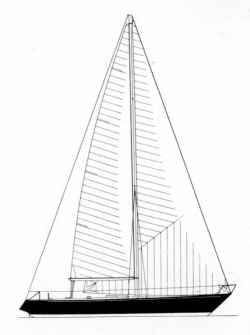

The pace slows

The future of the Onion Patch is uncertain. With little prospect of ever attracting a number of top-flight boats from overseas with the present organisation, one wonders how much it is all worth. Unlike the Admiral's Cup, it is run and co-sponsored by a number of clubs—the New York Yacht Club, the Seawanaka Corinthian Yacht Club on Long Island, the Ida Lewis Yacht Club in Newport and the Royal Bermuda Yacht Club. It deserves to be bigger and would be if two or three good European teams made the effort to enter.

In America itself hard feelings nearly always occur after the home team is arbitrarily selected by a four-man committee. The alternative is to open up the Onion Patch series to any three-boat team. States, yacht clubs or even just three drinking buddies could then form their own team just for the fun of it. The national team could still be selected, or better still be determined by means of trials, to race against the foreign teams which would certainly come if they felt some serious, enthusiastic effort was backing the series.

The S.O.R.C. too has always been the winter sunshine series for American yachtsmen, many of whom commute to the races each week. But now they are feeling the financial squeeze and many big boats, as well as a number of small ones, are having to stay at home.

With the general decline of the economy in the U.S. during 1974 has come diminished boat-building activity. Custom yards around the country are finding themselves without any large-boat orders and, in some cases, no boats at all to build. What building there's been concentrated on Two Tonners as American yachtsmen prepared themselves for the Two Ton World Championship and the Canada's Cup, both held on Lake St. Clair, off Detroit, Michigan. New Hood, Carter and Peterson designs were building in aluminium and wood and the Two Ton action on the Great Lakes during the summer '75 looked like being the most competitive seen anywhere.

There is renewed interest in sending an effective Admiral's Cup team to Britain for 1975. Ted Turner's new German Frers designed 49-footer *Tenacious*, a near sister to *Recluta III*, Jesse Philips' new S. and S. 54 ft. *Charisma*, Chuck Kirsch's *Scaramouche*, almost a definite for the team, a new 54 ft. Bill Lapworth aluminium design from the West Coast sailed by sailmaker Burke Sawyer, and a slightly modified *Salty Goose* are all battling for berths in Britain. *Scaramouche* was undergoing bow modifications at the Palmer Johnson yard in Racine during the 1974/75 winter.

It would be good to see some of the other newer U.S.A. yachts making the Transatlantic Race crossing, perhaps with an eye on laurels in the 50th anniversary Fastnet—79-footers such as Eric Ridder's *Tempest*, Jim Kilroy's *Kialoa* and Huey Long's *Ondine* plus Joe Wright's 58 ft. *Siren Song* and Homer Denius's new 60 ft. Morgan design.

There is a general 'wait and see' feeling among American yachtsmen both in response to the slowing economy and to the rapid advancement of speed in the smaller sized boats. Many owners are still reeling from three short years of One Ton activity which saw as many as four hot One Ton designs come and go before the Peterson *Ganbare*-type settled down as a consistent winner.

The announcement of the Massachusetts Institute of Technology programme to study the relationships between design and performance has also caused an undetermined amount of disquiet. Although the M.I.T. study was instigated by the North American Yacht Racing Union in response to the complaint that yachts were not being fairly handicapped under the I.O.R. rule, yachtsmen are now wondering what effect the study will have on the future of the current handicap rule. Will the M.I.T. study indicate the desirability of a completely new rating rule or will the I.O.R. be modified once again to incorporate new data?

Still further clouding the water is the current position being taken by the Cruising Club of America that numerous modifications must be made to the I.O.R. or the club will come up with its own version of the rule. Even though the C.C.A. administers only one ocean race in the U.S.A.—the Bermuda Race—the chances are that whatever this club does might be emulated throughout the country, as was the case during the days of the C.C.A. rule. Some owners undoubtedly feel their boats might rate better under any new handicap system and are therefore reluctant to plunge into a new boat.

The economy, the rapid progress of the level rating classes and the possibility of a change in the handicap system have all conspired to slow the rapid growth of racing fleets that existed during the early 1970s. There will no doubt be a decline in offshore activity followed by a resurgence when the economy rallies and rule stability is enforced.

Further evidence of a cooling of the American fervour for offshore racing was exhibited during the most recent S.O.R.C. when only 78 boats completed the six-race series instead of the 100 to 110 boats that made the Circuit in the early 1970s. The '75 S.O.R.C. was won by Dennis Conner in his Doug Peterson-designed One Tonner *Stinger* and top fleet positions were dominated by One Tonners. For the third year in a row the best efforts of the big boat sailors were not enough to overcome the very competitive One Ton Class, and big boat owners realize their prospects won't improve in the future. This feeling can have only an adverse effect on new big boat construction.

The 1975 United States Admiral's Cup team was selected by a committee in March '75 on the basis of the performances of the boats in the S.O.R.C. Because the decision to use the Circuit for trials was not made until October 28, 1974, Chuck Kirsch was unable to get his *Scaramouche* from Wisconsin to Florida in time and therefore she was not considered. Of the boats that were, Ted Turner's 49 foot *Tenacious*, which won two S.O.R.C. races and won every event in Class B, was selected along with Ted Hood's new 40 foot Two Ton rating *Robin* which finished fifth overall (the highest non-O.T.C. boat) in the S.O.R.C. and first in Class C. Third boat selected was Jesse Philips' 54 foot *Charisma*, an S. and S. design, which finished third in Class B behind *Tenacious* and World Ocean Racing Champion Wally Stenhouse's old 49 foot warhorse *Aura*. A poor Lauderdale race put *Charisma* behind *Aura* and the general feeling was that the new *Charisma* could save her time on *Aura* in most conditions and should therefore be picked.

Statistics

ADMIRAL'S CUP
Winning teams

1957 Great Britain
Myth of Malham (John Illingworth and Peter Green)
Uomie (Selwyn Slater)
Jocasta (Geoff Pattinson)
1959 Great Britain
Myth of Malham (John Illingworth and Peter Green)
Griffin II (R.O.R.C., sailed by Major Gerald Potter)
Ramrod (Selwyn Slater)
1961 U.S.A.
Windrose (Jakob Isbrandtsen)
Figaro (Richard Nye)
Cyane (Henry B. du Pont)
1963 Great Britain
Noryema III (Ron Amey)
Clarion of Wight (Dennis Miller and Derek Boyer)
Outlaw (Max Aitken)
1965 Great Britain
Firebrand (Dennis Miller)
Quiver IV (Ren Clarke)
Noryema IV (Ron Amey)
1967 Australia
Mercedes III (Ted Kaufman)
Balandra (Robert Creighton-Brown)
Caprice of Huon (Gordon Ingate, sailed by Gordon Reynolds)
1969 U.S.A.
Red Rooster (Dick Carter)
Carina (Dick Nye)
Palawan (Thomas J. Watson, Jr.)
1971 Great Britain
Cervantes IV (Bob Watson)
Morning Cloud (Edward Heath)
Prospect of Whitby (Arthur Slater)
1973 Germany
Saudade (Albert Büll)
Rubin (Hans-Otto Schumann)
Carina III (Dieter Monheim)

SOUTHERN CROSS CUP
Winning teams

1967 New South Wales, Australia
Mercedes III (Ted Kaufman)
Moonbird (Norm Brooker)
Calliope (Charlie Middleton)
1969 New South Wales, Australia
Ragamuffin (Syd Fischer)
Mercedes III (Ted Kaufman)
Boambillee (Vince Walsh)
1971 New Zealand
Pathfinder (Brin Wilson)
Runaway (John Lidgard)
Wai-Aniwa (Ray Walker, sailed by Chris Bouzaid)
1973 Great Britain
Prospect of Whitby (Arthur Slater)
Quailo III (Donald Parr)
Superstar (Alan Graham and Dave Johnson)

S.O.R.C.
Winning yachts

1941 *Stormy Weather* (William Labrot) and *Gulf Stream* (Dudley Sharp) tie
1947 *Ciclon* (A. Gomez-Mena and M. Bustamante, Cuba)
1948 *Stormy Weather* (Fred Temple)
1949 *Tiny Teal* (Palmer Langdon and Dick Bertram)
1950 *Windigo* (Walter Gubelmann)
1951 *Belle of the West* (Will Erwin)
1952 *Caribbee* (Carleton Mitchell)
1953 *Caribbee* (Carleton Mitchell)
1954 *Hoot Mon* (Worth Brown, Charles Ulmer, Lockwood Pirie)
1955 *Hoot Mon* (Worth Brown, Charles Ulmer, Lockwood Pirie)
1956 *Finisterre* (Carleton Mitchell)
1957 *Criollo* (Luis Vidana, Cuba)
1958 *Ca Va* (Jake Hershey and Robert Mosbacher, Jr.)
1959 *Callooh* (Jack Brown and Bus Mosbacher, Jr.)

1960 *Solution* (Thor H. Ramsing)
1961 *Paper Tiger* (Jack Powell)
1962 *Paper Tiger* (Jack Powell)
1963 *Doubloon* (Joe Byars)
1964 *Conquistador* (Fuller E. Callaway III)
1965 *Figaro IV* (Bill Snaith)
1966 *Vamp X* (Ted Turner)
1967 *Guinevere* (George Moffett)
1968 *Red Jacket* (Perry Connolly)
1969 *Salty Tiger* (Jack Powell and Wally Frank)
1970 *American Eagle* (Ted Turner)
1971 *Running Tide* (Jakob Isbrandtsen)
1972 *Condor* (Hill Blackett)
1973 *Muñequita* (Jack Valley and Click Schreck)
1974 *Robin Too II* (Ted Hood)
1975 *Stinger* (Dennis Conner)

ONION PATCH
Winning teams

1964 U.S.A.
Reindeer (E. Newbold Smith)
Prim (Sonny Neff)
Shearwater (Thomas Young)
1966 Great Britain
Firebrand (Dennis Miller)
Noryema IV (Ron Amey)
Assegai (Mike Vernon)
1968 U.S.A.
Thunderbird (Vince Learson)
Robin (Ted Hood)
Inverness (Bob McCullough)
1970 U.S.A.
Carina (Dick Nye)
Equation (Jack Potter)
Bay Bea (Pat Haggerty)
1972 U.S.A.
Charisma (Jesse Philips)
Yankee Girl (David Steere)
Aura (Wally Stenhouse)
1974 U.S.A.
Scaramouche (Charles Kirsch)
Dynamite (Llywd Ecclestone)
Harpoon (Mark Ewing)

Index